EXPLORING THE WORLD OF
J. S. BACH

Germany, ca. 1720. Johann Baptist Homann, *Postarum seu Veredariorum Germaniam et Provincias Adiacentes. Neu vermehrte PostCharte durch gantz Teutschland . . . revised edition* (Nuremberg). Detail.

EXPLORING THE WORLD OF
J. S. BACH
A TRAVELER'S GUIDE

ROBERT L. MARSHALL
AND
TRAUTE M. MARSHALL

Published in cooperation with the American Bach Society

University of Illinois Press
Urbana, Chicago, and Springfield

This publication is sponsored by the American Bach Society and produced under the guidance of its Editorial Board. For information about the American Bach Society, please see its website at www.americanbachsociety.org.

Library of Congress Cataloging-in-Publication Data
Names: Marshall, Robert Lewis, author. | Marshall, Traute M., 1942– author.
Title: Exploring the world of J.S. Bach: a traveler's guide / Robert L. Marshall and Traute M. Marshall.
Description: Urbana, Chicago, and Springfield : University of Illinois Press, 2016. | "Published in cooperation with the American Bach Society." |
Includes bibliographical references and index.
Identifiers: LCCN 2015047399 (print) | LCCN 2015048837 (ebook) | ISBN 9780252040313 (cloth : alk. paper) | ISBN 9780252081767 (pbk. : alk. paper) | ISBN 9780252098574 (ebook)
Subjects: LCSH: Bach, Johann Sebastian, 1685–1750—Homes and haunts—Germany. | Germany—Description and travel. | LCGFT: Guidebooks
Classification: LCC ML410.B13 M272 2016 (print) | LCC ML410.B13 (ebook) | DDC 780.92—dc23
LC record available at http://lccn.loc.gov/2015047399

CONTENTS

FOREWORD

It is with great pleasure that the American Bach Society, in collaboration with the University of Illinois Press, publishes *Exploring the World of J. S. Bach: A Traveler's Guide*. The Society's first venture into special publications, *The Organs of J. S. Bach: A Handbook*, issued in 2012, proved to be such a happy undertaking that the Society's Editorial Board quickly settled upon the idea of creating a companion volume, a guide to the Bach sites in Germany.

That a new sites guide, in English, was needed was apparent for many of the same reasons that spurred the publication of the organ handbook. The opening of Thuringia and Saxony after the fall of the Socialist government in 1989 and the reunification of Germany the following year have suddenly made the region where Bach lived and worked easily accessible to tourists for the first time in almost half a century. The rapid restoration and reconstruction of towns, churches, and palaces known to Bach and the establishment of new, visitor-friendly museums also call out for an up-to-date guide. While a number of books discussing the Bach sites are available in German and ostensibly could be translated into English, none capture the full range of recent developments such as the rebuilding of the Church of our Lady in Dresden (the site of Bach's triumphant organ concert before the Elector's musicians in 1736), the reimagining of the facade of the University Church in Leipzig (where Bach performed the Trauer-Ode, *Laß Fürstin, laß noch einen Strahl* in 1727), or the re-creation of the Royal Palace in Potsdam (where Bach improvised on Silbermann fortepianos before Frederick the Great in 1747). In addition, no existing guides incorporate the most recent findings of Bach research, a field that has flourished in the past twenty-five years with the opening of long-inaccessible archives in the former East Germany and Russia and the renewed efforts of the Bach Expedition team of the Leipzig Bach Archive. For all of these reasons, the Editorial Board concluded that an entirely new handbook was required, rather than the translation of an existing German guide. But who would write it?

By happy coincidence, distinguished Bach scholar and past president of the American Bach Society Robert L. Marshall and his wife Traute expressed interest in the project at an early stage of development. One cannot imagine a better set of tour guides. Robert, winner of the Kinkeldey Prize from the American Musicological Society and the Deems Taylor Award from ASCAP, is well known for his exacting scholarship and game-changing essays. *The Compositional Process of J. S. Bach* opened the world of source studies to American musicologists when it appeared in 1972, and articles such as "Bach the Progressive" and "Organ or Klavier? Instrumental Prescriptions in the Sources of Bach's Keyboard Works" altered the way we think about Bach and the performance of his works. Traute, a native German, is an equally seasoned writer, editor, and translator. Her German translations of Charles Rosen's *The Classical Style* and James Lyon's *Brecht in America* have become standards in the German-speaking world, and her *Art Museums PLUS: Cultural Excursions in New England* takes the precise guidebook approach desired for the present undertaking. It was clear from the start that the Marshalls, blessed with broad experience, impressive Bach credentials, and a rich sense of humor were the perfect team to produce a handbook on the German Bach sites.

Also auspicious for the present project was the American Bach Society's long-standing ties with the University of Illinois Press. For almost two decades now the Society and the Press have collaborated on publications such as *Bach Perspectives, About Bach*, and *The Organs of J. S. Bach*. With the strong support of then-Director William Regier, the savvy guidance of then-Senior Acquisitions Editor Laurie Matheson, and the elegant design work of Jim Proefrock (so evident in the organ handbook), the project was able to move forward in a smooth, efficient, and effective way. It has been a delight to join forces once again with the UIP team.

What the Marshalls have provided is far more than a straightforward guide to the Bach sites. In the course of discussing the activities of Bach in 51 German towns, they present an up-to-date overview of Bach biography, one that incorporates the very latest discoveries of Bach research. With substantial discussions of the architecture and art of the individual buildings and museums, the Marshalls also provide a concise study of Medieval, Renaissance, and Baroque art history. And by drawing on early guides to the postal and travel routes, they give us a sense of just how much time Bach spent in transit, and just how arduous many of his journeys actually were. Who would have thought that the trip from Leipzig to Kassel, a quick ride of less than three hours on the Intercity train today, took Bach at least a week in 1732, with overnight stops that probably included stays in Weißenfels, Erfurt, and Gotha? Although Bach did not venture abroad, it is obvious from the present guide that he spent much more time on the road than previously thought, traveling from town to town within Germany.

But most importantly, by drawing on critical details, the Marshalls convey a vivid picture of Bach's daily life. In 1730, disgruntled by deteriorating conditions for music-making in Leipzig, Bach reminisced to his school chum Georg Erdmann that he had been supremely happy in Köthen and had planned to spend the rest of his days there. The present volume shows that his employer in Köthen, Prince Leopold, spent the equivalent of almost $422,000 on a single stay at the Spa in Karlsbad. Why wouldn't Bach have been happy in such an environment of luxury, as a prized and graciously supported keyboard virtuoso in the Prince's retinue?!

Exploring the World of J. S. Bach: A Traveler's Guide, then, serves as a worthy companion to *The Organs of J. S. Bach.* It paints a broad portrait of Bach's life and career and the political and cultural milieu that he was compelled to navigate. It surveys the cities, towns, and villages in which he made music, telling us what these sites were like in his time and what they are like today. In short, it presents a vibrant description of Bach's world, in his day and ours. In their quest to track down the places where the great St. Thomas Kantor walked and worked, the Marshalls leave no Bach memorial tablet unturned. And in the process, they make a convincing case for some new ones.

George B. Stauffer
General Editor, American Bach Society

PREFACE

This book is a hybrid creature, combining in varying degrees the qualities of a biography, a reference work, and a tour guide. Its central focus is on all the towns we know—or have reason to presume—Johann Sebastian Bach lived in or visited: fifty-one in all.

Our inclination is to be comprehensive. That is, we prefer to err on the side of inclusion. But the volume will certainly not be complete, since it is now clearer than ever that Bach must have taken many trips that until now remain undocumented. For example—and most pertinent to the larger purpose of this book—in a newly discovered letter dated May 16, 1744, and published for the first time in 2007 (Langusch 2007), Bach mentions that he was away from Leipzig for "almost five weeks"—an absence hitherto unknown. Even more recently, in 2013, a document came to light in which a former student at the St. Thomas School, one Gottfried Benjamin Fleckeisen (1719–86), asserted that for "two entire years"—apparently covering the period 1744–46—he "had to perform and direct the music" in Leipzig's main churches of St. Thomas and St. Nicholas "in the place of the Kapellmeister." These are strong indications that Bach probably took many trips that are unknown to us, especially during the last decade of his life.

The book's biographical discussions, while relating the essential facts of Bach's life and career associated with a particular place, will emphasize recent findings not yet widely known beyond scholarly circles. But most historiographical writing, including biography, if it is to be more than a dry recitation of facts, dates, and statistics, will inevitably entertain conjecture and speculation. At times we report the testimony of local historians (clearly identified as such) regarding, for example, the precise location of the detention cell in the Weimar palace where Bach was incarcerated for almost a month in late 1717, or the identity of the consistory building in Arnstadt where, between August 1705 and November 1706, he was formally reprimanded on several occasions. Such conjectures, based on long-standing local tradition, while risky, are not necessarily wrong.

This survey describes sites that Bach would have seen as well as sites that the modern visitor can see. Often they are the same, but sometimes they are not. Several of the places that figured prominently in the life of Johann Sebastian Bach no longer exist. Some had already disappeared in the eighteenth century, others in the nineteenth and twentieth centuries. Among the more notable cases: the devastating fires in Ohrdruf (1753) and Weimar (1774) in the eighteenth century; the deliberate demolition of the St. Thomas School in 1902; the ravages of World War II; and the demolition, also in Leipzig, of the St. Paul's (University) Church in 1968 by the East German government. Most recently, in November 2013, a fire broke out in the Ehrenstein Palace in Ohrdruf.

On the other hand, the last few years have offered an especially propitious occasion to embark on this project. In the quarter century since the reunification of Germany a major effort has been underway to restore, rehabilitate, and renovate historic sites and landmarks in the former German Democratic Republic—specifically, the states of Thuringia, Saxony, Saxony-Anhalt, and Berlin-Brandenburg, which constitute the heart of "Bach Country." The same region was also the heart of German culture for most of its history until quite recent times: as the cradle of the Lutheran Reformation and, later on—especially in the cities of Weimar, Leipzig, and Berlin—as the host for the major centers of the nation's preeminent literary, musical, and intellectual developments.

The towns and regions of "Bach Country" are well aware of their cultural heritage—most emphatically its Bach (and Luther) connections. There are at least six museums dedicated to Bach or the Bach family: one each in Eisenach, Köthen, Leipzig, and Wechmar, and two in Arnstadt. This esteem is reflected further in the numerous statues and monuments dedicated to Bach and in plaques on buildings marking where Johann Sebastian Bach may (or may not) have lived or stayed.

The book consists of two main Parts. The eight chronologically arranged chapters of Part One offer in effect a brief biography, while describing the towns in which Bach resided from his birth in Eisenach in 1685 to his death in Leipzig in 1750. Part Two, by contrast, is organized like an encyclopedia, with alphabetical entries. It surveys the forty-three towns Bach is known to—or presumed to—have visited. The latter are indicated with an asterisk. The arguments supporting those presumptions in any individual case vary considerably in strength and are duly presented in the course of the entry.

Individual chapters and entries can range in length from little more than two hundred words (Stöntzsch) to well over six thousand (Leipzig). Since, as is the case with encyclopedia entries, there is no expectation that they will be read in direct sequence, some relevant points of information occasionally appear in more than one. The resulting "redundancy" is intentional and meant to assure that each entry is self-contained and self-sufficient.

The organization of the individual essays generally falls into two sections—often marked with explicit subheadings. The first section sets out Bach's connection with the town and briefly relates the town's political and cultural history, concentrating on those events and institutions most pertinent to Bach but also raising points of larger cultural and historical interest to a modern reader.

The biographical and historical discussions, in an effort to re-create something of the experience of an inhabitant or traveler in eighteenth-century Germany, include specific information regarding locations, distances, and travel routes. For the convenience of the prospective modern traveler, distances between the endpoints of one of Bach's journeys are given in both kilometers and in miles. By consulting eighteenth-century maps, we suggest the towns Bach may have passed through en route to his destinations. The purpose of this exercise is to enlarge our knowledge of the places he would probably have visited and experienced. It is quite likely, for example, that Bach passed through the towns of Dessau and Wittenberg on his trip in 1719 from Köthen to Berlin; Jena and Meissen on his trip from Weimar to Dresden in 1717; Zwickau and Plauen, perhaps, on his trips from Köthen to Karlsbad; Wolfenbüttel and Brunswick, perhaps, on his trek from Arnstadt to Lübeck—all places normally not associated with Johann Sebastian Bach but with considerable artistic or cultural interest. Future research may reveal whether in fact he ever visited any of them. Whether he had the interest, patience, or "eyes" to "see" them in a deeper sense, will no doubt never be known.

In calculating the value of the currency, we have taken the conversions published in Wolff 2000, p. 539, and assumed that over the course of the fifteen years since its publication, the values have inflated by a third. The value of one thaler, accordingly, assessed at about $72.00 in 2000, is assumed to have been worth about $96.00 in 2015 currency, the florin/gulden $84.00, the groschen $4.00.

The second section of the typical entry (frequently bearing the heading "Landmarks") describes those surviving edifices—churches, town halls, palaces and residences—which are known or thought to have played a role in Bach's life and experience, briefly recounting their history and calling attention to any notable architectural or stylistic features. We also call attention to any other major artistic and historical highlights that a visitor would not want to miss and, when appropriate, provide information relating to major musical figures other than J. S. Bach or regarding events for which a town is well known.

A major asset of the book, we hope, is its generous inclusion of images drawn from a variety of sources—modern and historic photographs, historic engravings, paintings and other artworks; the subjects range from conventional views of building exteriors and internal spaces to reproductions of items of particular biographical or artistic significance: a pulpit sculpture, altar piece, baptismal font. With few exceptions, illustrations of organs have not been included, since they are comprehensively presented in *The Organs of J. S. Bach: A Handbook* (referenced here as: Organs)—in many respects a counterpart to the present volume. The principal criterion governing the selection of an image has been its specific relevance and importance in the life of Bach, its larger historical or cultural interest, and its aesthetic value and power.

As for the modern traveler: We are confident that this volume will prove useful for anyone embarking on a tour of Bach Country by identifying the relevant sites in the first place, drawing attention to the specific landmarks and points of interest from the composer's time that still survive, and describing their historical, biographical, and cultural significance. It falls short of a full-fledged travel guide, however, in that it does not provide itineraries, city maps, or practical tourist tips. Maps 1 and 2 give the potential visitor an initial and helpful orientation regarding the proximity and clustering of towns. With Arnstadt as a center, for example, one can readily take day trips to the towns of Dornheim, Langewiesen, and Gehren. Similarly, Erfurt can serve as a convenient core for an excursion to Gotha and hence to Wechmar and Ohrdruf as well as to Weimar. From Leipzig, the towns of Kleinzschocher, Störmthal, Zschortau, Wiederau, Halle, and Weißenfels are in easy reach.

Anyone planning to visit any of the towns described in this book would be well advised to consult in advance the town's website via the internet. Upon arriving at the destination, the traveler's first station should be the local tourist information bureau (typically located on or near the town square and marked by a large capital "I"), where abundant materials are readily available. These usually include street maps pinpointing the exact locations of cultural points of interest, public transportation availability, and guided tours, along with the opening times of cultural landmarks and current admission fees.

The initiative for this book came from the Editorial Board of the American Bach Society and its general editor at the time, George B. Stauffer, who perceived the need and the desirability for an introduction and a guide to the historic places where Johann Sebastian Bach lived and worked, one tailored to the needs and interests of the English-speaking Bach enthusiast. The purpose would be to identify those places, sketch their history, and recount the roles they played in the composer's life. In introducing them to the international reader—and potential traveler—the book is particularly committed to describing those specific venues where Bach was active: drawing attention to the stylistic hallmarks and cultural significance of those landmarks that have survived, and accounting for those that have not survived.

In carrying out this agenda, we visited all the sites described in this volume. In doing so we were immensely fortunate in receiving advice from a number of highly informed individuals: residents with unique knowledge and intimate familiarity with their towns or institutions, who generously took the trouble to offer us personal, expert, guided tours of the landmarks, imparting invaluable insights and perspectives not readily available (if at all) in conventional published sources—and often enough granting us privileged access to places normally off-limits to the casual visitor.

In this regard we mention, with fond appreciation: Peter Bühner (former mayor, Mühlhausen), Myriam Eichberger (Liszt School of Music, Weimar), Jörg Hansen (director, Bach-Haus, Eisenach), Maria Hübner (Bach-Archiv, Leipzig), Otto Klein (Weißenfels), Elmar and Renate von Kolson (Wechmar), Knut Kreuch (mayor, Gotha), Christian Ratzel (Köthen Kultur und Marketing), Edgar Ring (Museum Lüneburg), Henrike Rucker (director, Heinrich-Schütz-Haus, Weißenfels), Lothar Scholz (pastor, St. Agnus's Church, Köthen), Daniel Senf (pastor, St. Nicholas's Church, Zschortau), Manfred Ständer (administrator, Stadtverwaltung Kultur und Tourismus, Ohrdruf), Ingeborg Streuber (Historisches Museum and Bach-Gedenkstätte Köthen), and Peter Wollny (director, Bach-Archiv, Leipzig).

The authors are also indebted to a number of friends, colleagues, authorities, and specialists who readily responded to their queries or otherwise provided valuable information or material: Gabriele Benning (Hohenlohe-Zentralarchiv, Neuenstein), Wolfgang Brandis (archivist of Lüneburg monasteries, Wienhausen), Lynn Edwards Butler (Vancouver), Jan-Christian Cordes (Stadtarchiv der Stadt Lüneburg), Peter Cramer (director, Schlossmuseum, Ohrdruf), Raymond Erickson (New York), Burkhard Foltz (Hannover), Thomas Fritzsch (Freyburg an der Unstrut), Monika Frohriep (Spenglermuseum, Sangerhausen), Frauke Gränitz (Stadtarchiv Leipzig), Georg Heeg (Köthen), Margit Kaye (map collection, Yale University Library), Erika Krüger, (abbess, Kloster Ebstorf), Robin A. Leaver (Dover, N.H.), Kerala Snyder (New Haven), Eberhard Spree (Leipzig), Thomas Ufert (Leipzig), Helge Wittmann (Stadtarchiv Mühlhausen).

Jörg Hansen, who was uncommonly prompt, patient, and generous in his responses to our repeated requests (not least with reference to historic images in the possession of the Bach-Haus, Eisenach) also took the trouble to comment on the Eisenach chapter of this volume. We also received helpful comments on chapter drafts from Peter Bühner, Mary Oleskiewicz (Boston), Edgar Ring, and Henrike Rucker.

Don O. Franklin (Pittsburgh), Mary Dalton Greer (Cambridge, Mass.), Mark Kroll (Boston) and George B. Stauffer (New Brunswick), admired colleagues and dear friends all, were kind enough to read the entire manuscript and offer important suggestions.

We wish to express our appreciation to the late Martin Petzoldt (Leipzig), eminent Bach scholar, theologian, and longtime chairman of the Neue Bach-Gesellschaft for providing the model and setting the standard for the present work with his exemplary publication, *Bach-Stätten: Ein Reiseführer zu Johann Sebastian Bach.*

Finally, our deep thanks to the American Bach Society and Stephen Crist, its current president; George Stauffer, once again; as well as the current members of the ABS Editorial Board for entrusting us with this project and providing us with the necessary material support to assure its successful completion; and to Laurie C. Matheson, Director of the University of Illinois Press, along with her colleagues Jennifer Clark, Nancy Albright, and Dustin Hubbart, for shepherding the volume into print.

INTRODUCTION

"Bach Country" is mostly defined by the three modern German states Saxony, Saxony-Anhalt, and Thuringia. These states encompass the area in which Bach and the majority of the extended Bach dynasty lived and thrived. The terms *Sachsen*, *Thüringen*, and *Anhalt* were used in Bach's time, but political reality was far more complicated.

States

THURINGIA. The medieval landgraves of Thuringia ruled from a number of highly fortified castles, some of which appear in this book (the Wartburg near Eisenach, the Runneburg in Weißensee, the Neuenburg near Freyburg later used by the dukes of Weißenfels). These were not only military but also cultural centers, serving, for example, as the stage for the medieval minstrels, writers of epics and songs. Sizable towns dating from that period include Mühlhausen, Waltershausen, and Weißensee.

The long-ruling Ludowingian dynasty ended in 1247 with the death of the last landgrave, Heinrich Raspe. Most of Thuringia's holdings were absorbed by the Wettin dynasty, while the western part formed the new realm of the landgraves of Hesse. By 1482 Thuringia as a political entity ceased to exist, but the cultural identity of the region continued to be regarded as "Thuringia."

SAXONY. The heartland of the later duchy of Saxony was the Meissen *March* (*march* or German *Mark* refers to a border region), already important in the twelfth century owing to the rich silver deposits around Freiberg. After the Thuringian War of Succession, 1247–64, Margrave Henry the Illustrious of Meissen (a town located ca. 25 km/15 miles northwest of Dresden) received the major portion of the extinct landgraviate of Thuringia. In 1423, the margraves of Meissen (belonging to the Wettin dynasty) received the duchy of Saxony-Wittenbrg and with it the electorate; that is, they cast one of the seven votes that elected the emperor of the Holy Roman Empire. The Wettins thereupon ruled over an expanse of territories that, taken together,

1. Map of Thuringia, ca. 1680. Different colors represent different principalities; capital "S" designates Saxony (*Sachsen*)—e.g., "S.-Weimar," "S.-Jena." (Names not so marked—e.g., Mühlhausen, Reuß—were not Saxon principalities.) Note: many principalities consisted of noncontiguous holdings.

would encompass the present state of Saxony, most of modern Thuringia, and the southern part of Saxony Anhalt.

As early as 1485, the brothers Ernst and Albrecht (English: Albert) divided the realm ("the Leipzig Partition"). Ernst and his heirs ruled the central area—with Wittenberg as the capital—and held the electoral power. Albrecht received the eastern part, with Dresden as his capital. From then on—until the dissolution of all German kingdoms and duchies in 1918—the basic division into the Ernestine and Albertine lines remained in force. In 1548, however, as a consequence of the Schmalkaldic War—which was a disaster for the Ernestine elector, Johann Friedrich I (r. 1532–47)—the duchy of Saxony-Wittenberg, along with the electorate, were ceded to the Albertine duke Moritz (r. 1547–53) and his heirs.

In the exercise of a politically unfortunate—but culturally highly fruitful tradition—the Ernestine rulers frequently divided their territories among their sons. The practice resulted in the creation of numerous small principalities, often financially hardly viable, but ruled by princes who felt in keen competition to have an appropriate court establishment. Whenever one of those rulers died without a male heir, the principality would be divided among other family members and combined with their holdings. The result was the patchwork map of central Germany and the abundance, to this day, of castles, palaces, hunting lodges, summer palaces, and parks. The practice also led to the creation of numerous musical establishments, as each court vied with the others for talent and prestige. These miniature principalities have been derisively called *Duodezfürstentümer*—best translated, perhaps, as "pocket-size principalities." The many well-known hyphenated names of rulers—for example, Queen Victoria's consort, Duke Albert of Saxe-Coburg-Gotha—reflect this state of affairs. The Albertine line, for its part, had observed the practice of primogeniture. The rule was broken just once: namely, by Johann Georg I (r. 1611–56), whose death resulted in the creation of three "secundogeniture" duchies: Saxony-Weißenfels, Saxony-Merseburg, and Saxony-Zeitz. All played a role in Bach's life.

ANHALT. Owing to its smaller size, Anhalt, a separate principality from Saxony, has played a much smaller historical role. It, too, was divided many times (Anhalt-Köthen, Anhalt-Dessau, Anhalt-Bernburg, and others), but only the court of Köthen played a role in the life of Johann Sebastian Bach. In contrast to staunchly Lutheran Saxony, the religion of Anhalt was Calvinist. Owing to its faith—and to its geographical proximity to Brandenburg—Anhalt maintained good relations with Brandenburg and the Prussian monarchs who were repeatedly at war with Saxony.

Towns

The towns of Bach Country naturally fall into distinct groups according to their history, economy, and the role they played within each principality.

PRINCELY SEATS (RESIDENZSTÄDTE). Princely seats ranged in size from the splendid court of the elector of Saxony in Dresden to the small, village-size princely residence of Ohrdruf. All share one common attribute: the presence of a palace—usually located within the capital (Dresden, Weimar) or at the edge of the town—but even then in easy walking distance (Arnstadt, Weißenfels). Palaces whose origins extend back to the Middle Ages often still preserve older elements; invariably however, they were remodeled, extended, or newly built during the Baroque era. Versailles was the model and even princes with limited resources tried to emulate its splendor—or at least its appearance: plaster or wood painted to simulate marble, while building programs stretched out over many years waiting for the necessary money to become available. In the meantime, within the symmetrical exterior of a large-scale palace, entire wings remained unfinished.

The presence of a ruler meant significant income to these towns, since a lavish court style and entertainments required manpower, materials, and services. In a number of residences (Gotha, Weißenfels), the court chapel was integrated into the palace architecture. In others, the town church also functioned as the court church. In the latter instance, a glass-enclosed, heatable balcony located at the rear or on the side of the chancel was added for the comfort (and exclusive use) of the ruling family. Such arrangements survive in Arnstadt (Bach Church) and in Eisenach (St. George's). A self-respecting prince required within his realm a summer palace as well as one or several hunting lodges, preferably located close to the capital. Wilhelmsthal (near Eisenach), and Ettersburg and Belvedere (both near Weimar) offer examples. Every palace contained a park. Many were extremely elaborate; few have survived. The capitals of undivided principalities often maintained smaller palaces for the rulers' younger brothers or, as in the cases of Arnstadt and Köthen, for a widowed consort. Princes occasionally maintained secondary residences in their realm: Sangerhausen fulfilled that function for the dukes of Weißenfels, Eisenach for the dukes of Weimar.

The populations of princely residences largely depended on the court for their livelihood, since such towns were generally not commercial hubs. The loss or dissolution of a court establishment, accordingly—whether owing to the death of a ruler without male offspring or to the decision to move to another town—meant calamity for the townspeople.

MERCHANT TOWNS. Many north-south and east-west trade routes, some dating back to medieval or even Roman times, traversed Saxony and Thuringia. The major rivers of the region (Oder, Neisse, Elbe, Saale) flow north; east-west routes therefore required crossing points: either ferry services or bridges. Many of these crossing points evolved into commercial hubs (Erfurt, Görlitz, Halle, Dresden, Naumburg). A location on a major route, however, could have disadvantages, as well: during wartimes armies used them, spreading bloodshed, pestilence, plunder, and destruction. A few merchant towns had the status of imperial cities; that is, they were subject not to the local ruler within whose realm they were situated but directly to the emperor. Mühlhausen, Hamburg, and Lübeck enjoyed this status. Major merchant towns jealously defended their independence from their de facto rulers. Leipzig, for example, managed to prevent the Saxon elector from building a residence there, obliging him to rent quarters from a rich merchant whenever he visited.

Town government typically consisted of elected representatives of the property-owning classes (town councilors, *Ratsherren*), who in turn elected a mayor. The town hall (*Rathaus*), usually an impressive building, reflected the citizens' pride and the city's importance. It typically has a tower, from which the town musicians would perform daily at set hours. The town hall is invariably located at the central square (*Marktplatz*), which was the site for regular fairs and markets. Important trading towns also required a weighing station (*Waage*) to calculate customs fees, along with inns to accommodate travelers' needs.

Major towns typically enclosed within their walls one or more monasteries. Erfurt, a bishop's seat with fourteen monasteries, was known as the "Thuringian Rome." Every monastery supported a church and every monastic order had its mission. The Dominicans emphasized preaching; their churches, accordingly, are often called *Predigerkirchen*—literally, preachers' churches (Erfurt, Eisenach, Mühlhausen). The Augustinians were scholars. (Martin Luther was an ordained priest in the Augustine convent in Erfurt and later a professor of theology in Wittenberg.) Mendicant orders—the Franciscans, for example—engaged in charitable work. Their churches are distinguished by the absence of a steeple and bells—visibly attesting to their vows of poverty. Erfurt's Church of the Barefoot Friars (*Barfüsserkirche*) is a representative example. These designations, however, were just popular nicknames; in fact, all churches were named for saints or for the Virgin Mary. Town districts, for their part, maintained their own parish churches for the lay population. Smaller towns supported just one principal church, known simply as the "town church" (*Stadtkirche*).

After the Reformation, existing churches usually retained their original saints' names; newly erected (Protestant) churches were often designated *Trinitatis-* or *Kreuzkirche* (Trinity Church or Church of the Holy Cross) in order to emphasize their dogmatic difference from Catholicism. The new church architecture often followed the precedent established by the court chapel in Torgau—the earliest post-Reformation example—which Luther himself had approved and consecrated. The Torgau chapel served specifically as the model for the Court Chapel (*Hofkapelle*) in Dresden. The new Protestant church is distinguished by the presence on three sides of single, double or even triple balconies; the location of the baptismal font in the chancel in front of the altar (rather than in separate baptisteries); and frequent round or square building shapes that enable all the parishioners to be close to the altar and to the pulpit. Renovations of Gothic church interiors during the Baroque period typically entailed the addition of balconies. To a significant extent, the codification of Protestant church design was the work of the architectural theorist, Leonhard

Christoph Sturm (1669–1719), as set forth in his *Architektonisches Bedencken von der Protestantischen kleinen Kirchen Figur und Einrichtung . . .* (Architectural reflexions about the shape and furnishing of small Protestant churches, Hamburg, 1712). A feature peculiar (and perhaps unique) to church architecture of the Bach region is the occasional vertical "stacking" of altar, pulpit and organ—a visual metaphor for the centrality of the triad consisting of the Eucharist, the word of God, and the praise of God through music. The Gotha court chapel and the town church of Waltershausen exemplify the new design.

The secularization of the monasteries in the wake of the Reformation—in particular, the confiscation of their holdings—enriched the local rulers. Monastery schools were often converted into town schools. The St. George's School in Eisenach

2. Torgau, Court chapel: The model for Protestant church design, consisting of a simple table altar, the organ above it, and double rows of balconies.

and the St. Michael's School in Lüneburg, both of which Bach attended as a boy, as well as the St. Thomas's School in Leipzig had been monastery schools.

VILLAGES. Although Bach never lived in a simple rural village, he visited or performed in several: he was married in Dornheim, conducted organ examinations in Störmthal and Zschortau, and performed compositions of his own in honor of the local lord in Wiederau and Kleinzschocher.

Musical Life

Daily life in Bach Country was permeated by music. Even small village churches boasted church bells, a one-manual organ, and an organist and/or kantor who also served as a teacher. Every school offered singing instruction. Several church services took place each week—services that included organ playing, choir, and congregational singing. Church bells called parishioners to the service, announced special occasions (joyful and sad), and sounded alarms.

Larger towns supported one or more Latin Schools, which trained a boys' choir to perform at weddings and funerals, engage in street singing for alms, sing at private functions (for money), as well as participate in the regular church services. Ensembles of bells of various sizes were rung in different combinations depending on the occasion to communicate specific information. Although many bells were melted down during the course of numerous wars, several ensembles from Bach's time have survived. Recordings of bell ensembles can be heard on internet websites. (The website *Geläute und Glocken aus Thüringen*, accessible via *youtube*, features, among others, bells from Erfurt, Weimar, Altenburg, Waltershausen, and Arnstadt).

Civic occasions, such as the installation of a new town council, or the inauguration of a new lord (whether a local squire or a king), demanded a musical homage. Musical performance, similarly, embellished any ruler's birthday, wedding, or funeral.

The so-called "town pipers" (*Stadtpfeifer*) were accomplished musicians expected to master several instruments, including—despite their title—stringed instruments. They constituted the town's resident small orchestra, performing at civic and church functions, supplying regular tower music from the town hall, and serving as watchmen to call the alarm in the event of fires or the approach of enemies. Musicians learned their trade through an apprentice system. J. S. Bach, like many other members of the Bach family, taught, housed, and fed several apprentices at any given time. The apprentices, in turn, assisted in musical duties, among them copying manuscripts. Unlike "beer-fiddlers" who typically played in taverns or at outdoor fairs and dances, town pipers were respected and privileged tradesmen.

The profession of *kantor* in Lutheran Germany during the eighteenth century was not the same as that denoted by the English *cantor*. Kantors were not primarily singers, nor exclusively choir directors. They were, above all, educators—usually (unlike J. S. Bach) university graduates typically with a degree in theology. Kantors were expected to teach religion and Latin, as well as music, at the Latin School; they typically ranked third in the school hierarchy—below the headmaster (*rector*) and assistant headmaster (*conrector*).

Travel: Routes and Maps

In Bach Country towns were still encircled by medieval walls; gates marked the departure points from which roads led to the next town and beyond. A road and its gate were typically named for the next town (or for a church nearby); many of those historic names are still used. Gates closed at night; anyone seeking admission after hours had to pay a token fee. Written records were kept of any nonresident who passed through a gate; merchants' goods were registered at the gate and then weighed at the weigh station where the customs charges were calculated. Although major streets within a town were paved, beyond the gate they usually became dirt roads. The regions of North and East Germany were notorious for their bad roads.

During the first quarter of the eighteenth century, August the Strong was instrumental in organizing and upgrading the road and postal system of Saxony. Local governing bodies became formally responsible for maintaining local stretches of road. Routes were measured, maps created, and markers installed at one-mile, half-mile, and quarter-mile intervals. The length of the "Saxon" mile (known also as the "German" and "Imperial" mile) was 9,062 meters (ca. 9 km/5.6 miles). Obelisk-shaped

3. Grimma, Distance marker: Crowned with royal emblems and coat of arms.

stone markers located at gates or in the center of town, gave vital travel information according to an ingenious system.

The face of a four-sided signpost lists the numbered post stations and distances—calculated in hours (not miles)—going west from Grimma: the stations of the first route—from "1. Leipzig" to "7. Erfurt"—lasted thirty-five and five-eighths hours and crossed the border after Naumburg from Electoral Saxony (*Kursachsen*) into Saxony-Jena. An alternative northern route (described below the horizontal line) diverged after "1. Leipzig." It passed through "2. Merseburg," and crossed into Hesse. A third alternative, passing through Leipzig to Halle, took fourteen hours. Similar listings on the remaining three sides of the post indicate the routes and destinations going in other compass directions.

The letters *Gr* indicated that a border (*Grenze*) had to be crossed. Every town listed—usually situated two-to-three Saxon miles apart—was a post station with facilities for changing horses and overnight accommodations—the innkeeper often serving as the postmaster. Many inns today are still named *Zur Post* (At the Post Station). A comparison of listed hours and spatial distances reveals that an "hour" was the equivalent of 4.5 km/2.8 miles—essentially what a sturdy walker could accomplish. This, then, was the pace that Bach presumably kept, whether traveling on foot or by post coach. Assuming a steady march of six to six-and-a-half hours a day (plus restorative pauses), the daily distance traveled could hardly have exceeded 30 km/18.6 miles.

Travel and postal service by horse would have been substantially faster than that. There is no indication, however, that Bach ever traveled on horseback. August the Strong established a new, separate, express connection between Dresden and Leipzig—the site of three important annual fairs, which the monarch typically attended. The ambitious project entailed major road improvements such as the construction of three stone bridges designed by the leading Dresden architect Daniel Pöppelmann (1662–1736). All three still survive; the largest—the Grimma bridge—was partially destroyed in the flood of 2002.

In light of the hazards, the necessary investment of time, and the hardships of travel, it is surprising how much and how far Bach traveled. The presumed routes taken by Bach, as proposed in this book, are based on two contemporary road maps. One is the *Postarum seu Veredariorum Stationes per Germaniam et Provincias Adjacentes. Neu vermehrte PostCharte durch gantz Teutschland . . . Verbesserte Auflage* (Post and Express Stations throughout Germany and Neighboring Provinces . . . Improved Edition), first published in Nuremberg in 1709 by Johann Baptist Homann (1664–1724), see frontispiece. (The revised edition was issued before the death of the publisher; later editions appeared under the imprint of Homann's heirs.) The second

4. Grimma, Mulde River: stone bridge with marker. The elaborately sculpted marker pays tribute to the royal sponsor. Intertwined gold letters, "FAR," designate Fridericus Augustus Rex, Saxon elector and king of Poland.

map consulted, the *Neue Chursächsische Post Charte* (New Electoral-Saxon Post Map), by Adam Friedrich Zürner (1679–1742), was first published in 1718.

August the Strong, having seen earlier maps that Zürner had created, appointed him to prepare an accurate map for all the districts of Saxony, based on an ingenious measuring wagon of his invention that recorded distances by clicks on a wheel. Zürner began the work in 1713; he presented the finished map to the king in 1718. In the ensuing years it was revised numerous times and served as the basis for later maps. (The edition at our disposal was published in 1753.) The stone markers and distance columns mentioned above were installed as part of Zürner's comprehensive mapping effort.

Epilogue: Re-creating Bach's Move from Köthen to Leipzig Today

Trying to follow Bach's routes is rarely easy but not impossible. Although many bike and hiking trails, as well as roads, have fanciful historical names (Salt Road, Copper Road, *Via regia*), they are mostly promotional designations; modern autobahns and city expansions have obliterated, straightened, or subsumed most old roads. In attempting, for example, to retrace Bach's move from Köthen to Leipzig (71 km/44 miles, probably a three-day journey), the authors were able to note these way stations (along with others) on the Zürner map: Köthen—Prosigk—Gölzau—Radegast—Zörbig—Landsberg. The "Leipziger Strasse" in Köthen did, indeed, lead to Leipzig; but the historic towns along the route are avoided by new circumventing roads, designed so that through-traffic never touches the town centers. To visit them, the modern traveler must therefore turn off the modern road and head for a town's church tower by whatever road seems to lead there.

Having once arrived in a historic town—especially a small town less touched by development—it is easy to imagine oneself back in Bach's time. One notes the sturdy Romanesque or Gothic stone church surrounded by a cemetery (such cemeteries were abandoned in expanding towns during the eighteenth and nineteenth centuries, replaced by new ones outside the city walls). The main street—often named *Kirchstraße*, *Hauptstraße*, or *Schulstraße*—may (as in Radegast) still be paved with cobblestones. An old inn and a post office may in fact occupy the same locations—and the same buildings—used then. One sees a town hall and a small market square, perhaps (as in Zörbig and Landsberg) adorned with replicas of the historic distance columns. Zörbig still preserves remnants of the old town wall and the "Halle Tower" (*Hallescher Turm*), part of the now-lost gate, from which the road to Halle would have led. According to a local informant, the road, south of Radegast, would pass a stone monument bearing a rhymed inscription thanking "Dear [Duke] Christian" [of Saxony-Merseburg] for having built a dam in 1688 through a once-hazardous swamp.

The landmark could only be found, however, by avoiding the main road at the end of the village and taking a bicycle path instead—one following the historic road that passed over "Dear Christian's" dam. The Bach family, too, after crossing the "border" between Anhalt and Saxony, must have passed by this same point. Beyond Landsberg, the urban sprawl of greater Leipzig had swallowed up whatever historic road may once have passed there.

Literature: Jeschke 2006; Gränitz 2007; Rose 2011.

Website: www.wikipedia.org/wiki/Leipziger_Stadttore (G) provides a richly illustrated description of Leipzig's city gates and their function, history, and architecture.

The website www.mapy.mzk.cz (E, G) gives access to an excellent collection of Central European historic maps, scanned at high resolutions allowing enlargements down to minute details.

NOTES ON USAGE

THE GENEALOGY AND THE OBITUARY. Two indispensable early sources that form the basis for all serious biographical treatments of Johann Sebastian Bach and the Bach family are J. S. Bach's own "Origin of the Musical Bach Family" (*Ursprung der musicalisch-Bachischen Familie*), compiled in 1735, and the obituary for him coauthored by his son Carl Philipp Emanuel and his one-time student Johann Friedrich Agricola, written in 1750 and published in 1754 in Lorenz Mizler's *Musikalische Bibliothek*. They will be cited throughout as "the Genealogy" and "the Obituary," respectively. The original text of the Genealogy appears in *Bach-Dokumente*, Volume 1 (BDOK I), as No. 184; an English translation is published as No. 303 in *The New Bach Reader* (NBR). The original text of the Obituary appears in *Bach-Dokumente*, Volume 3 (BDOK III), as No. 666; the English translation in NBR, as No. 306.

PLACE NAMES IN BOLDFACE. With the exception of the eight principal towns treated in Part One, names of towns mentioned in the course of an entry are printed in boldface type if there is an independent entry for them in this volume.

BIRTH, REIGN, AND DEATH DATES. Birth and death dates are provided in parentheses for every person mentioned in the text after its first appearance in any entry, for example, Georg Böhm (1661–1733). The only exceptions are world-famous figures (Goethe, Napoleon) and instances where the dates would unduly clutter the text (for instance, in connection with the names of organ builders where the dates of instruments are given in the same sentence). The index, however, provides birth and death information, where known, for every person. In the case of rulers, the main text indicates the dates of their reign—Frederick the Great (r. 1740–86)—while the index gives their birth and death dates—Frederick the Great (1712–86).

ORTHOGRAPHY. Three frequently occurring terms are rendered here as *kantor*, *kapelle*, and *kapellmeister*—i.e., with modern German spellings, but lowercase in regular roman type—since they are both exceedingly common in this volume and yet designate functions and institutions unique to the historic context. The common monetary units *groschen*, *gulden*, and *thaler* are handled in the same way. Less common German terms such as *Hausmann, Kurrende, Stadtpfeifer* are capitalized, italicized, and defined. The names of churches, palaces, and other major edifices are given initially in both English and German, thereafter only in English.

WEBSITES. All the websites cited were last accessed on October 7, 2015. The letters G and E after the reference indicate whether the website is in German, English, or in both languages.

Map 1. Bach-related towns in Germany

Legend:
- ■ Towns where J. S. Bach lived
- ▲ Towns certainly visited by Bach
- ● Towns presumably visited by Bach

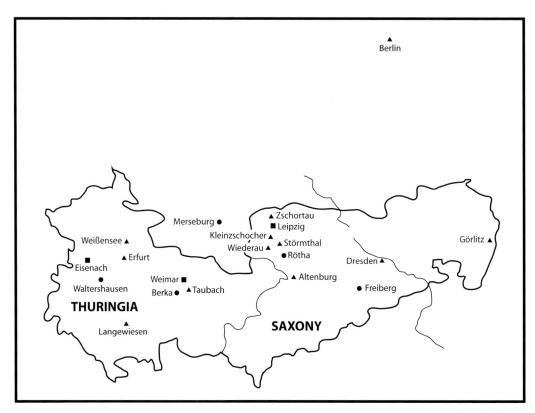

▲ Berlin

▲ Zschortau
Merseburg ● ■ Leipzig
Weißensee ▲ Kleinzschocher ▲
Wiederau ▲ ▲ Störmthal
▲ Erfurt ● Rötha
Eisenach ■ Görlitz ▲
Waltershausen ● Dresden ▲
Weimar ■
Berka ● ▲ Taubach ▲ Altenburg
● Freiberg
THURINGIA
SAXONY
▲ Langewiesen

■ Towns where J. S. Bach lived
▲ Towns certainly visited by Bach
● Towns presumably visited by Bach

Map 2. Detail of Thuringia and Saxony with additional Bach-related towns

EXPLORING THE WORLD OF
J. S. BACH

PART ONE

J. S. BACH'S PRINCIPAL RESIDENCES (CHRONOLOGICAL)

Chapter 1

EISENACH (1685–95)

In October of 1671, Johann Ambrosius Bach (1645–95), a native of **Erfurt** and one of the town musicians there, set out for Eisenach, a town with a population of ca. 6,000, located some 70 km/43 miles to the west. With him were his wife, Maria Elisabeth (née Lämmerhirt, 1644–94—also an Erfurt native) and their infant son, Johann Christoph (1671–1721).

At about the time of Ambrosius's arrival, Eisenach, still recovering from the devastation of the Thirty Years War, was beginning to recover its commercial importance as part of the medieval *via regia*, which, in Germany, led from Aachen in the west via Frankfurt am Main, Eisenach, **Gotha**, and Erfurt to Leipzig and points further east. In the twelfth and thirteenth centuries Eisenach had been the main residence of the Ludowingian landgraves. Beginning in 1263, the Wettin dynasty, whose origins can be traced back to 1030, became the rulers of Thuringia; Saxony was added to their domain in 1423. The landgraviate ended in 1440. Henceforth, Thuringia was no longer an independent political entity but purely a geographical region mainly ruled by Saxony. In 1485, the brothers Ernst (r. 1464–86) and Albert (Albrecht in German, r. 1464–1500) divided their Wettin inheritance, creating the Ernestine and Albertine branches. Eisenach, like most of the region of Thuringia, became part of the Ernestine branch.

Eisenach, along with Weimar and Coburg, was one of the duchies created in 1572 with the further partition of the Ernestine branch. Over the course of the next two centuries the duchies were repeatedly divided and reconfigured in a variety of combinations. In 1672, Johann Georg I (r. 1672–86) became the ruler of the duchy of Saxony-Eisenach. His successors were Johann Georg II (r. 1686–98), Johann Wilhelm III (r. 1698–1729, resident in Jena from 1690), and Wilhelm Heinrich (r. 1729–41). In 1741, with the death of Wilhelm Heinrich, who left no heirs, the duchy of Eisenach was absorbed by Weimar and became part of Saxony-Weimar-Eisenach.

5. Eisenach, Johann Ambrosius Bach: Oil portrait (ca. 1685–90) attributed to Johann David Herlicius (d. 1693), Eisenach court painter. J. S. Bach's father, a town musician, is represented in traditional craftsman's clothing. Visible in the distance: Wartburg Castle.

Johann Ambrosius Bach was a versatile instrumentalist, especially skilled as both a violinist and trumpeter. In Eisenach, he took up simultaneous positions as court trumpeter and *Hausmann*, that is, director of town music. In settling in Eisenach he joined his first cousin, Johann Christoph Bach (1642–1703), who, since 1665, had been organist at the town's principal church, St. George's, as well as organist and harpsichordist in the court kapelle of Duke Johann Georg I of Saxony-Eisenach. Until that time Eisenach had played a relatively minor role in the activities of the musical Bach family, certainly in comparison with the towns of **Wechmar**, **Erfurt**, and Arnstadt.

In 1684, after thirteen years of service to the duke, Ambrosius requested permission to return to Erfurt in order to accept a favorable position there as director of the municipal band. His petition was rejected. Had it been approved, his eighth and last child would, like his parents, have been born and raised in Erfurt. Instead, Johann Sebastian Bach was born in Eisenach on March 21, 1685, in a house almost certainly located on the Fleischgasse (now Lutherstrasse 35, long since replaced by a modern building), which Ambrosius had purchased in 1675 and held until his death. Two days later, the boy was baptized in St. George's Church.

At about the age of five or six, Sebastian began to learn the rudiments: reading, writing, arithmetic, and religion. He may have received this instruction at a "German School"—perhaps one run by a family neighbor in the Fleischgasse, Franz Hering (d. 1708). At all events, Sebastian enrolled in the fifth class (*Quinta*) of St. George's Latin School for the 1692–93 school year, remaining there until the death of his father in February 1695—less than a year after the death of his mother in May 1694—left him an orphan. In the wake of the family's dissolution, Sebastian and his brother, Johann Jacob (1682–1722), were obliged to move to the town of Ohrdruf, located 46 km/28 miles southeast of Eisenach, where they were taken in by their oldest brother, the recently married twenty-four-year-old Johann Christoph, then the organist at St. Michael's Church.

Decades later, in September 1732, Bach may have passed through Eisenach again on his journey from Leipzig to **Kassel** and arranged at that time for the Eisenach cellist and court painter, Antonio Cristofori (1701–37), to execute the portrait of Bach's wife, Anna Magdalena. The oil painting, once in the possession of C. P. E. Bach, is now lost (Maul 2011). No other visits of Bach to Eisenach are documented.

Telemann and Eisenach

From 1708 to 1712, Georg Philipp Telemann (1681–1767) was active in Eisenach as kapellmeister at the court of Johann Wilhelm III. During this period, he composed and performed several cycles of church cantatas on texts of Erdmann Neumeister (1671–1756). J. S. Bach, then residing in Weimar, may have met Telemann through his cousin, Johann Bernhard Bach. In later years, Bach in Leipzig performed a number of church cantatas that Telemann had composed in 1719/20 for the Eisenach court, which by then he was serving as visiting kapellmeister. During the same period (1716–25) Telemann continued to compose serenatas in homage to the duke, works that would have been performed either at Wilhelmsthal or in the Eisenach town palace.

In December 2012, a small stele was erected on the Georg Philipp Telemann Square, just off the market square. It bears an inscription that reads "Here he created the new form of the Protestant church cantata."

Landmarks

Churches

ST. GEORGE'S CHURCH (GEORGENKIRCHE). Eisenach's principal church, which served as both the city and the court church, is named after and dedicated to the town's patron saint. The most prominent features of the church's exterior—the neo-Baroque tower, the facade's decorations and the portal—were added around 1900. A ducal loge, from which court members attended services,

6. Eisenach, St. George's Church: Interior (after the renovation of 2014).

was added in 1717; it is located on the right wall of the chancel. The interior of the three-aisled hall church as it now appears—with three levels of surrounding galleries—mostly dates from the second half of the sixteenth century, after the structure had sustained considerable damage during the Peasants' War (1525). The interior recently (2014) underwent a thorough renovation and now displays a brilliant white and gold color scheme with a salmon-red trim. As part of the renovation, the sarcophagi of the ducal family of Saxony-Eisenach, who were buried in the church's crypt from 1665 to 1741, have been thoroughly restored and are now accessible to the public in a ground-level hall located in the church tower.

The baptismal font at which Johann Sebastian was baptized on March 23, 1685, still survives. It is prominently positioned today at the foot of the altar near the pulpit, the latter dating from 1676.

For well over a century, from 1665 until 1797, beginning with Johann Christoph Bach—the temperamental "uncle" (actually first cousin, once removed) much admired by J. S. Bach and described by him in the Genealogy as "a profound composer"—members of the Bach family held the position of organist at St. George's almost continuously. The organ of St. George's Church, dating from 1696 to 1707, was built by Georg Christoph Stertzing (ca. 1650–1717), following a disposition proposed by Johann Christoph Bach. At the time of its completion, it was the largest organ in Thuringia with four manuals, each with a chromatic range from C to e³, 58 stops, and a fully chromatic pedal board compass from C to e¹. Of Stertzing's instrument, only the original case survives.

Johann Pachelbel (1653–1706) was court organist in Eisenach for one year (1677–78), performing at services both in St. George's Church and in the kapelle. In 1680 he stood godfather to Johann Sebastian's short-lived sister, Johanna Juditha (1680–86). Later that decade, as organist at the Prediger (Preachers) Church in Erfurt, Pachelbel was the teacher of Sebastian's older brother, Johann Christoph.

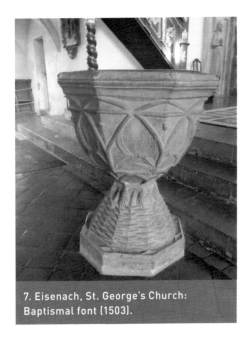

7. Eisenach, St. George's Church: Baptismal font (1503).

A series of thirteenth-century gravestones lining the walls of the chancel bears witness to the early history of Eisenach: the period of the Ludowingian dynasty (ca. 1030–1247) and the landgraviate of Thuringia (1130–1440). The gravestones include images of Ludwig "the Springer" (r. 1056–1123), founder of the dynasty, and of Ludwig IV "the Saint" (*der Heilige*, r. 1217–27), husband of Saint Elisabeth of Thuringia (1207–31). These figures play a role in Wagner's *Tannhäuser*, whose subtitle reads: "The Song Contest on the Wartburg" (*Der Sängerkrieg auf der Wartburg*), referring to the medieval castle above Eisenach.

ST. GEORGE'S LATIN SCHOOL (LATEINSCHULE ST. GEORGEN), DOMINICAN MONASTERY, MARTIN-LUTHER-GYMNASIUM. From 1692 to 1695, Johann Sebastian Bach attended St. George's Latin School. Two centuries earlier, from 1498 to 1501, Martin Luther (1483–1546) had been a student at the same school, although it was located at the time in a different building. By Bach's time, the Latin School had been moved into a former Dominican monastery, dating from 1230; Luther had urged that it be used as a school. Surviving sections of the old monastery building are now integrated into Eisenach's high school

(Martin-Luther-Gymnasium). The monastery church (*Predigerkirche*) currently houses a museum of sacred sculptures collected from Thuringian churches and monasteries.

The school materials used by Bach included the 1,000-page *Eisenachisches Gesangbuch* (Eisenach Hymnbook, 1673), which made available to him early on the texts of the extensive repertoire of Lutheran congregational chorales. Their principal musical source, containing over 300 settings of the chorales, was the *Cantionale Sacrum* (*Gotha Cantional*, 1646–48). As a student, Bach was no doubt a member of the *chorus symphoniacus*, which performed polyphonic music at St. George's under the direction of the kantor, Andreas Christian Dedekind (d. 1706).

CEMETERY. Adjacent to the Dominican monastery and just outside the partially surviving city wall is the former town cemetery, now a park. Bach's parents, as well as other family members, were buried here. Although their graves are lost, a marker in the form of a tombstone commemorates their resting place. The park encloses the Church of the Cross (Kreuzkirche), built in 1693—at just the time that Bach was attending the Latin School. From his vantage point in the school building, he would have witnessed the ongoing construction of the church that was destined to be the venue, shortly after its completion, for the funeral services of both his parents.

JOHANN AMBROSIUS BACH HOUSE. Between 1671 and 1674 Johann Ambrosius and his family lived in a house located at Ritterstraße 11. Known as the Ambrosius-Bach-Haus, it still stands and faces the rear of the stately *Bachhaus*.

BACH MUSEUM (BACHHAUS). Long erroneously considered Bach's birth house, the low-slung yellow house at Frauenplan 21 dates from the mid–fifteenth century. It was selected in 1907 by the New Bach Society (*Neue*

8. Eisenach, Johann Ambrosius Bach house: The residence of J. S. Bach's parents, 1671–74.

9. Eisenach, *Bachhaus*: The mid-fifteenth-century structure is the oldest and largest museum dedicated to J. S. Bach. A modern annex was added in 2007.

Bachgesellschaft) as the first official Bach museum. Decades earlier the town had raised funds—partly through benefit concerts by Franz Liszt, Clara Schumann, Engelbert Humperdinck and others—to erect a statue of Bach. It was unveiled in 1884 at a ceremony that included a complete performance of the B-minor Mass under the direction of Joseph Joachim (1831–1907). The statue, executed by Adolf von Donndorf (1835–1916), stood at the time in front of St. George's. It was moved in 1938 to its current location, to the right of the Bach Museum, as part of a redesign of the area around the museum.

In entering the exhibition area from the visitor lobby, one passes the original entrance door belonging to Bach's Leipzig apartment in the St. Thomas School. It was salvaged when the Thomas School was demolished in 1902. Expert members of the museum staff offer hourly live demonstrations and performances on five different keyboard instruments in the *Instrumentensaal* (instrument room). The upper floor of the original house contains period rooms, original artifacts, and

10. Eisenach, Old mint building: Residence of J. S. Bach's uncle, Johann Christoph Bach (1642–1703), the "profound composer."

instruments organized according to four topics: "A Baroque Life," "Town Musicians," "Wives and Children," "Residential Quarters."

A new wing, inaugurated in 2007—connected to the original building and designed by Berthold Penkhues, a student of the American architect, Frank Gehry—offers conceptual exhibits illustrated with original pictures and documents and touching on such subjects as the changing images of Bach over time, historiography, biography, and performance practice traditions. The museum stages a special exhibition each year, usually accompanied by a scholarly catalog.

JOHANN CHRISTOPH BACH RESIDENCE. A narrow house with a steeply pitched roof, located a few steps beyond the Dominican Monastery Church on the street *An der Münze* (At the Mint), was the domicile of the "profound composer." A plaque on the wall commemorates the former St. George's organist—arguably the Bach family's most talented composer before Johann Sebastian.

MARKET SQUARE: COURT RESIDENCES AND TOWN HALL (RATHAUS). The court where both Johann Christoph and Ambrosius Bach were active was housed in a complex of buildings across from St. George's Church at the south side of the main market square. Some had previously existed as private homes. Two buildings from Bach's time still survive in the square: the so-called *Residenzhaus*, featuring a distinctive round tower, and the *Creuznacher Haus*, named after an early owner. A new palace, the Town Palace (*Stadtschloss*), a typical Baroque, four-wing edifice built in the 1740s (and, like its counterpart, incorporating previously existing buildings), occupies the north side of the market square. It now houses the Eisenach tourist information bureau and the Thuringia Museum.

11. Eisenach, Wartburg Castle: Construction of the historic fortress and margraves' residence began in 1067.

The Town Hall (*Rathaus*), a Renaissance structure dating from the sixteenth century, occupies the east side of the square. From its tower, Ambrosius Bach, in his role as town musician (*Stadtpfeifer*)—in collaboration with his apprentices—played trumpet calls twice a day.

Additional Sites

WARTBURG. Located at the crossroads of important commercial routes, Eisenach required the protection of a fortress—hence the construction, by Ludwig I the Springer, of the Wartburg, the ancestral castle. Building began in 1067. The imposing and iconic structure served as a center of power and culture during the ensuing period of the Thuringian landgraviate. Ludwig's grandson, Ludwig II (r. 1140–72), founded the town of Eisenach and added the Wartburg *Pallas* (royal residence) to the fortress. A gem of late-Romanesque architecture, it functioned as the residence, administrative center, and site of feasts and entertainments. These included recitations by medieval minstrels, among them the most famous minstrel of all: Walther von der Vogelweide (1170–1230).

In 1521/22 Martin Luther, under the name "Junker Jörg," (Squire Jörg) lived in the castle, shielded from the wrath of the emperor and the church by his sovereign, Elector Frederick III the Wise of Saxony (r. 1486–1525). During this time Luther translated the New Testament into German, rendering the foundational text of the Christian faith accessible to laymen and creating the basis for the Lutheran concept of the "general priesthood of all believers." Convinced of the unequaled power of music to inspire religious feeling, Luther insisted that the laity participate in church services by singing congregational hymns (chorales) in their native language. His educational agenda, accordingly, gave music a role second in importance only to theology in the school curriculum. The high level of musical literacy and competence achieved thereby in Thuringia and Saxony undoubtedly provided the basis for the extraordinary flowering of music in the German-speaking world in the following centuries up through Bach's time and beyond—a cultural phenomenon unthinkable without Luther's transformative influence.

MARTIN LUTHER HOUSE. During his years as a student at the Latin School, 1498–1501, the future Reformer lived in the home of the Cotta family. According to a popular anecdote, they had taken the young man in after Ursula Cotta, wife of the prosperous patrician and *Bürgermeister*, Conrad Cotta, had been delighted when she heard the young man singing as a member of the school *Kurrende*, the traditional chorus consisting of indigent boys who made the rounds singing for alms. The spacious half-timbered house, located near the market place, and one of the oldest in Eisenach, is thought to have been their residence.

WILHELMSTHAL PALACE (SCHLOSS WILHELMSTHAL). Located 7 km/4 miles south of Eisenach, the palace was originally a hunting lodge. Later named for Duke Johann Wilhelm III, the architect Johann Mützel (1647–1717) converted the property into a summer residence in the years 1709–15. The cluster of buildings, surrounded by gardens, is notable for its elegant Telemann Hall (1714), one of the oldest surviving freestanding concert halls and currently the venue for occasional concerts.

The Palace ceased to function as a princely residence after Eisenach reverted to Weimar rule in 1741. During Goethe's years of service to the Weimar duke Carl

August (r. 1758–1828), he often accompanied the court on its summer sojourns in Wilhelmsthal. In 1777, however, he preferred to escape the courtly turmoil and withdrew to the nearby Wartburg castle.

———————————————————

Literature: NBR; Keiser 1994; Oefner 1995; Badstübner 2007; Oefner 2008 (?); Wollny 1999; Wolff 2000; Petzoldt 2000; Butler 2008; Maul 2011; Eisenach 2011; Organs; Rathey 2016; Leaver 2016.

Website: www.bachhaus.de (G, E).

12. Ohrdruf, Town view, early nineteenth century: Ehrenstein castle tower (right);
St. Michael's Church (center), rebuilt after the 1808 fire, still lacking its high tower;
St. Trinity's Church (left), outside the town wall.

CHAPTER 2

OHRDRUF (1695–1700)

Sometime after the death of their mother Elisabeth in May 1694 and their father Johann Ambrosius in February 1695, the nine-year-old Sebastian Bach and his thirteen-year-old brother Johann Jacob (1682–1722) left their childhood home in Eisenach and traveled 46 km/28 miles southeast to Ohrdruf, a town with a population at the time of ca. 2,500. They were to live there with their oldest brother, Johann Christoph (1671–1721), organist since 1690 of St. Michael's Church, Ohrdruf's principal church. Christoph had married in October 1694 and had become a father in July 1695, presumably at about the time that his young brothers enrolled as students in the local Latin school.

Johann Jacob returned to Eisenach the following year, where he became an apprentice to Johann Heinrich Halle, his father's successor as director of the town musicians. Sebastian, however, remained in Ohrdruf until March 1700, when he left for Lüneburg "in the absence of free board" (NBR, no. 8). Apparently the financial source for his room and board—a subsidy traditionally paid by the ruling count of Hohenlohe—was no longer forthcoming. Johann Christoph's modest annual salary of some 70 gulden (that is, less than $6,000, plus in-kind payments) was presumably insufficient to provide for Sebastian in addition to Christoph's own family, which by then consisted of his wife and two children—even though it was augmented by Sebastian's earnings as a member of the *chorus musicus*. The so-called street, or *Kurrende*, singing by the chorus could be lucrative: Sebastian may have earned close to 20 thalers ($1,900) per year owing to this activity. The chorus sang in the Sunday and feast day services as well as on special occasions. In addition, at certain times of the year the students sang in the streets, following a prescribed route with no fewer than eighteen stations. The money earned from these activities was distributed among the students.

Ohrdruf, one of the oldest documented settlements in Thuringia, can trace its origins back to 724/25 when St. Boniface (ca. 675–754), the "Apostle of the

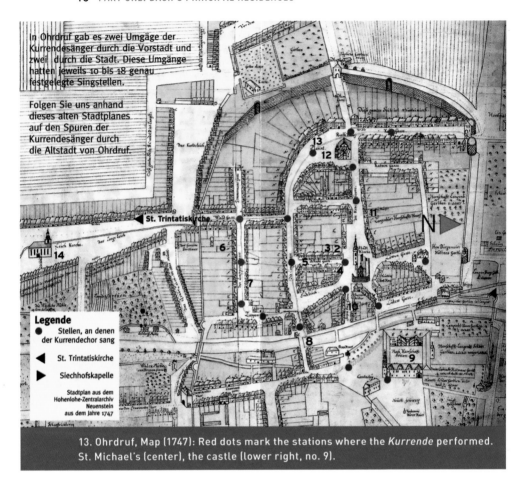

In Ohrdruf gab es zwei Umgäge der Kurrendesänger durch die Vorstadt und zwei durch die Stadt. Diese Umgänge hatten jeweils 10 bis 18 genau festgelegte Singstellen.

Folgen Sie uns anhand dieses alten Stadtplanes auf den Spuren der Kurrendesänger durch die Altstadt von Ohrdruf.

St. Trintatiskirche

N

Legende
- Stellen, an denen der Kurrendechor sang
◄ St. Trintatiskirche
► Siechhofskapelle

Stadtplan aus dem Hohenlohe-Zentralarchiv Neuenstein aus dem Jahre 1747

13. Ohrdruf, Map (1747): Red dots mark the stations where the *Kurrende* performed. St. Michael's (center), the castle (lower right, no. 9).

Germans," founded a Benedictine monastery there as part of an effort to Christianize the Saxon population and incorporate it into the Frankish empire. The monastery chapel, St. Michael's, was the precursor to St. Michael's Church. The original monastery school, similarly, was the precursor to the *Lyceum illustre Ordruviense*—the Latin school founded in 1560 by Georg II, count of Gleichen, and attended 135 years later by Johann Sebastian Bach.

By the time Sebastian had left the school in 1700 it had largely recovered the fine reputation it had lost earlier owing to the scandalous behavior of one of the teachers, Johann Heinrich Arnold (1653–98), kantor of St. Michael's. In

1697, Arnold was dismissed and replaced with Elias Herda (1674–1728), who several years earlier had been a pupil at the Lüneburg St. Michael's School and may have helped pave the way for Sebastian to transfer there. At all events, Sebastian acquired a solid foundation in vocal music, theology, Latin, arithmetic, geography, and science during his years at the lyceum. He was consistently among the youngest and top-ranked students in his classes.

Johann Christoph Bach, for his part, had no formal academic education. In 1685, at the age of fourteen, he began a three-year apprenticeship with Johann Pachelbel (1653–1706), then organist at the Dominican Preachers' Church (*Predigerkirche*) in **Erfurt**. Pachelbel, a native of Nuremberg, passed on to his student the Central German organ tradition, of which he was the leading representative. In 1690, Johann Christoph accepted the appointment as organist at St. Michael's in Ohrdruf and remained there for the rest of his life. Two of his sons succeeded him in the position after his death in 1721: Johann Bernhard (1700–43), and, after him, Johann Andreas (1713–79).

In Ohrdruf, Sebastian no doubt expanded the knowledge of organ building and maintenance he had acquired in Eisenach. The organ of St. Michael's underwent prolonged repairs during his stay. Even more significantly, according to the Obituary, Sebastian "laid the foundations for his playing of the clavier under the guidance of his eldest brother, Johann Christoph" (NBR, no. 306). The Obituary, whose principal author was C. P. E. Bach, also relates the famous anecdote that Sebastian had surreptitiously copied out, by moonlight, "a book of clavier pieces by the most famous masters of the day—Froberger, Kerl [*sic*], Pachelbel"—that his brother, "for who knows what reason . . . [had] denied him" and locked behind the grillwork door of a music cabinet. The tale is almost certainly an elaborate exaggeration—one perhaps perpetrated by J. S. Bach himself—of some underlying incident. It is a variant of a common legend found in the biographies of other musicians of the time, notably those of Telemann and Handel: "the tales of young musicians who circumvented family opposition by studying secretly at night" (Rose 2011, 210). Sebastian may have wished "his children to know and understand how he had heroically overcome all obstacles set in his path" (Gardiner, 79). In any event, the relationship between the brothers must have been reasonably friendly in later years. In early September 1713, Bach presumably returned to Ohrdruf from Weimar in order to serve as godfather for his namesake, Johann Christoph's short-lived son, Johann Sebastian Jr. (The infant died after just two months.) Moreover, Bach taught (and no doubt housed) two of his older brother's sons: Johann Bernhard was his pupil in Weimar and Köthen from 1715 to 1719; Johann Heinrich (1707–83) served as one of Sebastian's principal copyists in Leipzig for almost three years (1724–27).

The veracity of the "moonlight" story is cast into further doubt by the discovery in 2005, in the Weimar Duchess Anna Amalia Library, of the earliest known document in Bach's hand: a copy, written in tablature notation, of Dietrich Buxtehude's demanding chorale fantasy, *Nun freut euch, lieben Christen g'mein* (BuxWV 210). The manuscript dates from Sebastian's Ohrdruf period and attests above all to his early familiarity with and perhaps ability to play, before the age of fifteen, a challenging example of the virtuosic North German organ style. Whether the manuscript was written out with the approval of his brother or clandestinely, its existence may be evidence of Sebastian's determination to complete his schooling not in Ohrdruf but in Lüneburg, where not only a stipend awaited him but also the presence of the great organist Georg Böhm (1661–1733).

Of even greater historical, if not biographical, importance than the recently discovered tablature manuscript are two musical anthologies consisting mostly of organ and keyboard compositions by North German composers, including unique copies of works by Böhm, Buxtehude, Reinken, and others. The volumes are known as the "Möller Manuscript" and the "Andreas Bach Book"—the names of previous owners (the latter Johann Christoph's youngest son). Johann Christoph was the principal scribe of both collections, compiling them over the course of a decade beginning ca. 1703. In many instances, he presumably copied sources provided to him by Johann Sebastian, who may well have brought many of them back from his 1705/6 sojourn in Lübeck. The manuscripts contain over one hundred compositions, including twenty-eight by J. S. Bach, among them the earliest autograph scores of his own works.

LANDMARKS

Churches

ST. MICHAEL'S CHURCH (MICHAELISKIRCHE). The town of Ohrdruf experienced devastating fires in 1753 and again in 1808, followed by heavy bombing during World War II that left almost no buildings from Bach's time standing. Of St. Michael's Church only the tower survives. Its lower sections are part of the original fifteenth-century church; a small chapel currently houses an exhibit; the church library occupies the space above it.

The shape of the church destroyed in the war is depicted in an outline drawn in the pavement around the tower. Bach, however, would not have recognized that silhouette—a Baroque building erected 1754–60 after the fire of 1753 (and rebuilt again after the fire of 1808). The church he knew was a small Gothic hall church with a pointed steeple. A Bach memorial sculpture located in front of the tower represents the church tower, organ pipes, and cabinet lattice door through which

Bach allegedly retrieved forbidden manuscripts. The abstract metal sculpture, unveiled in 1999, bears an inscription consisting of Beethoven's famous tribute: "Nicht Bach, Meer sollte er heissen" ("Not brook, ocean should be his name"—a pun on the name Bach, which in German means brook).

TRINITY CHURCH (TRINITATISKIRCHE). The town's second church, the Trinity Church, which stood outside the city walls, was largely spared from the town's fires. Johann Christoph Bach played at the consecration of this church—a Baroque hall church built 1709–14, that is, after Sebastian had left Ohrdruf. Recently restored, it now regularly hosts concerts, including the biennial *Ohrdrufer Bachtage* (Ohrdruf Bach Days).

EHRENSTEIN PALACE (SCHLOSS EHRENSTEIN). The only surviving building in Ohrdruf that can be linked—if only indirectly—to Bach is the Ehrenstein Palace, a four-wing castle located across the Ohra river, just steps from the town center. Built in 1550–75 on old foundations and expanded in 1610–16, the Renaissance structure was the residence of the counts of Gleichen until 1631, when the county fell to the Hohenlohe dynasty. On July 30, 1699, a ceremony was held there to honor the memory of the recently deceased Count Heinrich Friedrich von Hohenlohe (1625–99). Twelve street singers (*Kurrende*)—Sebastian Bach no doubt among them—dressed in black, arrived at the castle with their preceptors; they performed two pieces of music, and sang a hymn. After a formal procession to St. Michael's Church, they sang additional chorales before and after the funeral sermon, which was delivered by Superintendent Johann Abraham Kromayer (1665–1733). After the solemnities, bread was distributed in the castle to the poor: among them, most likely, the *Kurrende* singers. (Kromayer's printed sermon still survives, as do two annual cycles of liturgical sermons, in manuscript, preserved in the St. Michael's church library. They may well be the only extant contemporary sermons Bach is certain to have heard preached by their authors (Marshall and Marshall 2015).

Although the castle was never the main residence of the Hohenlohes, they used it occasionally, and in 1760 they rebuilt parts of it in Baroque style. After decades of neglect, renovations that had begun in 1971 were about to undergo final inspection when, in November 2013, a fire destroyed the entire roof construction of two wings. Among the parts destroyed or damaged were museum rooms housing a unique collection of rocking horses and dolls—many items were completely lost. (In the early twentieth century Ohrdruf had been a leading center for the production of children's toys.) The museum also displayed detailed wooden models of historic buildings, including the three incarnations of St. Michael's Church. Fortunately, these and other Bach-related items were saved—among them the original class lists containing valuable information about Bach as a young student.

14. Ohrdruf, Ehrenstein Castle: central court.

CEMETERY. Since singing at funerals was part of Bach's obligations, he would have visited the Ohrdruf cemetery. Now a park, it was the resting place of all the Ohrdruf Bachs, the last buried in 1859. A memorial in tribute to them, crafted from a surviving funerary monument and standing near the park entrance, was dedicated in 2013.

Additional Sites

None of Ohrdruf's school buildings, the kantor's residence, or the town hall have survived as they were known to Bach. A house on the Johann-Sebastian-Bach-Strasse (formerly Schulgasse) bears an old plaque erroneously claiming that Johann Christoph Bach's residence had stood on that spot. In fact, his residence was located in the Lappengasse, now Vollrathstrasse, at No. 5. The current house occupying that location bears a corrected plaque.

During World War II a concentration camp—a satellite of Buchenwald—was located just outside Ohrdruf. On April 4, 1945, it was the first such facility liberated by the allied armies. Eight days later, on April 12, 1945, Generals Omar Bradley, George S. Patton, and Dwight D. Eisenhower visited the infamous place.

Literature: NBR; Löffler 1949/50; Schulze 1979; Schulze 1984b; BuxWV; Schulze 1985; Hill 1987; Petzoldt 2000; Wolff 2000; Ständer and Marschik 2000; Maul-Wollny 2007; Rose 2011; Gardiner 2013; Wolff GMO, accessed November 15, 2014; Marshall 2015.

CHAPTER 3

LÜNEBURG (1700–1702)

In the spring of 1700, at about the time of his fifteenth birthday, Bach set out with his schoolmate Georg Erdmann (ca. 1682–1736) from Ohrdruf in Thuringia to Lüneburg in Lower Saxony, a trek of ca. 375 km/233 miles. Bach had been living in the house of his oldest brother Johann Christoph. Now both he and Erdmann had received stipends allowing them to enroll as scholarship students at the Latin School of St. Michael's Monastery. The two teenagers may have passed through **Gotha** and Mühlhausen—towns that would play a role in Bach's future—and then to Duderstadt, Seesen, Goslar, Wolfenbüttel, Brunswick, **Celle**, and finally, Lüneburg. (Alternative routes are also possible.)

Lüneburg, part of the duchy of Brunswick (Braunschweig)-Lüneburg in Lower Saxony and historically an affluent Hansa city, derived its wealth during the Middle Ages in great part from producing salt, an indispensable commodity, obtained by means of solution mining. At the time of Bach's arrival, Lüneburg had a population of about 9,500; that is, it was considerably larger than Eisenach (ca. 6,000)—not to mention Ohrdruf (ca. 2,500), the towns that the young Bach would have known best. The residence of Duke Georg Wilhelm of Brunswick-Lüneburg-Celle (r. 1655–1705) was located not in Lüneburg but in Celle, some 85 km/53 miles to the south.

It is not known whether the two youngsters made the journey from Ohrdruf on foot, as Bach would do so proudly five years later on his pilgrimage from Arnstadt to Lübeck (an even longer journey). Nor is it known precisely when or why Bach returned to his native Thuringia in 1702. In response to a question put to him by the biographer, J. N. Forkel, C. P. E. Bach wrote, "I do not know what took him from Lüneburg to Weimar" (NBR, no. 395). Since Bach auditioned for the organist position at St. James's Church (*Jakobikirche*) in **Sangerhausen** in the latter half of 1702, he had evidently returned to his native orbit by then. Sometime after mid-December he began his service as a court musician in Weimar. His whereabouts in the surrounding time period are unknown.

Only one official document referring to Bach survives from his time in Lüneburg. Written by August Braun (d. 1713), kantor of St. Michael's Church, it records two payments to Bach of twelve groschen (ca. $48) each for the period from April 3 to May 29, 1700, for his participation in the activities in the *Mettenchor* (matins choir). This included singing the *Kurrende*, that is, making the rounds of the town along a specified route, singing for alms. His friend Erdmann received the same payment.

The long-standing assumption that Bach and Erdmann had been recommended for the Lüneburg scholarships by their Ohrdruf mentor Elias Herda (1674–1728), a fellow Thuringian who had himself been a pupil at the St. Michael's

15. Lüneburg, St. Michael's Church: Woodcut (1882) by Friedrich Kallmorgen, including the adjacent building of the former *Ritterakademie*.

School, has recently been called into question (Maul-Wollny 2007). At all events, in Bach's time there were actually two schools connected to St. Michael's Monastery, which was part of a former Benedictine monastery adjacent to the church. The monastery, first mentioned in 956 and occupying this location since the fourteenth century, was located to the north of the church; it was transformed into a Latin school after the Reformation. In 1656, it became a *Ritterakademie*, a residential school for sons of the aristocracy. The neighboring *Partikularschule*, on the southeast side, was a nonresidential school for commoners like Bach and Erdmann. Its students were obliged to find private accommodations in the town. It was demolished in 1782.

Although the living arrangements and instruction were separate, the students of both institutions shared the same faculty, classrooms, and a curriculum that consisted of religion, Latin, Greek, arithmetic, logic, and rhetoric. Bach would have learned Latin from the works of Virgil, Cicero, and Horace, and Greek from the New Testament. He may also have acquired some French from the resident aristocratic students at the *Ritterakademie*, where French was the official language. The elite academy's curriculum also included the natural sciences, dancing, riding, and fencing.

No doubt one of the school's greatest attractions for Bach was its extraordinary library of choral music. Consisting of over 1,100 works, it contained compositions by seventeenth-century German and Italian composers, including Monteverdi (1567–1643), Carissimi (1605–74), the Thomaskantors Sebastian Knüpfer (1633–76) and Johann Schelle (1648–1701), and, most notably, Heinrich Schütz (1585–1672). To the extent that these works were part of the active performing repertory of the church choir, Bach would have heard and performed the pieces here for the first time. Bach's activities in the main chorus, the *chorus symphoniacus*, began as a singer. But "some time thereafter," according to the Obituary, "as he was singing in the choir, . . . there was once heard, with the soprano tone that he had to execute, the lower octave of the same. He kept this quite new species of voice for eight days. . . . Thereupon he lost his soprano tones and with them his fine voice" (NBR, 299–300). He may have participated in the church services thereafter as an instrumentalist playing the violin or the organ or both.

Among the most important influences on Bach's musical development during the Lüneburg years was unquestionably his contact with Georg Böhm (1661–1733), organist at St. John's Church (*Johanniskirche*) and a leading composer of the North German school. The long-standing assumption that Bach must have been a pupil of Böhm's is now a certainty, thanks to the recent discovery of a manuscript in Bach's hand of the Fantasia on *An Wasserflüssen Babylon*, the largest, most demanding, and most famous work of Johann Adam Reinken (1623–1722), the Hamburg master. Bach's notation at the end of the manuscript reads: "Copied in the home of Georg Böhm in 1700 in Lüneburg." One plausible interpretation of this comment is that Bach was both living with and taking lessons from Böhm, perhaps from the time of his arrival in the city.

A fellow Thuringian who had grown up near Ohrdruf, Böhm presumably had numerous personal and musical connections with members of the musical Bach family and may have been aware in advance of Sebastian's coming to Lüneburg. In a letter of January 1775 to Forkel responding to a query regarding early influences on his father, C. P. E. Bach mentioned that his father had, among others, "loved and studied . . . the Lüneburg organist Böhm" (NBR, no. 395). (Before the last three words Philipp Emanuel had originally written "his teacher Böhm" but immediately crossed it out.) Although there is no compelling evidence that any of Bach's surviving works were composed during his Lüneburg years, the stylistic influence of Böhm's harpsichord suites and chorale partitas for organ can be observed in Bach's works in these genres apparently dating from his Arnstadt, Mühlhausen, and early Weimar periods.

The French style is strongly discernible in many of Böhm's compositions (along with Central and North German elements). It was popular in the duchy of Brunswick-Lüneburg, largely owing to the taste of Eleonore d'Olbreuse (1639–1722), the Huguenot mistress and later wife of Duke Georg Wilhelm. After the edict of 1684, welcoming émigré French Huguenots to the duchy, the court became a veritable French colony. The ducal couple maintained a French kapelle at Celle, their principal residence, and one of the court musicians, Thomas de la Selle, was also a dance master at the *Ritterakademie*. The Obituary reports that during the Lüneburg period Bach "had the opportunity to go and listen several times to a then famous band kept by the Duke of Celle, consisting for the most part of Frenchmen," and that he thus "acquired a thorough grounding in the French taste" (NBR, no. 300). Although the implication that Bach traveled to Celle has been challenged, its plausibility is supported by the fact that the then-octogenarian duke and his kapelle evidently never visited Lüneburg during Bach's years there. Moreover, during solemn official visits to Lüneburg such as the *Erbhuldigungen* (that is, formal reciprocal affirmations of loyalty) of 1666 and 1706, the musical entertainment was provided not by the court kapelle but by the host city. On these occasions Lüneburg took the opportunity to display its own musical resources such as the school choirs and town musicians. It would seem, then, that to hear the court kapelle,

Bach must have traveled to Celle, presumably in the company of Thomas de la Selle. An alternative scenario is explored in the entry for Celle in this volume.

The Obituary also reports that "from Lüneburg [Bach] journeyed now and again [NB] to Hamburg, to hear . . . Johann Adam Reinken." These much shorter trips (56 km/35 miles), presumably undertaken on foot, provided Bach with the opportunity to hear the great organs of the Hamburg churches and above all to observe and perhaps meet the venerable Reinken, who had been organist of the Church of St. Catherine's (*Katharinenkirche*) since 1663. Reinken's influence on Bach's early style was at least as significant as Böhm's.

LANDMARKS

The historic core of Lüneburg appears much the same today as it did in Bach's time. Largely untouched by World War II, the old town suffered few fires over its history owing to its mostly brick architecture. During the Middle Ages, the city was a major producer and exporter of salt, which was essential for the preservation of fish caught in the Baltic and North Seas. It shipped the product either from its harbor on the Ilmenau and via the Elbe River to Hamburg or via a canal built in the fourteenth century to Lübeck and the Baltic. Full-size replicas of historical ships and a crane from 1797 are on display in the harbor area.

TOWN HALL (RATHAUS). The Main Square (*Marktplatz*) is dominated by the Baroque facade of the town hall, which consists of a complex of large buildings dating back to the medieval and Renaissance eras. A number of magnificent historic rooms are housed within: the Judgment Hall (*Gerichtslaube*), with fourteenth- and fifteenth-century floors, painted ceilings and walls, and glass windows; the Princes' Hall (*Fürstensaal*), adorned with late medieval paintings of Lüneburg princes; and the Council Chamber (*Ratsstube*), outfitted with wood panels and carvings. All attest to the wealth, confidence, and civic pride of old Lüneburg.

ST. JOHN'S CHURCH (JOHANNISKIRCHE). Böhm's church is an excellent example of the North German "brick Gothic" style. It was built over the course of two centuries in two main stages: 1289–1370 and 1460–70. In contrast to the traditional French Gothic basilica form characterized by a high central aisle, St. John's displays the typical German design of the hall church: its three aisles and two additional rows of side chapels are all approximately equal in height. Although the interior was completely renovated in the nineteenth century, a number of significant early artworks are housed in it: a late Gothic carved altar; a sixteenth-century baptismal font; and above all, the main altar, a large-scale fifteenth-century, two-sided carved triptych with 47 elements depicting the stations of the cross, the crucifixion, saints, prophets, apostles, and an unusual series devoted exclusively to female figures.

The organ of St. John's, originally built by the Dutch masters Hendrich Niehoff and Jasper Johansen in 1551–53 and enlarged by Friedrich Stellwagen in 1651–52, was a three-manual instrument with forty stops at the time of Bach's sojourn. The lack of an independent pedal division (a feature typical of Dutch organs) was rectified at Böhm's request by Mathias Dropa only in the years 1712–15, that is, after Bach's departure.

16. Lüneburg, Georg Böhm house: On Papenstraße 13, a narrow medieval lane of modest dwellings. The St. John's Church organist is identified on the attached plaque as a Bach precursor.

On a side street near the church a row house, Papenstrasse 13, bears a plaque designating it as the place where Georg Böhm died (1733). Contemporary documents indicate that from 1699 to 1711 Böhm lived near St. Michael's Monastery, at Neue Sülze 8. It is here that Bach may well have lived for a time.

ST. MICHAEL'S CHURCH (MICHAELISKIRCHE). The three-aisle brick Gothic hall church dates from 1376 to 1418, replacing the original tenth-century Benedictine church and monastery that had been destroyed in a recent uprising. The tower, which assumed its present form in 1750, houses the oldest chimes in Germany, originally made ca. 1491. An oil painting of the church interior by Joachim Burmester, ca. 1700, includes a depiction of the three-manual organ originally built in the sixteenth century by Jacob Scherer and his son Hans. As a member of the matins choir, Bach may have played the church's

17. Lüneburg, St. Michael's Church: Interior, depicted by Joachim Burmester (ca. 1700). Many artworks shown were removed in the late eighteenth century.

second organ, a positive originally built in 1662 and enlarged in 1701 by Johann Balthasar Held, an apprentice of Arp Schnitger and a Lüneburg native. The church's large modern organ, dating from 1931, retains the case of the organ built in 1708 by Matthias Dropa, another Arp Schnitger student.

ST. NICHOLAS'S CHURCH (NIKOLAIKIRCHE). Lüneburg's third Gothic church served the harbor district. It is a narrow basilica, with a central nave four times as high as it is wide, culminating in a rare eight-point star vaulting. The church's altar was inherited from the Church of St. Lambert, which was demolished in the nineteenth century after the depletion of the salt deposits beneath it caused the ground to collapse.

Literature: Homann; NBR; Reinecke 1907; Fock 1950; Walter 1967; Petzoldt 1985; Wolff 1986a; Zehnder 1988; Zehnder 1995; Petzoldt 2000; Wolff 2000; Maul-Wollny 2007; Organs; Yearsley 2012.

Websites: www.lueneburg-erleben.de (G, E; panoramic videos of all major sights). www.youtube.com/watch?v=BkNeqoTogh8 (six-bell set of St. John's).

CHAPTER 4

ARNSTADT (1703–7)

No town celebrates its status as a Bach site more enthusiastically than Arnstadt. The name of the church where the composer served as organist for four years was officially changed in 1935 to *Bachkirche* (Bach Church). The town hosts an annual Bach festival; a statue of the young Bach stands in the town square opposite the town hall; Arnstadt has not one but two Bach museums; commemorative plaques (occasionally of questionable accuracy) are affixed to several buildings suggesting that they played a noteworthy role in the life of the composer.

Contexts

On August 9, 1703, at the age of eighteen, Bach became the organist of the New Church (*Neue Kirche*) in Arnstadt where he would remain for just under four years. This was Bach's first substantial paid position. His previous and very first job, as a low-rank servant ("the lackey Baach" [*sic*]) at the Weimar court, had lasted barely six months. About a month earlier, by July 13th, he had tested and inaugurated the New Church's new organ built by Johann Friedrich Wender (1655–1729) of Mühlhausen, one of Thuringia's leading builders. The instrument, under construction since 1699, had just been completed—two years late. Bach's examination (carried out singlehandedly, not as part of a committee) marked the beginning of his long friendship with Wender. The Weimar court organist, Johann Effler (d. 1711), may have recommended his young colleague for the assignment, or Bach may have been acting as a last-minute substitute for Effler. This circumstance might explain why he was presciently described in the pertinent Arnstadt document as "Court Organist to the Prince of Saxony-Weimar." Bach would only assume this position five years hence, when, in 1708, he in fact became Effler's successor (Wollny 2005). Bach was offered the organist position at the New Church with no further audition, even though a local candidate, Andreas Börner, had applied for it as well. Börner, however, was appointed organist of Arnstadt's Our Lady's Church (Liebfrauenkirche) on the same day.

The Wender organ was presumably one of the attractions that Arnstadt held for Bach. Another may have been the town's growing importance as a cultural and musical center. Possibly the oldest town in Thuringia (its existence mentioned in 704), it was, at the time of Bach's employment, a prosperous town of 3,800 to 4,000 residents. In 1681, Arnstadt came under the rule of Count Anton Günther II of Schwarzburg-Sondershausen at Arnstadt (r. 1697–1716), a result of a division of the territory between two brothers.

In 1683, the count, together with his wife, Auguste Dorothea of Brunswick-Wolfenbüttel, took up residence in Neideck Castle, where they amassed important collections of paintings, coins, and books, and recruited notable artists and literary figures to the court. Among the latter was the poet Salomo Franck (1659–1725), who would be Bach's colleague in Weimar and one of his principal librettists. From 1683 to 1701, the court kapelle, consisting of twenty-two musicians, was under the leadership of Adam Drese (1620–1701), who had previously served in that capacity in Weimar. (His successor as Weimar kapellmeister was his cousin, Johann Samuel Drese (1644–1716), under whom Johann Sebastian Bach would serve as concertmaster.)

In addition to Weimar, Arnstadt maintained close relations with the musical establishments at Köthen and Leipzig, as well as **Celle**, **Gotha**, and **Halle**—all of which played larger or smaller roles in Bach's future career.

Political relations, however, between Weimar and Arnstadt were often tense in the early years of the eighteenth century, evidently a consequence of Emperor Joseph I having bestowed upon Count Anton Günther and his brother, in 1697, the title of "Princes of the Holy Roman Empire." In 1705, and again in 1711, in fact, the Weimar dukes sent forces to occupy Arnstadt.

Arnstadt Bach Dynasty

Bach was no doubt drawn to Arnstadt as well by the strong relationship that had prevailed for generations between the town and the musical Bach family. Arnstadt is located at the center of Thuringia and at the heart of Bach Country. By the time of Sebastian's arrival the association of the Bach name with the musical profession in Arnstadt was so strong that it was virtually a synonym there for the word *musician*. That is a reasonable inference, at all events, from a petition written in the name of Bach's stepmother a month after the death of his father, Johann Ambrosius, in 1695. The widow, in requesting a pension from the Eisenach town fathers, related that after the death of her brother-in-law, Johann Christoph Bach (1645–93, Ambrosius's twin brother) in Arnstadt two years earlier, "the Noble

18. Arnstadt, Neideck Castle Tower: The castle's only surviving remnant. A corner of the consistory building is visible at right.

Count and Lord of that place" wondered "in these words: whether there was not another Bach available . . . for he should and must have a Bach again" (NBR, no. 7). That "noble count" was Anton Günther II.

The family presence in Arnstadt began with Caspar Bach (ca. 1575–after 1640)—a bassoonist and watchman in Arnstadt from 1620 to 1633. The Arnstadt Bach dynasty took root, however, only about a half-century before Sebastian's appointment in 1703, with the arrival of the brothers Christoph (1613–61) and Heinrich Bach (1615–92). Both brothers remained there for the rest of their lives. Christoph Bach (Johann Sebastian's grandfather) served as a court and town musician from 1654; Heinrich was town musician and organist at Arnstadt's

19. Arnstadt, Neideck Castle: Watchman's apartment, presumably the residence of J. S. Bach's ancestor Caspar Bach.

two main churches (the Upper and Lower Churches) for over fifty years, beginning in 1641. (See Figure 1.)

Of Christoph Bach's three musical sons, two were associated with Arnstadt: Johann Ambrosius (1645–95)—Sebastian's father—was a *Stadtpfeifer* there until 1667; his identical twin brother, Johann Christoph, a violinist, was a court and town musician in Arnstadt from 1671 until his death.

Heinrich Bach had three sons as well, all with Arnstadt connections. Johann Christoph Bach (1642–1703), described by J. S. Bach in the family Genealogy as a "profound composer" (*profonder Componist*), was organist at the Arnstadt court chapel for two years (1663–65) before leaving for Eisenach. Johann Michael (1648–94) succeeded him at the chapel, remaining there until 1673 when he became town organist in **Gehren**. J. S. Bach described him in the Genealogy as "like his brother an able composer" (*gleich seinem ältern Bruder, ein habiler Componist*). Heinrich's third son, Johann Günther (1653–83), an instrument maker, spent his entire brief life in Arnstadt, serving from 1682 as assistant organist to his father.

From Sebastian Bach's own generation, his older brother, Johann Christoph (1671–1721), with whom he lived for five years after the death of their parents, had briefly substituted for their old and ailing great uncle Heinrich in Arnstadt in 1689–90 before moving to Ohrdruf in 1690.

The extensive family network in Arnstadt included other notable individuals as well. Ambrosius Bach's second wife, Barbara Margaretha, née Keul (b. 1648), was the daughter of an Arnstadt mayor. Another Arnstadt mayor, Martin Feldhaus (1634–1720), a supporter of Johann Sebastian's, was married to a sister of Johann Michael Bach and was godfather to Sebastian's future wife (Michael's daughter), Maria Barbara (1684–1720).

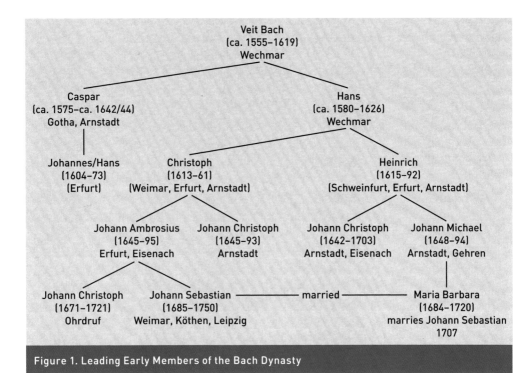

Figure 1. Leading Early Members of the Bach Dynasty

Finally, in light of this legacy, it is not surprising that the so-called Old Bach Archive (*Alt-Bachisches Archiv*), a collection of twenty vocal works composed by early members of the Bach family, originated in Arnstadt (Wollny 1998).

J. S. Bach in Arnstadt

Bach's official duties, along with looking after the upkeep of the organ, apparently consisted only of accompanying hymns and otherwise providing liturgical organ music for four services: the Sunday and Thursday sermons, the Monday prayer sessions, and the Wednesday vespers—a total of less than six hours a week. In light of this undemanding schedule, his salary was quite generous: 50 gulden (ca. $4,200) plus an additional 30 thalers (ca. $3,000) for room and board. Although there were apparently plans to institute concerted church music at the New Church at the time of Bach's appointment, those plans did not materialize.

Whatever formal teaching or training responsibilities Bach may have had with regard to students do not seem to have been made explicit.

Bach's employment in Arnstadt had begun auspiciously with his immediate appointment after the organ examination. His tenure thereafter, however, was troubled by a series of unpleasant incidents as well as stern reprimands from the church consistory. The first, an altercation with the student Johann Heinrich Geyersbach (b. ca. 1682), occurred on the night of August 4, 1705, when Bach, "as he walked home from the castle," was waylaid by Geyersbach and his fellow students at the "long stone," a bench, in the town square (BDOK II, no. 14; NBR, p. 44). Weapons were brandished, obscene insults were hurled, a hearing was held, no action was taken. The fact that Bach was coming from the castle suggests that he would have participated in court music-making there, even though that was not part of his official responsibilities.

Less than a half-year later, on February 21, 1706, Bach was reprimanded by the consistory for a long list of infractions, among them having overstayed a four-week leave of absence he had been granted so that he could travel to hear Dieterich Buxtehude in Lübeck "in order to comprehend one thing and another about his art." Bach stayed away for some sixteen weeks, from October through early February. At the same proceeding he was criticized for harmonizing the congregational chorales with "curious *variations*" and "strange tones" that "confused" the congregation; he was also taken to task for his inability to get along with the students and for not providing any concerted music, an obligation Bach did not think was his (BDOK II, no. 16; NBR, p. 46). On November 11, 1706, he was rebuked again: this time once more for his hostile relationship with the students but also for having allowed an "unfamiliar young lady" to make music in the choir loft (BDOK II, no. 17; NBR, p. 47)—a "young lady" who may in fact not have been his cousin and future wife, Maria Barbara Bach (Wolff 2000, 88). Five months later, on April 24, 1707, Bach auditioned in Mühlhausen for the post of organist at St. Blasius's Church.

There are no positively dated compositions from Bach's Arnstadt period. The nature of his duties suggests that many of his shorter organ chorale compositions were written at that time. These include the thirty-one pieces in the so-called "Neumeister Collection," BWV 1090–1120, along with a half-dozen *"passaggio"* chorales, such as his setting of *Allein Gott in der Höh*, BWV 715. Their often bold, "strange" harmonies and the flamboyant flourishes between the lines of the hymn are precisely the features that had upset the church consistory. Other settings reflecting seventeenth-century style presumably date from the Arnstadt years. Particularly intriguing is the conjecture that the Toccata and Fugue in D minor,

BWV 565, surely Bach's most famous organ work and clearly an early composition, was written in Arnstadt. Its unusual opening octave passages might have compensated for the lack of a sixteen-foot register on the manuals of the Wender organ (Wolff 2000).

The hymns Bach chose for his organ settings were no doubt influenced by the views of the Arnstadt clergyman and theologian, Johann Christoph Olearius (1668–1747), deacon and one-time pastor of the New Church and a leading hymnologist committed to the core chorale repertoire of the Reformation era. His edition of a hymnal, published in 1701, was presumably the one used by Bach in the New Church. Olearius's father, Johann Gottfried (1635–1711), was superintendent in Arnstadt at the time of Bach's employment and thus his immediate superior. In that capacity he participated in the February 1706 interrogation of Bach. The idea for Bach's Lübeck pilgrimage may have been suggested to the young musician by J. C. Olearius, who had a close relationship with the Lübeck superintendent at the time (Leaver 2016).

Although Bach evidently wrote no vocal compositions explicitly for the Arnstadt service, the Easter cantata, *Christ lag in Todesbanden*, BWV 4, which he is thought to have performed at his Mühlhausen audition on April 24, 1707, would have been composed in Arnstadt.

Landmarks

Churches and Cemetery

NEW CHURCH/BACH CHURCH (NEUE KIRCHE/BACHKIRCHE). Of Arnstadt's three churches, the New Church, where Bach was employed, was the newest and the lowest in rank. It was built in 1676–83, replacing St. Boniface's Church, which had burned down in 1581. The church served, in the words of one scholar, as "a kind of proving ground for newly ordained clergy, who usually held the position of pastor for no more than a year" (Leaver 2016).

A notable feature of the barrel-vaulted Baroque hall church is its tiers of galleries with the organ loft located above the choir loft. In Bach's day the interior, including the organ, would have been bare wood. It was not painted and gilded until 1776, at the time the current rococo pulpit and altar table were installed. A sculpted crucifixion group, now placed against the north wall, had been part of the original altar. Of the church's two present organs, one is closely modeled on the original two-manual Wender instrument, incorporating seven of the original stops and the case. It now occupies its original location on the third gallery and includes four bellows for mechanical pumping. A newer Romantic organ,

20. Arnstadt, New Church (Bach Church): J. S. Bach was organist here from 1703 to 1707.

dating from 1913 but renovated since, occupies the lower gallery, placed behind a grillwork.

UPPER CHURCH (OBERKIRCHE). Also known as the Church of the Barefoot Friars (*Barfüsserkirche*), this was Arnstadt's Main Church (*Hauptkirche*), which was attended by Arnstadt's rulers and leading citizens. The pastor was Superintendent Johann Gottfried Olearius. A large single-nave, barrel-vaulted church located south of the Market Place, the Upper Church dates from the mid–thirteenth century. The superintendent officiated at this church, which also offered concerted church music during the main services under the direction of the town kantor. The nobility were accommodated in a heated, glassed-in area. (Restoration of the church and the adjoining monastery is expected to be completed in 2017.)

LOWER CHURCH (UNTERKIRCHE). Built between 1200 and 1330, this is one of the largest and most impressive examples of Romanesque-Gothic architecture in Thuringia. Arnstadt's second-ranked church, it is also known as Our Lady's Church (*Liebfrauenkirche*) and as the Morning Church (*Frühkirche*). From the fourteenth through the seventeenth centuries, it served as the burial site for the Schwarzburg dynasty.

OLD CEMETERY (ALTER FRIEDHOF). Now a park, the old cemetery contains a monument in memory of the many members of the Bach family buried there.

Secular Architecture, Bach Family Residences

NEIDECK CASTLE (SCHLOSS NEIDECK). Little remains from the Schwarzburg dynasty's sixteenth-century castle apart from a single, earlier tower (60 meters high), in which the watchman Caspar Bach, the first musical Bach to settle in Arnstadt, presumably lived from 1620–33. The watchman's apartment, which in its simplicity is not unlike the prison cell a few stories below it, is open to the public. The Schwarzburg line died out in 1716 upon the death of Count Anton Günther II. The town of Sondershausen, located 80 km/49 miles to the north, became the seat of the ruling family of Schwarzburg-Sondershausen. The castle in Arnstadt, meanwhile, remained vacant, was used as a quarry, and eventually collapsed. The grounds where it once stood now contain models of the vanished castle and other historic buildings amid scattered ruined walls. The area is also used for open-air events and filmmaking. The moat that surrounded the castle is still visible, and large portions of the park survive.

GARDENER'S HOUSE (GÄRTNERHAUS). The gardener's house in the castle park displays a complete model of the old city of Arnstadt based on early paintings and documents. It reflects the appearance of the town "circa 1740." Most of the houses are half-timbered, in contrast to the classicistic plastered exteriors typical of the early nineteenth century. The diorama allows one to recognize many surviving buildings.

NEW PALACE (NEUES PALAIS). The New Palace, 1729–36, is located near the ruins of Neideck Castle. Built as a residence for the widow of Prince Günther I of Schwarzburg-Sondershausen (r. 1720–40), it now serves as the palace museum consisting of several collections, one of which is the permanent exhibit: "Bach in Arnstadt." Its highlights are a model of the New Church representing its original state, an oil painting of Johann Gottfried Olearius, and, above all, the original key-desk of Bach's Wender organ.

The museum also houses a "doll city" (*Puppenstadt*), *mon plaisir*, a major tourist attraction. This unique, informative collection, created by the princess and her staff, consists of fully furnished, oversize dollhouses depicting the life of a princely residence and town of the time in eighty-two scenes representing all social stations and vocations with scrupulously accurate replicas of tools, costumes, and furnishings.

CITY ARCHIVE/CONSISTORY. Across the Ritterstrasse from the *palais* is the Arnstadt city archive. Originally the castle stables, by Bach's time it was the venue in which the consistory (*Consistorium*) held its interrogations and issued its reprimands of the young composer.

TOWN HALL (RATHAUS). Located on the town square next to the Bach Church, the town hall, like the castle, dates from the late sixteenth century; its gables and decorations reflect Dutch influence. Across the square, directly facing the town hall, sits (or leans) the 1985 bronze statue by Bernd Göbel (b. 1942) of the young Bach gazing into the distance.

FELDHAUS RESIDENCE. Two houses located at the corner of Ledermarkt and Holzmarkt, once known as "*Zur goldenen Krone*" (At the Golden Crown) and "*Steinhaus*" (Stone House), have since been combined under a single roof. They belonged to the mayor Martin Feldhaus (1634–1720). One of the tenants was Maria Barbara Bach, Johann Sebastian's second cousin and future wife. It is likely that the pair met in Arnstadt. A plaque on the house dating from 1935 identifies it as the residence of Johann Sebastian Bach.

J. S. BACH RESIDENCE. The claim that J. S. Bach, too, lived in the Feldhaus residence has recently been challenged and a plausible case made for an alternative candidate: Kohlgasse 7, a house that had belonged to Bach's uncle (his father's identical twin brother), Johann Christoph. After Johann Christoph's death it continued to be occupied by his widow and their children. The argument

21. Arnstadt, Town Hall (1583–85): In the foreground, the provocative statue of the young Bach, perhaps at the location of the "long stone" (at which the notorious "Geyersbach Incident" took place).

that Sebastian resided at Kohlgasse 7 is based on testimony from the Geyersbach incident: specifically, the detail that Bach was attacked when he crossed the town square "as he walked home from the castle." If he had been living in the Feldhaus residence, Bach would not have crossed the town square to go home; but he would have done so, had he been living in the Kohlgasse (Friedel 2007).

This attractive conjecture cannot be corroborated, however, since documentation regarding tenants was not collected at the time. The house, at all events, has recently been restored and remodeled and, since 2004, constitutes *Das Bachhaus Kohlgasse 7*—a second Bach museum, in effect, mostly dedicated to early members of the musical Bach family.

FAMILY REUNION SITES. On the Riedplatz, near the Jacobsgasse, are two hotels, both of which claim to have been the venues where the Bach family, during Sebastian's youth, assembled for their annual reunions—joyous, music-filled occasions famously described by Bach's first biographer, Johann Nikolaus Forkel, but questioned in recent years (Schulze 1994). Of the two inns—*Zur Güldenen Henne* (At the Golden Hen) and *Zur Goldenen Sonne* (At the Golden Sun)—the latter bears a plaque stating the claim. It is doubtful

22. Arnstadt, residence of Johann Christoph Bach (1645–93, twin brother of Johann Ambrosius): Located at Kohlgasse 7, and perhaps where Sebastian once lived, it now houses a Bach family exhibit.

that either establishment has a valid case. The humorous, fragmentary, wedding *quodlibet* (medley), BWV 524, dating from 1707/8—possibly composed in Arnstadt, but more likely in Mühlhausen—is an example of the kind of music-making the family reportedly indulged in at these reunions.

Literature: *BDOK II; NBR; Schulze 1994; Wolff 1986b; Wollny 1998; Marshall 2000; Petzoldt 2000; Wolff 2000; Botwinick 2004; Wollny 2005; Friedel 2007; Billeter 2007; Leaver 2009; Erickson 2009; Organs; Wolff GMO, accessed November 15, 2014; Leaver 2016a.*

Website: www.preller-gottfried.de/html/bachkirche.htm (G).

23. Mühlhausen, Statue of the young J. S. Bach (2009) by Klaus Friedrich Messerschmidt.

CHAPTER 5

MÜHLHAUSEN (1707–8)

During the course of his single year's employment in Mühlhausen Bach crossed the threshold of immortality. This event is captured in the form of a charming life-size statue standing near the entrance to Bach's St. Blasius's Church, depicting the young genius placing a first foot on the pedestal erected to reserve his future place in the pantheon.

Mühlhausen, a prosperous commercial center since the Middle Ages, became an Imperial City of the Holy Roman Empire in the course of the twelfth and thirteenth centuries, accountable to no secular ruler other than the emperor. In 1198, Philipp of Swabia (1178–1208), the youngest son of Emperor Frederick Barbarossa, was elevated in Mühlhausen to the title of King of the Holy Roman Empire. The city was also a member of the Hanseatic League for a time in the fifteenth century. During the Reformation period, it was a center of social rebellion and the Peasants' War. In 1525, the radical reformer Thomas Müntzer (1489–1525), a preacher at St. Mary's church, and a leader of the rebellion, was beheaded near the city after the insurrection collapsed.

When Bach moved to Mühlhausen in June 1707 to assume the post of organist at St. Blasius's Church (*Blasiuskirche* or *Divi Blasii*), the town had been devastated just weeks earlier by a conflagration, the most recent of many. The city at the time was still recovering from the plague of 1682/83 that had carried off some 4,000 residents and from the fire of 1689, in which over 500 buildings were destroyed. The population of what was then the second largest city in Thuringia, after **Erfurt**, was probably no more than 7,000. On the other hand, it largely escaped the ravages of World War II. Called *Mulhusia turrita* (tower-rich Mühlhausen) owing to its fifty-nine church- and watchtowers, it still boasts large portions of the city walls and eleven historic churches.

Bach at the time had been an organist in Arnstadt for about four years. But the position had become increasingly untenable owing to his frequent confrontations with the local authorities. On Easter Sunday, April 24, 1707, Bach auditioned for the Mühlhausen position. Exactly one month later, on May 24, council member Dr. Conrad Meckbach (1637–1712), the former mayor, suggested that the position be offered to "the man named Pach from Arnstadt." While the council document (NBR, no. 22) indicated only that Bach had "played" at the audition, scholars have long assumed that he also performed the cantata *Christ lag in Todes Banden*, BWV 4, a complete setting of Martin Luther's famous hymn.

Bach's name may well have been proposed to the Mühlhausen authorities by the organ builder Johann Friedrich Wender (1655–1729), who was a Mühlhausen resident at the time. More pertinent, he was the builder of the organ at the New Church in Arnstadt, the instrument the eighteen-year-old Bach had inspected upon its completion in early 1703 and thereafter regularly played and serviced as the church's organist. There is little question that, despite a thirty-year age difference, Wender and Bach had developed a close relationship based on mutual admiration and respect, one that continued in the ensuing years.

Bach appeared before the council on June 14, 1707, to settle the details of his employment. By June 22, he had accepted the position and by August had begun his service. His salary was eighty-five gulden (ca. $7,500) per year, the same as it had been in Arnstadt (and twenty gulden more than that of his predecessor Johann Georg Ahle). The salary was augmented by in-kind payments in grain and wood, amenities he had not received in Arnstadt.

As the organist of St. Blasius's, Bach occupied the most important musical position in Mühlhausen, effectively serving as the town's music director with responsibilities not only for the two main churches, St. Blasius's and St. Mary's, but others as well. His duties consisted in providing the music for church services on all Sundays and feast days, as well as Tuesdays and Fridays. In addition to the organ, he had at his disposal professional town musicians and students of the Mühlhausen Latin School or *Gymnasium*. He also presumably could call on the assistance of his private pupils, including Johann Martin Schubart (1690–1721), who studied with Bach from 1707 to 1717 and followed him to Weimar, and Johann Caspar Vogler (1696–1763). Both later succeeded Bach as organists in Weimar.

Bach soon arranged for his marriage to Maria Barbara, née Bach (1684–1720), a native of **Gehren**, the daughter of the Gehren organist, Johann Michael Bach (1648–94), and Sebastian's second cousin. Both had been living in Arnstadt over the past few years, where they clearly developed a close relationship. The financial security provided by his new position in Mühlhausen now enabled Bach to take this step—especially since, that same autumn, he had come into an inheritance of fifty gulden (ca. $4,200) left to him by his Erfurt uncle, Tobias Lämmerhirt (1639–1707), his mother's brother. The young couple formally announced their betrothal on October 1 and took their wedding vows on October 17, 1707, in **Dornheim**.

Eight months later, on June 25, 1708, Bach asked to be relieved of his post in order to take up employment in the court chapel of the Duke of Weimar. In his written request to the town council, he famously expressed his "final goal" (*Endzweck*) of creating "a well-regulated church music to the glory of God without further vexation." He not only complained that he could live "but poorly" on his income but also lamented the poor state of church music in Mühlhausen, remarking that the church music to be heard elsewhere, indeed "in almost every township," was "often better than the harmony that is fashioned here." He claimed that he could not accomplish the duties of his office "without hindrance." The town council, acknowledging Dr. Meckbach's argument that "there was no holding him back," decided the following day to grant Bach's request, stipulating only that "he help bring to completion the project that had been undertaken" (NBR, nos. 32–33). By mid-July, Bach had moved to Weimar.

The project referred to was the renovation of the St. Blasius organ. Bach had submitted an extensive proposal regarding the organ on February 21, 1708 (NBR, no. 31), no doubt in consultation with J. F. Wender. Wender executed the renovation between

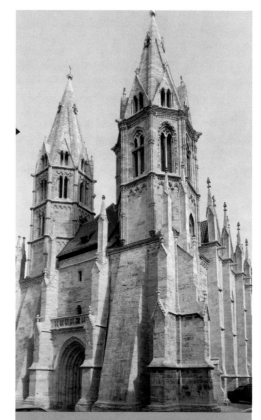

24. Mühlhausen, St. Blasius's Church: Built between the early-thirteenth and mid-fourteenth centuries. A three-aisle hall church with two octagonal towers on the west facade, one in late Romanesque, one in early-Gothic style. The French-influenced, high-Gothic nave and choir date from ca. 1345.

1708 and 1709 in accordance with Bach's proposal. Among other items, the proposal called for the addition of a third manual (*Brustpositiv*) and for an increase in the number of stops from 29 to 37, including a thirty-two-foot *Principal*, a sixteen-foot *Fagotto*, and a set of chimes. No documentation survives indicating when the renovation was completed, when the organ was inspected or consecrated, or whether Bach was present for those events. Perhaps he returned from Weimar on Reformation Day, October 31, 1709, for the consecration of the instrument, performing his setting of Luther's Reformation chorale, *Ein feste Burg ist unser Gott*, BWV 720. (According to a copy in the hand of Johann Gottfried Walther (1684–1748), this work calls for a registration that accords perfectly with the disposition of the renovated Blasius organ. The newly discovered chorale fantasy, *Wo Gott der Herr nicht bei uns hält*, BWV 1128, also conforms to the specifications of the remodeled organ.)

Exactly which of Bach's organ compositions were written during his Mühlhausen year is uncertain. We are better informed regarding his vocal works from that period. The obligation to compose church music was evidently implicit in Bach's contract. The earliest completely datable composition by Bach in any genre is the cantata, *Gott ist mein König*, BWV 71, written for the inauguration of the new town council on February 4, 1708. (It is preserved in a set of printed parts that mentions the precise date and place of the performance.) The annual event took place in St. Mary's Church, the official church of the Mühlhausen town council. The work was repeated the following Sunday at St. Blasius's Church as part of the regular service. (Bach also composed inaugural cantatas for the years 1709 and 1710, that is, after he had left Mühlhausen. The works are now lost. One of the inaugural celebrations may have provided him with the opportunity to examine and perform on the renovated organ.)

Another church work clearly belonging to the Mühlhausen period is the cantata, *Aus der Tiefen rufe ich, Herr, zu dir*, BWV 131, Bach's only setting of a complete psalm (Psalm 130). An autograph notation in the surviving score reports that it was written "at the request" of Georg Christian Eilmar (1665–1715), the pastor of St. Mary's Church. The psalm's penitential character suggests that the work may have been composed for a commemoration of the great fire of May 1707.

The cantata, *Nach dir, Herr, verlanget mich*, BWV 150, has recently been shown to date from Bach's Mühlhausen period: the composition's three aria texts contain an acrostic that spells out the name "Doktor Conrad Meckbach," Bach's advocate in the town council (Schulze 2010). The specific occasion for its composition is not clear.

The notable absence in these compositions of the newly fashionable recitatives and da capo–form arias taking root elsewhere suggests that other Bach cantatas that share those (and other telltale features) were composed during his Mühlhausen stay. The potential roster of cantatas belonging to Bach's Mühlhausen period includes, above all, the so-called *Actus tragicus: Gottes Zeit ist die allerbeste Zeit*, BWV 106. This powerfully expressive and theologically sophisticated composition is arguably the greatest of Bach's early church cantatas. It may have been written as a memorial for Bach's uncle Tobias Lämmerhirt, who had died in Erfurt on August 10, 1707. (Another plausible occasion was the funeral service for the venerable Mühlhausen mayor, Adolf Strecker (1624–1708), who died after a long illness on September 13, 1708.)

In early June 1735, twenty-seven years after he had resigned his post, Bach returned to Mühlhausen from Leipzig—a journey of some 200 km/124 miles—in the company of his third son, the ill-fated Johann Gottfried Bernhard (1715–39). The route may have passed from Leipzig through **Merseburg**, Eckartsberga, Kölleda, **Weißensee**, Bad Tennstedt, and Langensalza to Mühlhausen. The twenty-year-old son was to audition for the post of organist at St. Mary's Church. During the two-week visit J. S. Bach also made recommendations regarding the church's organ, then in the process of being rebuilt by Christian Friedrich Wender (1694–1740), the son of J. F. Wender (BDOK II, no. 365). On June 22, on his return trip to Leipzig, Bach examined the Town Church organ in Weißensee.

Johann Gottfried Bernhard's audition was successful. He served in the position, however, only until early 1737, when he resigned to become the organist at the Jacobikirche in Sangerhausen.

Landmarks

ST. BLASIUS'S CHURCH (BLASIUSKIRCHE/KIRCHE DIVI BLASII). The principal church of Mühlhausen's old town, the so-called "lower city," St. Blasius's Church was the site where emperors worshipped when in town. Medieval stained-glass windows depicting Biblical figures adorn the chancel. The north transept has a rosette window modeled on Notre Dame in Paris, but with modern glass. The altar, pulpit, and baptismal font date from the late fifteenth and sixteenth centuries and would have been known to Bach. Although the church's Wender organ no longer exists, the present instrument, built in 1959 by the firm Schuke Orgelbau, largely follows Bach's 1708 proposal.

The church has always served as the seat of the superintendent, effectively the head of the church government. During Bach's time the position was occupied by Johann Adolph Frohne (1652–1713), with whom the young organist evidently had a strained relationship.

ST. MARY'S CHURCH (MARIENKIRCHE). An extravagantly decorated, five-aisled Gothic hall church dating from the fourteenth century and distinguished by a 280-foot tower, St. Mary's is, next to the Erfurt cathedral, the largest church in Thuringia. As both the principal church of Mühlhausen's new town (the "upper city") and the official church for the town council, that is, the secular government, it functioned as the counterpart to St. Blasius's Church. In 1627, the Holy Roman Emperor Ferdinand II (1578–1637) held an electoral assembly in St. Mary's, an event embellished with the premiere of Heinrich Schütz's *Da pacem, Domine*, SWV 465, performed under the direction of the composer. The church's galleries suggested the work's polychoral scoring, a feature exploited by Bach some eighty years later in Cantata 71, written for the same venue.

The church's pastor during Bach's time was Archdeacon Georg Christian Eilmar, the counterpart and theological adversary to Superintendent Frohne. The two antagonistic clergymen exchanged pulpits from week to week. Eilmar, who had prevailed upon Bach to compose Cantata 131, not only was supportive of his musical efforts but evidently a good friend as well, serving as a godparent for Bach's first child, Catharina Dorothea, born in Weimar in December 1708.

TOWN HALL (RATHAUS), TOWN ARCHIVES. The original documents relating to Bach's Mühlhausen appointment are on public display in the

25. Mühlhausen, Town archives: Preserved in the town hall (1615), they retain the original wooden cases and drawers, organized by an intricate system of Greek and Latin letters and Zodiac signs. Original Mühlhausen documents, including Bach's signed appointment letter, are on display.

town archives. Also located in the town hall—a stylistic mélange of buildings built between the fourteenth and nineteenth centuries—is the large council hall (*Ratssaal*), with a wooden vaulted ceiling and now used for concerts and events. The smaller council chamber (*Ratsstube*) is adorned with rare Gothic wall paintings. The chancellery (*Kanzlei*), dating from 1570, is a small square room off the council hall. It was here that Bach presumably received and signed his letter of appointment.

MECKBACH HOUSE. A stately green house, formerly belonging to Mayor Meckbach, stands at Untermarkt 6, a few steps away from St. Blasius's. Bach may have resided here during his Mühlhausen tenure. In 1710, Conrad Meckbach's son, Paul Friedemann (1674–1731), served as a godfather (and name-giver) for Bach's first son, Wilhelm Friedemann (1710–84).

POPPERODE FOUNTAIN FESTIVAL (POPPERÖDER BRUN-NENFEST). This long-standing (since 1605) and ongoing Mühlhausen tradition, a religious feast of thanksgiving for the gift of water, was celebrated by local pupils at the Renaissance fountain pavilion located 4 km/2.5 miles west of the town center. The event normally took place in early June. It was canceled in 1707 owing to the great fire but resumed in 1708. Although no evidence exists, it is conceivable that Bach, like his predecessors, composed a simple strophic song for the occasion.

"BRÜCKENHOF" CHURCH (BRÜCKENHOFKIRCHE) (NO LONGER EXTANT). Bach had limited responsibilities in Mühlhausen for the services in the "Brückenhof" Church, a simple, one-aisle monastery church, formerly St. Mary Magdalene's Church of the Augustinian Convent (a nunnery). According

26. Mühlhausen, Popperode fountain house (1604): The loggia has stone benches and inspirational texts welcoming travelers. The spring, in Bach's time, was Mühlhausen's source for drinking water.

to his contract, he shared the duties in rotation with the organist of St. Mary's, Johann Gottfried Hetzehenn (1664–1735).

The organ, a small work with one manual and seven registers, was built 1701/2 by J. F. Wender. This was the same period during which Wender built the organ for the New Church in Arnstadt. The "Brückenhof" Church was demolished in 1884. Parts of its organ, however, survived and, in 1999, were incorporated into the restored organ of St. George's Church in the nearby town of Dörna, where Wender was baptized. The key-desk, worm-eaten and no longer usable, is now on display in the Bach Museum in Eisenach.

The Dörna church, surrounded by its cemetery, sits on a hillock above the village, ca. 7 km/4 miles northwest of Mühlhausen. The lower part of the tower belonged to the Romanesque building dating from 1119. The surviving Gothic nave and tower date from 1295.

ADDITIONAL SITES

Next to Johann Sebastian Bach the most famous historical figure connected to Mühlhausen is Thomas Müntzer (ca. 1489–1525). A museum devoted to his life and the history of the Peasants' War is located in the former Corn Market Church (*Kornmarktkirche*). Otherwise, the city's most celebrated and favorite son is John A. Roebling (1806–69), a Mühlhausen-born engineer who emigrated to the United States where he designed the Brooklyn Bridge. The town celebrates his memory with a statue, a memorial plaque affixed to his birth house, and periodic reunions attended by members arriving from Mühlhausen's sister city, Saxonburg, Pennsylvania. The town was founded by Roebling and a group of fellow *emigrés*.

Literature: NBR; Ernst 1987; Cowdery 1989; Kröhner 1995; Wolff 2000; Petzoldt 2000; Rathey 2006; Blaut-Schulze 2008; Schulze 2010; Organs.

CHAPTER 6

WEIMAR (1703, 1708–17)

Listed by UNESCO since 1998 as a "World Heritage Site," Weimar has done little to promote its Bach heritage. Instead, it is culturally dominated by the literary icons of the Classical period, above all, by Johann Wolfgang von Goethe, whose charismatic presence and influential role there from 1776 to his death in 1832 still defines Weimar's cultural profile for the world. The remainder of the celebrated literary triumvirate consists of Friedrich Schiller and Johann Gottfried Herder. Due tribute is also rendered to Friedrich Nietzsche, the Bauhaus, and the Weimar Republic. With regard to its musical heritage, Franz Liszt, rather than Bach, is the city's principal official representative.

The UNESCO-designated "Classical Weimar" includes eleven institutions, of which only one, the Town Church (or Herder Church; *Stadtkirche*, *Herderkirche*), has any connection with Johann Sebastian Bach. Only a determined sleuth will find traces of Bach in Weimar, although the composer spent some ten years of his professional life in this town, longer than anywhere else other than Leipzig. Moreover, Weimar was the birthplace of his two oldest, illustrious sons, Wilhelm Friedemann (1710–84) and Carl Philipp Emanuel (1714–88).

J. S. BACH IN WEIMAR

Bach's first professional engagement in Weimar lasted barely six months, from December 1702 or January 1703 through June 1703, whereupon he accepted an offer from Arnstadt. According to the Weimar court register, the seventeen-year-old was listed as "the lackey Baach" [*sic*] (NBR, no. 13). But the words of the family Genealogy indicate that he regarded himself as a "court musician, in Weimar, to Duke Johann Ernst" (NBR, no. 303, item 24).

Bach's second appointment in Weimar—this time as court organist—lasted over nine years, from July 1708 through December 1717. From March 1714 on, he also served as concertmaster.

The population of Weimar during Bach's years there numbered about 4,700, of whom about one-third were employed by the palace. The entire duchy of Saxony-Weimar numbered under 50,000. In accordance with an agreement dating to 1629, Weimar had two nominal rulers—a coregency that made for ongoing difficulties and tensions. Duke Wilhelm Ernst (r. 1683–1728), the childless, de facto ruler of the duchy and Bach's employer from 1708 on, resided in the main castle, the Wilhelmsburg. His younger brother, Duke Johann Ernst III (r. 1683–1707), a dissolute alcoholic, was the coregent and, in 1703, Bach's first employer. His residence was

27. Weimar, "Red Palace" (1574–76): The nickname's origin is unknown; the building's basic color is gray (only the window casings are red). Bach would regularly pass the Renaissance-era palace, which was connected to the Wilhelmsburg by a covered bridge, on his way to work.

the so-called Red Palace (*Rotes Schloss*), located just steps away from the main castle—and a stone's throw from Bach's residence.

Upon the death of Johann Ernst III in 1707, his oldest son, Ernst August I (r. 1707–48), became coregent with his uncle, Wilhelm Ernst, with whom relations eventually became strained in the extreme. From 1728 on—from Wilhelm Ernst's death until his own—Ernst August ruled alone. During the course of his twenty-year reign he introduced primogeniture and ended the dysfunctional coregency. His grandson, Carl August (1757–1828), would be Goethe's patron.

An overview of the Ernestine Weimar dynasty from 1620–1828, particularly as it bears on Bach's Weimar career, can be seen in Figure 2.

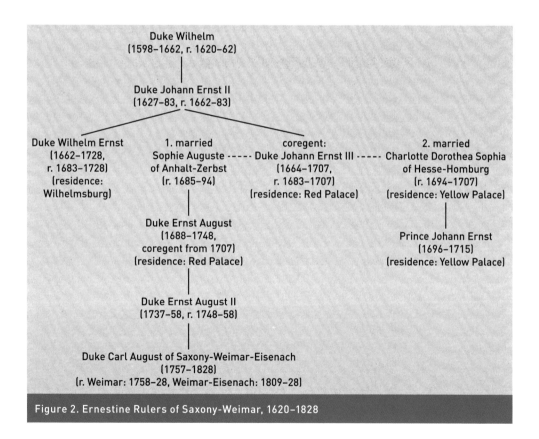

Figure 2. Ernestine Rulers of Saxony-Weimar, 1620–1828

Lackey and Chamber Musician

Little is known about Bach's first short employment in the service of Duke Johann Ernst III. He presumably played the violin in the duke's chamber orchestra; the concertmaster was Johann Paul von Westhoff (1656–1705), a celebrated violin virtuoso who had pioneered the performance of multiple stops. Bach may also have substituted occasionally for the court organist, Johann Effler (d. 1711), whose position he would inherit in 1708.

During the reign of Ernst August, Bach had no official role in the Red Palace. Like other servants, including the musicians, he was expected to serve both ducal households, albeit always upon the prior approval of the reigning duke. This condition, however, was regularly—apparently flagrantly—violated by the coregent, who in so doing put the musicians in a tenuous position: by obeying one ruler they almost invariably disobeyed the other. Penalties and punishments—often extremely harsh—ensued. Bach, too, was, caught in the middle of this tense situation.

Bach's activities for Ernst August, then, are unclear. One assumes that he performed and composed instrumental chamber music for the Red Palace. But with the exception of a single violin composition, the Fugue in G minor, BWV 1026, none survives. A lost trio sonata in G minor for oboe, viola da gamba, and continuo, dating from ca. 1714 and later reworked as the E-minor Organ Trio, BWV 528, has been postulated and partially reconstructed (Dirksen 2003).

Court Organist

During Bach's employment by Duke Wilhelm Ernst his principal role was that of court organist, and his main workplace was in the Wilhelmsburg palace. (He also participated in activities at the two town churches: the Town Church of SS Peter and Paul, and the St. Jacob's Church.) The palace church was a narrow rectangle (ca. 30 × 12 m/98 × 39 ft.), three stories high (20m/65ft); it had a balustraded opening in the ceiling, around which the kapelle of about fifteen musicians with their instruments (including the organ) and a small choir could be grouped. The music, in effect, "floated down" from above, from "heaven." The name for the church, *Weg zur Himmelsburg* (Path to the Heavenly Castle)—or simply *Himmelsburg*—confirmed that the unusual proportions of the space were conceived as an architectural allegory of the ascent into heaven. The sound, however, must have been somewhat muffled and diffused (Schrammek 1988). The altar, with its soaring obelisk resting on a platform supported by stylized palm trees, all in black and white marble and populated by dancing angels—was equally striking.

28. Weimar, *Himmelsburg*: Interior. Oil painting by Christian Richter (ca. 1660), showing the Compenius organ located in the ceiling space. Court musicians, including Bach at the organ, were invisible when performing.

Bach regularly played the organ from the dizzying perch in the ceiling and, beginning in March 1714, performed a monthly series of church cantatas from there as well. He initiated the project on Palm Sunday, March 25th, with the cantata, *Himmelskönig sei willkommen*, BWV 182, whose text could not have been more appropriate to the space. In doing so, Bach had finally launched as well the ambitious project he had proclaimed some six years earlier to be his "final goal": the creation of "a regular church music to the glory of God" (NBR, no. 32).

The organ Bach had at his disposal was a modest two-manual instrument in typical Thuringian style built 1657/58 by Ludwig Compenius and enlarged by Johann Conrad Weisshaupt in 1707/8, that is, before Bach arrived in Weimar. It had only twenty-four stops, featuring several string stops and a preponderance of eight-foot and other foundation registers, which gave the instrument the "gravity" of tone Bach seems to have preferred. In 1712/14, the local builder Heinrich Nikolaus Trebs renovated the organ under Bach's supervision.

The Obituary reports that Bach "wrote most of his organ works" during this period, a claim substantiated by later research. Almost the entirety of the *Orgelbüchlein* and of the early versions of the "Great Eighteen" organ chorales, along with many of the most celebrated large-scale preludes, toccatas, and fugues stem from this period.

Until 1715, Bach taught and performed with the half-brother of Ernst August, the precocious and short-lived Prince Johann Ernst (1696–1715), who also studied with Bach's friend and distant relative, Johann Gottfried Walther (1684–1748), organist at the Town Church. When the young prince returned to Weimar from Holland in the spring of 1713, he brought back samples of the modern Italian concerto style as developed by Vivaldi and others. Bach and his royal pupil studied and transcribed them for keyboard and organ. Bach's concertos BWV 592–96 and 972–87 were modeled after them, as were several concertos composed by the prince. The influence of the Vivaldian concerto form on Bach's compositional style thereafter was lasting and profound.

Concertmaster

In March 1714, Bach became court "*Concert*-Meister," a position subordinate to the vice-kapellmeister, specifically created for him "at his most humble request" (NBR, no. 51). It was no doubt his reward for having turned down an attractive offer from **Halle** in order to remain in Weimar. The new position carried the obligation to perform new works monthly. The regular monthly sequence was disrupted during the late summer and autumn of 1715, however, owing to an official period of mourning after the untimely death of Prince Johann Ernst. Bach composed more than twenty church cantatas over the course of the following years, among them some of his best known works: *Ich hatte viel Bekümmernis*, BWV 21; *Weinen, Klagen, Sorgen, Zagen*, BWV 12; and *Widerstehe doch der Sünde*,

BWV 54. Over half were settings of texts by the
Weimar court poet, Salomo Franck (1659–1725).
Conducting, perhaps, from the violin stand, Bach
led an ensemble, which perhaps consisted of some
fourteen musicians, including six professional
singers. (The exact number of participating per-
formers cannot be determined.) At Bach's insis-
tence, rehearsals were held, not in the apartment
of Kapellmeister Drese as hitherto, but in the
Himmelsburg.

Although Bach received regular salary
increases that rose steadily from 150 gulden
(ca. $12,600) in 1708 to 250 gulden (ca. $21,000) by
1714, he was denied the post of kapellmeister when
it became available upon the death of Johann
Samuel Drese (1644–1716) in December 1716. After
having first been offered to Telemann, the position was given instead to Drese's son, the vice-
kapellmeister, Johann Wilhelm (1677–1745). Apparently, Bach composed no further cantatas after
December 1716, ending with the last of the four
Advent cantatas. This may have been in response
to his having been passed over for the kapellmeister position. He would remain in Weimar for
another eleven months, during which time his
relationship with Duke Wilhelm Ernst continued
to deteriorate, as the composer apparently sought,
and eventually found, employment elsewhere.

Bach had received and accepted a firm offer
from Prince Leopold of Köthen (1694–1728) for
the position of court kapellmeister before he
formally requested release from his Weimar
position. The Weimar duke was furious. When
Bach again "too stubbornly forced the issue of his
dismissal," he was placed under arrest and kept
in the county judge's detention cell for a month,
after which he was given an "unfavorable discharge" (NBR, no. 68).

29. Weimar, "Bastille": One of several
such gatehouses, which were once
part of the castle. Bach passed
through this gate whenever he
attended court.

30. Weimar, Detention cell window:
To the left of the bastille portal (now
mostly hidden by trees).

Bach apparently used the month of isolation to develop the plan for *The Well-Tempered Clavier*. The music lexicographer Ernst Ludwig Gerber (1746–1819), whose father, Heinrich Nikolaus, had studied clavier with Bach in Leipzig in the mid-1720s, reported that "according to a certain tradition," Bach wrote the work "in a place where there was ennui, boredom, and the absence of any kind of musical instrument" (NBR, no. 370).

As far as is known, Bach never returned to Weimar after he left in 1717, no doubt owing at least in part to his dishonorable discharge. In contrast, he had not hesitated to return to other places of residence or previous appointment, specifically, Eisenach, Mühlhausen, and Köthen. (He even returned to Halle as early as 1716 for an organ examination despite his ethically questionable dalliance about accepting an appointment there in 1713/4.)

LANDMARKS

Of Bach's three workplaces in Weimar, the Wilhelmsburg with its *Himmelsburg* chapel no longer exists, and the Red and Yellow Palaces were damaged in World War II. While the exteriors of the latter appear much as they did in Bach's time, the interiors are entirely modern.

WILHELMSBURG. An isolated castle in Weimar is documented as early as the tenth century, and the town gradually developed around it. Over time, more elaborate structures were built on the site, expanded, and consumed by fires. After a conflagration in 1618, plans were made for a large four-wing, Italianate palace surrounding an interior courtyard. Construction began in 1619 with the church, which was consecrated in 1630. Following the disruption of the Thirty Years War, building resumed in 1651 under the culturally ambitious Duke Wilhelm (r. 1620–62), for whom the castle is named. The architect, Johann Moritz Richter the Elder (1620–1667), proposed a French-style three-wing chateau opening to the park that extends along the Ilm River. The Wilhelmsburg was the first major Italian-French–inspired Baroque palace built in central Germany. The preexisting church was integrated into the design, acquiring its final form, featuring the *Himmelsburg*, in 1658, when it was reconsecrated. The sole remnant of the medieval castle is the lower part of the tower.

The center of Bach's activities in Weimar, the Wilhelmsburg, was destroyed in the fire of 1774. Nothing remains of it except for the Renaissance gatehouse, now known as the "Bastille." The present castle tower bells, too, considered a major Baroque bell ensemble, are those Bach heard. The "Bastille" may have a connection with Bach's incarceration in the county judge's detention cell. The surviving

"Bastille," the old gatehouse, contains two such detention cells. Although there may have been others, the "Bastille" is the only one extant. At the least, it offers an idea of what such a place of detention looked like.

RED PALACE (ROTES SCHLOSS). Bach would regularly pass this Renaissance-era building on his way to the castle. The Red Palace served as the secondary ducal residence. Used today for administrative services related to the Duchess Anna Amalia Library (*Amalienbibliothek*), the building is distinguished by three tall gables and an artful portal adorned with colorful coats of arms. Its front extends along the Kollegiengasse—directly opposite the space once occupied by Bach's residence (now an empty lot) on Markt 16. A bust of Bach is located on the short, southern end of the Red Palace, within sight of what had been Bach's house.

YELLOW PALACE (GELBES SCHLOSS). The Yellow Palace faces the Green Market (*Grüner Markt*), in effect abutting the Red Palace. It was built by Johann

31. Weimar, "Yellow Palace" (1704): Located between the "Red Palace" and the castle gate, this Baroque-era building, too, stood on Bach's route to the Wilhelmsburg.

Ernst III as a residence for his second wife, Charlotte Dorothea Sophia of Hesse-Homburg (r. 1694–1707), and their son, the half-brother of Ernst August, Prince Johann Ernst. Bach gave instruction to the young prince in this building.

TOWN CHURCH OF SS PETER AND PAUL (STADTKIRCHE ST. PETER UND PAUL). A few blocks to the north of the town square (*Markt*) is Weimar's second center, defined by the Town Church, or Herder Church. A Gothic structure dating from 1498 to 1500, it has a pronounced overlay of Baroque elements (pulpit, balconies, decorations) that were added after Bach's departure. Johann Gottfried Herder preached here from 1776 until his death in 1803. During Bach's time the church was the focus of religious life for the townspeople. Johann Gottfried Walther (1684–1748) was the town organist here from 1707 to his death. The original organ no longer survives.

32. Weimar, Town Church: Interior. Five of Bach's children were baptized at the late-Gothic baptismal font.

During the sixteenth and seventeenth centuries the chancel of the Town Church served as the burial place for the early Weimar dukes. It was separated from the church by a wrought-iron screen. Visitors today can see (as Bach could only glimpse) the ducal funerary monuments as well as the altarpiece by Lucas Cranach the Elder (1472–1553), court painter to the Saxon electors and a Weimar resident. The painter's last work was made expressly for this church and embodies a veritable allegory of Protestant theological thought. Martin Luther and Cranach himself are portrayed in it.

Five of Bach's children were baptized here, beginning with his eldest son, Wilhelm Friedemann. Georg Philipp Telemann along with Bach's landlord, Adam Immanuel Weldig, served as godparents for C. P. E. Bach, also baptized here. (Whether Telemann, at the time kapellmeister in Frankfurt am Main, was physically present for the ceremony is unclear.) Bach himself served here as godfather for the sons of Johann Gottfried Walther and of the organ builder H. N. Trebs. Bach may have taught and practiced on the Town Church organ while the instrument in the *Himmelsburg* underwent renovations during the years 1712–14.

ST. JACOB'S CHURCH (JACOBSKIRCHE) AND CEMETERY. During the Middle Ages the area surrounding the Town Church functioned as the town cemetery. In 1530, a new cemetery was created at St. Jacob's Church, which at the time stood outside the city walls. By Bach's time, St. Jacob's church had become so dilapidated that in 1713 Duke Wilhelm Ernst had the church rebuilt with a new tower on its old walls to serve the residents of the surrounding suburbs. For the consecration ceremony, the entire court musical establishment took part in the procession. Bach was listed as no. 44, a reflection, no doubt, of his place in the court hierarchy. Only the organ case survives from Bach's time.

In 1817, the church interior was renovated in classicist style by Goethe's colleague, the court architect Wenzeslaus Coudray (1775–1845). The cemetery was converted into a park in the mid–nineteenth century, but many old tombstones were preserved. Some are now attached to the church walls. Among those interred here are Cranach, Johann Gottfried Walther, the poet Salomo Franck, and Bach's two deceased infant children: the twins Maria Sophia (February 23–March 15, 1713), and Johann Christoph (born and died February 23rd).

GREEN PALACE (GRÜNES SCHLOSS). An armory in Bach's time, the Green Palace (now colored pale pink) was rebuilt and enlarged in 1761–66 as a publicly accessible space for the ducal library and art collection, which had formerly been kept in the Wilhelmsburg. The building now houses the Duchess Anna Amalia Library, named for Duchess Anna Amalia (1739–1807) of Saxony-Weimar-Eisenach. A rococo-style, three-story-high oval atrium forms the center of the palace. Shelves containing the collections are arranged around this central structure. The design of the *Himmelsburg* chapel presumably served as its inspiration. The library also displays Duke Wilhelm Ernst's prize possession: the "life clock" (*Lebensuhr*), dated 1706. A lavishly decorated artifact with built-in chronological and biographical data cycles, it is regarded as one of the "wonders" of the palace. Bach presumably viewed it.

During the 1774 fire in the Wihelmsburg palace, many of J. S. Bach's compositions, perhaps including numerous now lost instrumental chamber works, no doubt went up in flames. A far more recent conflagration (2004), this time in the upper floors of the Duchess Anna Amalia library, destroyed about 50,000 volumes. By happy coincidence several manuscripts had been removed shortly beforehand for an exhibition, among them a hitherto unknown aria by Bach composed in 1713 as a birthday ode for Duke Wilhelm Ernst: *Alles mit Gott und nichts ohn' ihn* ("Everything with God, nothing without Him"), a translation of the Latin motto of the Weimar Dukes), BWV 1127 (Maul 2005).

BACH'S WEIMAR RESIDENCE. From the standpoint of J. S. Bach's biography, the state of affairs prevailing at Markt 16, the address where, according to tax records, Bach and his family resided, is altogether regrettable. The Bachs occupied quarters in the house of Adam Immanuel Weldig (1667–1716), pageboy master and falsettist from at least 1709 on (BDOK II, no. 45). In 1713, after Weldig moved to **Weißenfels**, the house was acquired by Prince Johann Ernst and then, after his death, by his mother Charlotte Dorothea Sophia. Bach's first six children were born in this residence. He also taught his private students here, among them his successors as Weimar court organist, Johann Martin Schubart (1690–1721) and Johann Caspar Vogler (1696–1763). Another student was Philipp David Kräuter

33. Weimar, Wall at Markt 16: Tax records reveal that Bach and his family lived at this address. The remains of his former residence, damaged during World War II, were demolished in 1988/89 and replaced by a parking lot.

(1690–1741), an Augsburg native who later served as kantor and music director of the Church of St. Anna there. Kräuter presumably gave local residents of this Bavarian town, Leopold Mozart among them, their first exposure to Bach's church music.

In 1803, the property at Markt 16 was integrated into the adjoining hotel *Zum Erbprinzen* (At the Crown Prince). This section of the hotel was destroyed in 1945. The remainder, severely damaged during World War II, was completely demolished in 1988/89. A portion of the front wall still stands and bears a plaque commemorating Bach and his two most famous sons. The entire area is currently a parking lot for the Hotel Elephant, itself an historic landmark. In preparing the area for its present use, the cellar of Markt 16 was filled in. Having survived the bombing, the cellar still exists—albeit unseen. At present, efforts are underway by an organization called "Bach in Weimar" to rectify the apparently deliberate neglect of Bach's Weimar connections and to make meaningful use of the gaping hole behind the wall where Bach had once lived. The society's website (www.bach-hausweimar.de) offers specific proposals for the construction of a worthy "Bach House" in its original location. (The website discusses other Bach sites in Weimar as well and includes a computer-generated virtual tour of the no-longer-extant *Himmelsburg*.)

ETTERSBURG PALACE (SCHLOSS ETTERSBURG) AND TIEFURT. As part of his court duties Bach may have visited two additional venues in the environs of Weimar. The first, Ettersburg Palace (about 8 km/5 miles to the northeast), was built 1706–12 as a hunting lodge for Duke Wilhelm Ernst. A coat-of-arms relief above the entry features the duke's motto, *Omnia cum Deo et nihil sine eo.*

Even closer to Weimar, in the village of Tiefurt, stands the second: an old village church that bears the ducal coat of arms with the date 1716. Above the entry, a sign reads *Weg zur Himmelsburg* (Path to the Castle of Heaven), an unmistakable indication that the pyramid-shaped altar resting on palm trees was intended to evoke the original in the Himmelsburg. Although no organ was available in Bach's time, performances by the court kapelle may well have taken place in the church.

ADDITIONAL SITES

Other music-related sites in Weimar include the Liszt Museum, the summer residence of Franz Liszt (1811–86) from 1869 until his death. A Liszt statue, in Carrara marble, is located close to the park on the Ilm River. Johann Nepomuk Hummel (1778–1837), court kapellmeister in Weimar from 1819, is buried in the Historic

Cemetery of Weimar (*Historischer Friedhof Weimar*); his house at Marienstrasse 8 is marked by a plaque. The Franz Liszt Conservatory (*Hochschule für Musik Franz Liszt)* is housed in the Royal Residence (*Fürstenhaus*) of 1774, which served both as the temporary home of the ducal family after the castle fire and as Goethe's workplace in his role as privy council to the duchy.

As mentioned at the outset, the major cultural focus of Weimar is on its literary heritage. The residences of Goethe, Schiller, and Nietzsche all serve as museums. The city also maintains several institutions connected with the activities and personalities associated with the modernist Bauhaus school of architecture, which was founded in Weimar in 1919 by Walter Gropius (1883–1969).

CITY PALACE (STADTSCHLOSS), MUSEUM. After the fire of 1774 a new palace was built on the ruins of the former Wilhelmsburg. Goethe presided over the building commission. The palace today houses the Art Museum of Weimar (*Kunstmuseum Weimar*) containing a significant collection of canvases by Lucas Cranach the Elder (1472–1553) and Albrecht Dürer (1471–1528). The palace's historic rooms reflect the aesthetics of early-nineteenth-century classicism and serve the veneration of Weimar's literary golden age: one room each is dedicated to Goethe, Schiller, and Christoph Martin Wieland (1733–1813).

Literature: Jauernig 1950; NBR; BDOK II; BDOK V; Stauffer 1980; Schrammek 1988; Cowdery 1989; Glöckner 1988; Baselt 1994; Stinson 1996; Stinson 2001; Rampe 2002; Dirksen 2003; Maul 2005; Koch 2006; Mende 2008; Wolff 1997; Glöckner 1997; Rich 2009; Organs; Wolff 2000; Wolff GMO, accessed November 15, 2014; Leaver 2016.

Website: www.bachhausweimar.de (G, E).

CHAPTER 7

KÖTHEN (1717–23)

On October 28, 1730, in an uncharacteristically personal letter to his childhood friend, Georg Erdmann, the disaffected *Director Musices* and kantor at the St. Thomas School indicated that he wished to "seek his fortune elsewhere." Referring to his prior service as kapellmeister in Köthen, Bach famously declared that "there I had a gracious Prince, who both loved and knew music, and in his service I intended to spend the rest of my life" (BDOK I, no. 23; NBR, no. 152). As it happened, he spent fewer than six years at Köthen, from December 1717 through May 1723.

Bach's Köthen period began after his release on December 2, 1717, from a month's detention in Weimar, and after he had passed through Leipzig. There, on December 16, he inspected the newly rebuilt organ in the University Church, proudly signing his report "Joh: Seb: Bach. Kapellmeister to the Prince of Anhalt-Köthen" (NBR, no. 72).

Köthen ("Cöthen" in Bach's time), the capital of the principality of Anhalt-Köthen situated to the north of Saxony (ca. 167 km/103 miles northeast of Weimar), was an independent Calvinist state with strong ties to Calvinist Prussia and the Netherlands. The principality at the time had about 10,000 inhabitants, the capital city itself about 3,000. Köthen's cultural ambitions were already established during the reign of its first prince, Ludwig (1579–1650), who cofounded the Fruit-Bearing Society (*Fruchtbringende Gesellschaft*), which was committed to the refinement of the German language and literature.

Bach's "gracious prince," Leopold (1694–1728), assumed the throne in December 1715 after coming of age, thus ending the regency of his Lutheran mother, Princess Gisela Agnes (1669–1740), who had ruled since the death in 1704 of her husband Prince Emanuel Leberecht (1671–1704). Bach and the prince presumably met for the first time in January 1716 at the wedding, in **Nienburg**, of Leopold's younger sister, Eleonore Wilhelmine (1696–1726) to Duke Ernst August of Weimar

34. Köthen, Prince Leopold: Oil portrait (ca.1724) attributed to Johann Christoph Müller. The portrait hangs in the palace "potentate's room," where the prince's cuirass (visible in the portrait) is displayed.

(1688–1748), while the composer was still in the employ of the Weimar court. The prince's official coronation took place four months later, in May 1716. But even before taking power, Prince Leopold, a passionate music lover who sang bass and played the violin as well as the harpsichord and viola da gamba, had begun to revitalize the court's musical establishment, which had been founded by his father in 1691 but had languished during his mother's regency.

As a student at the aristocratic *Ritterakademie* in **Berlin** (1707–10) the prince came to know and admire the outstanding court kapelle of the Prussian king, Friedrich I (r. 1701–13), himself a Calvinist, who served, at the request of Emanuel Leberecht, as young Leopold's de facto guardian in order to blunt the Lutheran influence of his mother. Leopold spent the following three years abroad on the "Cavalier's Tour," during which he visited Holland, England, France, Italy, Vienna, and Prague, attending opera performances and acquiring a substantial collection of French and Italian music. Much of the Italian stay was spent in the company of the future **Dresden** kapellmeister, Johann David Heinichen (1683–1729).

After the death of Friedrich I, his son and successor, Friedrich Wilhelm I "the Soldier King" (r. 1713–40), quickly dissolved the **Berlin** kapelle. The dowager princess, Gisela Agnes, at the urging of her son, proceeded to recruit six of the dismissed musicians for Köthen. They formed the core of the reinvigorated musical forces of the Köthen court. Two more musicians were appointed in 1716, soon after Leopold's accession, one of them the gamba virtuoso Christian Ferdinand Abel (1682–1761). In August 1717, following the departure of the kapellmeister, Augustin Stricker (one of the Berlin musicians), the prince offered Bach the position, announcing the appointment on August 5. Bach's salary—twice that of his pre-decessor—began almost at once. Bach's wife, Maria Barbara, their four children, Maria Barbara's older sister, Friedelena Margaretha, and a housemaid, apparently left for Köthen at that time. Bach, however, could not disentangle himself from Weimar until December.

Perhaps the last musician to join the kapelle during Bach's tenure was the soprano, Anna Magdalena Wilcke, a daughter of the **Weißenfels** court trum-peter, Johann Caspar Wilcke. Bach presumably made her acquaintance there and recruited her for Köthen, where she arrived in the spring of 1721 at the age of nine-teen. Her salary of 300 thalers ($28,800) was second only to that of Kapellmeister Bach's 400 ($38,400), suggesting that she was acknowledged to be an exceptionally talented singer.

Anna Magdalena Wilcke's arrival at the Köthen court occurred slightly less than a year after the death of Bach's first wife, Maria Barbara, in July 1720 at the age of thirty-five. Johann Sebastian at the time had been in **Karlsbad** (now Kar-lovy Vary) as part of Leopold's entourage and only learned of her death when he returned home on July 7th, soon after her burial. In September 1721, Anna Magda-lena and Johann Sebastian Bach served together as godparents at a chapel service, an indication that they were already engaged. They were married on December 3, 1721, "at home," observing the custom for a widowed spouse. Nine days later, Prince Leopold of Anhalt-Köthen married the nineteen-year-old Friederica Hen-rietta of Anhalt-Bernburg (1702–23), described by Bach in his letter to Erdmann as an *amusa* (unartistic) and causing the Prince's loss of interest in music.

In point of fact, the gradual decline of the kapelle's budget, along with a reduction in the number of salaried musicians (from seventeen to fourteen), had begun by 1720 and had accelerated by 1723. Evidence of Bach's growing sense of unease with the situation appears as early as November 1720, when he applied for the position of organist at St. James's Church in **Hamburg**. The March 1721 dedication of the autograph score of the Brandenburg Concertos to the margrave of Brandenburg may be a further indication of Bach's interest in leaving Köthen. (Bach's having provided music for the birthday of Prince Johann August of **Zerbst** in August 1722, a time following the sudden departure of the previous kapell-meister that spring and before the appointment of the new Zerbst Kapellmeister, Johann Friedrich Fasch, in September, may be yet another.) All these events ante-dated Leopold's marriage to the *amusa*. In December 1722, Bach applied to Leipzig for the position of Thomaskantor, vacant since the death the previous June of Johann Kuhnau (1660–1722). In April 1723, after having been chosen as Kuhnau's successor, Bach petitioned Prince Leopold for his release. He departed Köthen that month and on May 22, 1723, assumed his new position in Leipzig and moved into his quarters at the St. Thomas School.

Bach had no successor in Köthen: he retained the title of kapellmeister until the death of Prince Leopold in November 1728. At the memorial ceremony for the prince in March 1729, Bach is described as the "former Kapell-Meister" (BDOK II, no. 258). In the intervening years Bach returned to Köthen on several occasions for guest appearances at court: in July 1724 (with Anna Magdalena), December 1725 (for the prince's birthday and other events, again with Anna Magdalena), and in January 1728 (for an unspecified occasion, perhaps the traditional New Year's cantata). He was presumably also present in 1726 (or 1725) for the performance on November 30th of *Steigt freudig in die Luft*, BWV 36a, a birthday cantata for the prince's second wife, Charlotte Friederica Wilhelmina, whom Leopold had married in June 1725. In September 1726, Bach dedicated a manuscript copy of the Keyboard Partita in B-flat, BWV 825, to the couple's newborn son, describing the suite's movements as his "slight musical firstborns" (*geringe Musicalische Erstlinge*). He included also a self-authored poem of homage to the infant (BDOK I, no. 155; NBR, no. 128). The partita later appeared as the opening work in Part I of the *Klavierübung*, published in 1731 and designated on the title page as "Opus I" (NBR, no. 155). Even after the prince's death Bach's music continued to be cultivated in Köthen, most notably by his former student in both Köthen and Leipzig, Bernhard Christian Kayser (1705–58), who later appears to have served as organist at both the court church and at St. Agnus's Church.

During his years at the Calvinist court, Bach was under no obligation to compose church music, apart from an annual New Year's cantata. Otherwise, the only vocal music he was expected to provide regularly was a "serenade" celebrating the prince's birthday on December 10. Only one example of each genre survives: the cantata, *Die Zeit, die Tag und Jahre macht*, BWV 134a, composed for New Year's Day, 1719, and the birthday cantata, *Durchlauchtster Leopold*, BWV 173a, presumably composed in 1722. In the latter work, the two soprano arias were no doubt sung by Anna Magdalena; they reveal a voice of considerable agility. Several cantatas dating from Bach's Weimar years—BWV 21, 172, 132, and 199—are known to have been re-performed during the Köthen period, though not necessarily by Bach himself or in Köthen. Cantata 21, *Ich hatte viel Bekümmernis*, however, was apparently performed in the town's main Calvinist venue, St. Jacob's Church, perhaps in May 1721. Unlike the practice in other Calvinist towns, instruments were occasionally employed here in church music. The occasions for the other cantata performances are not known.

Bach's Köthen years witnessed above all the production of some of his most important chamber music and keyboard compositions. The unaccompanied violin sonatas and partitas, BWV 1001–6, were presumably conceived for the premier *Cammer Musicus*, the violinist Joseph Spiess (d. 1730), and they survive in an autograph manuscript from 1720. The unaccompanied cello suites, BWV 1007–12, appear to have been written for the cellist Carl Bernhard Lienicke (d. 1751). The sonatas for violin and harpsichord probably date from this time as well. The Brandenburg Concertos, BWV 1046–51, although dedicated to the margrave Christian Ludwig of Brandenburg (1677–1734), who apparently never bothered to acknowledge them or have them performed, were put into final form by March 1721. They were most likely composed over several years, perhaps extending back to the Weimar period. Assuming they were performed in Köthen, they attest to the extraordinary virtuosity of Bach's court musicians.

The keyboard works dating from the Köthen years include the French and possibly also the English Suites for harpsichord and the first volume of the *Well-Tempered Clavier*, dating from 1722. The year 1722 also appears on the title page of the fragmentary *Klavierbüchlein* for Anna Magdalena Bach. The volume begins with the earliest version of five of the French Suites, BWV 812–16, entered into the album by the composer with numerous formative corrections. Early versions of eleven of the preludes from the *Well-Tempered Clavier* and the Two- and Three-Part Inventions and Sinfonias, BWV 772–801, are found in the *Klavierbüchlein* for Wilhelm Friedemann Bach. According to the title page, the *Klavierbüchlein* was begun on January 22, 1720, two months after Friedemann's ninth birthday. Its first entries describe the rudiments of notation, ornamentation, and proper keyboard fingering and reflect the book's didactic function. The famous Chromatic Fantasia and Fugue, BWV 903, appears to date from around 1720 as well.

The full extent of Bach's compositional activity in Köthen is unknown. On the one hand, at least fifty volumes of instrumental music documented by bookbinder receipts are lost. No doubt many of them contained compositions by Bach that were left in Köthen after the composer had moved to Leipzig, in accordance with prevailing custom, On the other hand, a number of surviving instrumental compositions traditionally assigned to Köthen, such as the violin concertos and trio sonatas, may have been written during the Leipzig period for the Collegium Musicum.

LANDMARKS

PALACE (SCHLOSS). Despite Köthen's small size and its growing economic problems, Leopold maintained a lavish court establishment for as long as possible. Surrounded by water, only two wings of the palace were built up; the south wing

35. Köthen, Palace: Residential wing. The princely suites were serviced from the then-open balcony.

(with towers) contained the princely living quarters. The moated Renaissance castle was transformed into a Baroque palace by adding artwork, fine furniture, damask wall coverings, and other luxurious refinements. The formal French gardens boasted artificial islands, a labyrinth, and an orangerie. They do not survive. The castle forecourt contained a tiltyard for jousting and a riding house with stables. The Grand Hall (*Grosser Saal*) on the third floor of the palace, known since its thorough renovation in 1822 as the "Hall of Mirrors" (*Spiegelsaal*), was the venue for larger concerts. Chamber music performances and private musical instruction, on the other hand, presumably took place in Leopold's private rooms.

The princely couple each inhabited a suite of four rooms on the second floor. The suite occupied by the princess now serves as the Bach Memorial Museum and is organized as follows:

Room 1. The Red Room houses the "Gallery of Potentates," consisting of over-life-size oil portraits: among them Leopold, his relatives, his sister's husband (Bach's former patron) Duke Ernst-August of Saxony-Weimar, and Friedrich I of Prussia.

Room 2. The Köthen Room displays materials pertaining to Leopold's early education, his "Cavalier's Tour" of 1710–13, and the Köthen court in Bach's time.

Room 3. The Bach Room contains twenty-seven instruments including a replica of the "grand" two-manual harpsichord by the maker Michael Mietke (d. 1719) that Bach had personally escorted to Köthen in 1719 from Mietke's Berlin workshop. Its acquisition may have inspired the composer to expand the original harpsichord cadenza of the Fifth Brandenburg Concerto to sixty-five measures. On the occasion of this **Berlin** visit, Bach may have met the margrave of Brandenburg. Other items on display include a bill for eight buckets (264 quarts) of Rhine wine costing eighty-four thalers ($8,064), most likely incurred by Bach for his wedding with Anna Magdalena in December 1721 (BDOK II, no. 111).

Room 4 is a picture and curiosity gallery.

The palace ceased to function as a princely residence in 1853. Thereafter, its contents were sold off to cover debts. As a result, the exhibition pieces on display are mostly "of the time." With the aid of a surviving inventory from 1729, however, it has been possible to repurchase a few originals. The same inventory provides valuable information about the musical instruments that belonged to the kapelle in Bach's time.

The small palace chapel served the prince and his family. The children of all court employees were required to be baptized in this venue. Accordingly, Bach's only son born in Köthen (and the last child from his marriage with Maria Barbara), Leopold Augustus, was baptized here in November 1718. Prince Leopold and his brother Augustus Ludwig were among the godparents. The child died less than a year later.

The forecourt of the palace housed the stables and a riding hall. The riding hall has been refashioned into a conference center with a concert/lecture hall—the *Johann-Sebastian-Bach-Saal*; the various conference rooms are named after Bach family members. The former stables now house the town's music school, "Johann Sebastian Bach." Other wings of the castle contain the city archives, a major ornithological collection, a prehistorical museum, and an exhibit relating to the Fruit-Bearing Society.

ST. AGNUS'S CHURCH (AGNUSKIRCHE). As a Lutheran, Bach belonged to the small parish that stood under the patronage of Leopold's Lutheran mother, Gisela Agnes. Her husband had formally granted Lutherans complete religious freedom and ordered the construction of a new edifice, the Church of St. Agnus. Bach's children attended the school attached to the church. On occasion, he may have played the organ, an instrument built 1707/8 by Johann Heinrich Müller with a pedal compass reportedly extending up to f′—in Bach's time, a rare occurrence. Only this instrument, apparently, along with the **Weißenfels** palace organ, was able to accommodate the pedal solos in Bach's Toccata in F, BWV 540. A full-length portrait of Princess Agnes (including an image of the church in

36. Köthen, St. Agnus's Church: Consecrated 1699 (the name undoubtedly an allusion to Prince Leopold's Lutheran mother, Gisela Agnes). Built for a religious minority, the small church lacks a spire and is integrated into the adjoining buildings on Stiftstraße.

37. Köthen, St. Agnus's Church: Bach and his wife took communion from this gold chalice, still in use. The register of communicants lists Bach and his wife (above the horizontal line).

the background) by the famous Berlin court painter, Antoine Pesne (1683–1757), hangs to the left of the altar. The interior of the plain Baroque hall church was heavily renovated in the mid– and late nineteenth century, at which time balconies were added. A few original church benches from Bach's time are preserved on the organ balcony.

ST. JACOB'S CHURCH (JACOBS-KIRCHE). Dominating the central market square, the three-aisle Gothic hall church, mainly built 1400–1430, was not completed until 1514. Its highly visible double spires connected by a bridge (a Köthen landmark), however, are a nineteenth-century addition. St. Jacob's was the town and court church, as well as the burial site for the princely family. Köthen—and, accordingly, St. Jacob's Church—embraced the Lutheran Reformation as early as 1525. The imposition of the Calvinist faith in 1596 by the ruling family led to the removal of much of the church's medieval furnishings. In 1866–69, the interior was refashioned once again, this time in neo-Gothic style, and a large organ by Friedrich Ladegast (1818–1905) was installed in 1877. Forty imposing coffins holding the remains of the princely family of Anhalt-Köthen are located in the crypt under the altar. Bach had personally known ten of them.

Prince Leopold died on November 19, 1728, a few days before his thirty-fourth birthday. His mother outlived him by twelve years. Bach's *Trauermusik* (funeral music) for the prince was performed in St. James's Church on March

24, 1729, under the direction
of the composer. The composition, *Klagt, Kinder, klagt es
aller Welt*, BWV 244a, is now
lost. It was derived from movements of Bach's 1727 funeral
ode for the electress Christiane,
*Laß, Fürstin, laß noch einen
Strahl*, BWV 198, and from the
St. Matthew Passion, BWV
244. It can be largely reconstructed from those works.

BACH'S KÖTHEN RESI-
DENCES. While it is quite
clear where Bach worked and
worshipped in Köthen, it is
less certain where he lived. No
fewer than eight locations have
been proposed. An extensive
computer-based analytical

38. Köthen, Bach's likely first residence: Until 1719, Bach probably lived in a spacious apartment in a building on the Schalaunische Straße. No longer extant (shown in the center of this 1884 drawing).

study of inventories, tax lists, town maps, home-ownership lists, etc.—736 documents in all—published online in 2008 by the Köthen-based software company
Georg Heeg, produced the following, necessarily tentative, conclusions: (1) Bach,
like his predecessor Kapellmeister Augustin Stricker, was the tenant (*Haus-
genosse*) of a private individual (unlike other musicians, who were home owners
or rented from the prince's properties); (2) Bach's residence was large enough to
accommodate his family (along with at least one servant), students who lived in
his household, and rehearsals of the court kapelle that took place there; (3) Bach's
first home was facing the Holzmarkt at Schalaunische Strasse 44. One of Köthen's
largest houses, it was owned by the merchant Johann Andreas Lautsch (d. 1741).

Finally, Heeg reports that from 1719 to 1723 the Bach family resided in the so-
called "Baroque Quarter." Bach was the first tenant in this new property, which,
like his first residence, was owned by merchant Lautsch. This *Bach-Haus*, unlike
his first residence, still stands; and the street is still called Wallstrasse. The house
is not open to the public. A few steps away, at Wallstrasse 31, stands the so-called
New Palace (*Neues Schloss*), which served as the town residence of Leopold's
younger brother until he acceded to the throne in 1728.

ABEL RESIDENCE. In 2014 Georg Heeg identified the residence of
Bach's colleague, the gamba virtuoso, Christian Ferdinand Abel. Located at

39. Köthen, Bach's likely second residence: Located at Wallstraße 25/26 and part of a large-scale urban expansion established in 1719 by Prince Leopold. The project required the construction of a new city wall (hence the street's name). The street widens in front of the house (at right) into a small plaza (*Bachplatz*) with a bust of the composer.

Springstrasse 8, close to the palace, the house (now an old-age home) was the birthplace of Abel's son, Carl Friedrich (1723–1787). Bach's sonatas for viola da gamba and harpsichord, BWV 1027–29, assuming they date from the Köthen period, would presumably have been composed for Abel senior, the prince's gamba instructor. The younger Abel, the most significant musician born in Köthen, was arguably the greatest gamba player of the eighteenth century as well as an outstanding composer. Although he resided in Leipzig for a period from 1743, it is uncertain whether he ever was a pupil of J. S. Bach's, as sometimes claimed. From 1759 until his death, he lived in London where in 1764 he founded the renowned Bach-Abel concerts with Sebastian's youngest son, Johann Christian (1735–82), who settled in the English capital in 1762.

CEMETERY. The cemetery where Bach's first wife was buried no longer exists. The area is now called Peace Park (*Friedenspark*), a public green space; it contains a plaque commemorating Maria Barbara Bach.

Literature: *BDOK I; BDOK II; NBR; Rust 1878; Hoppe 1985; Smend 1985; Glöckner 1997; Hoppe 1997; Zimpel 1998; Hoppe 2000; Wright 2000; Wolff 2000; Petzoldt 2000; Maul-Wollny 2003; Talle 2003; Hübner 2004; Organs; Erickson 2009; Reul 2011; Beißwenger 2012; Yearsley 2013; Leaver 2016a.*

Website: *www.heeg.de (G).*

CHAPTER 8

LEIPZIG (1723–50)

Bach spent well over half of his professional life in Leipzig. Until he arrived in the city on May 22, 1723, at the age of thirty-eight he had spent a total of twenty years—from 1703 to 1723—at his previous positions in Arnstadt, Mühlhausen, Weimar, and Köthen. He would spend the remaining twenty-seven years of his life occupying one of the most prestigious positions a church musician in Lutheran Germany at the time could attain. His title and his duties were twofold: Music Director for the City of Leipzig and Kantor of the St. Thomas School. He was offered the post only after two other candidates had turned it down: Georg Philipp Telemann (1681–1767), then music director for the city of **Hamburg**, and Christoph Graupner (1683–1760), then court kapellmeister in Darmstadt.

Bach had been in Leipzig before. In December 1717, in transit from his prior position at Weimar to his new one in Köthen, he conducted an examination of Johann Scheibe's new organ in St. Paul's Church (also known as the University Church), at the time the largest organ in Saxony. He submitted a critical yet balanced report on December 17th (NBR, no. 72). Bach's next documented visits to Leipzig were in connection with his application for the Thomaskantor position. On February 7, 1723, he performed two audition cantatas, *Jesus nahm zu sich die Zwölfe*, BWV 22, and *Du wahrer Gott und Davids Sohn*, BWV 23. After his selection and written acceptance of the position in April, he returned to Leipzig the following month. On that occasion he submitted to (and passed) a rigorous theological examination, presumably conducted in Latin, and administered by the superintendent, Salomon Deyling (1677–1755), together with a professor of theology from the university. It confirmed the composer's command of, and reliability with respect to, Orthodox Lutheran teaching. On May 5th, Bach signed the official contract in the town council chamber. He was formally installed as kantor of the St. Thomas School on June 1st by the pastor of St. Thomas's Church, Christian Weiss Sr. (1671–1736).

CONTEXTS

In addition to the lofty professional status, Leipzig offered Bach and his family other attractions. It was not only a prosperous metropolis but also a significant intellectual and cultural center with one of the most distinguished universities in Germany.

Political and Religious History

The Saxon city of Leipzig, situated at the crossroads of numerous ancient north-south and east-west trade routes, was founded in 1160. By the Renaissance, it had become a major commercial center rivaling Hamburg and Frankfurt am Main. Its early affluence was propelled not only by its favorable location but also by the discovery of silver and other valuable metals in the hills of the Ore Mountains region (*Erzgebirge*) located south of the city.

Contrasting with the medieval character created by the city's thirteenth-century walls and the original Gothic churches, Leipzig's appearance was substantially modified in later centuries. In the early sixteenth century, the Holy Roman Emperor Maximilian I (r. 1486–1519) granted the city trade privileges that attracted investment from the powerful Augsburg banking family, the Fuggers. By the mid-1550s, the city's prosperity was outwardly marked by monuments of Renaissance architecture such as the town hall (*Rathaus*) and the municipal weighing station (*Waage*).

Lutheranism had been established in Leipzig in 1539. In the next few years church and monastery properties were confiscated and placed under the jurisdiction of the secular government, that is, the town council. Monastery buildings belonging to the Augustinian St. Thomas's Church, the Franciscan Barefoot Friars' Church (*Barfüsserkirche*), and the Dominican St. Paul's Church were all secularized, the last given over to the university in 1544.

About 150 years later, and some 50 years after the end of the Thirty Years War (1618–48), the religious identity of Saxony was notably affected when Friedrich August I (August the Strong, 1670–1733) embraced the Catholic faith in 1697, just three years after his installation as elector, in order to acquire the Polish crown as King August II. His wife, Christiane Eberhardine of Brandenburg-Bayreuth (1671–1727), however, remained a devout Protestant and insisted that her children be raised in her faith. Perhaps in response to the monarch's conversion, Leipzig's Protestant character, if anything, intensified from the 1690s on.

40. Leipzig, Town Square: Town Hall (right) and "Old Weighing Station" (left). The rectangular structure of the town hall includes an off-center octagonal tower capped by a rounded Baroque crown. The town pipers' balcony is visible below the tower clock.

Commerce and the Fairs

Leipzig was besieged five times during the Thirty Years War and occupied for a time by Swedish troops. Soon afterward, during the plague of 1680, its population dropped from over 17,000 to 14,000. The city embarked thereafter on a spectacular and rapid economic recovery driven by the merchant and professional classes. The ruling Wettin family had granted the city substantial autonomy from the capital, Dresden, enabling it to profit from its geographical position. A manufacturing boom ensued, nourished by the influx of immigrants, notably the Huguenots driven from France after 1685. Leipzig's publishing industry steadily grew so that by the late seventeenth century the city had surpassed Frankfurt am Main as the center of the German book industry. Moreover, by 1700 it eclipsed Frankfurt as Germany's leading host of trade fairs.

Banking on its prosperity, Leipzig installed an underground sewage system in 1700 and introduced street lighting the following year. By 1714 there were some seven hundred municipal street lights that replaced private lanterns and, in the words of a chronicler, "remarkably checked" the commission of "many sins, especially those against the Fifth, Sixth and Seventh Commandments."

At the time of Bach's arrival, seventy-five years after the end of the Thirty Years War, Leipzig was the second-largest city in Saxony, after Dresden. Between 1700 and the early 1750s, its population increased from some 20,000 to over 32,000—its highest point in the eighteenth century. By the mid–eighteenth century, the writer and critic Gotthold Ephraim Lessing (1729–81) could describe Leipzig as "Little Paris."

The principal outward symbol of Leipzig's prosperity and commercial importance were the international trade fairs, which took place three times each year: at New Year's, Easter, and St. Michael's Feast (September). Each fair lasted three weeks, and special booths were constructed for the sale of goods. They complemented shops located in the permanent arcades that constituted part of the new architectural style. By royal decree, the fairs were protected from competition within a radius of some seventy miles. Since the fairs were an important source of tax revenue for the royal family, the Saxon electors were major benefactors of the city and patrons of cultural events during the fair seasons—none more so than the culture-loving monarch, August the Strong.

After having reached an apex in the early 1750s, Leipzig's fortunes began to fade soon after Bach's death, however, especially after the outbreak of the Seven Years War (1756–63), which left the city burdened with a crippling war debt of ten million thalers ($960 million), to be paid to victorious Prussia.

Government

Neither a princely residence nor an "imperial free city," Leipzig was technically subject to the monarchical rule of the Saxon electors resident in the capital, Dresden. The effective governing body, however, was the town council (*Stadtrat*). Consisting of thirty-three leading citizens, mostly businessmen and lawyers, council members were elected for life. The council conducted the city's business, which included oversight of the main churches. Structurally, it was organized into three subgroups, each with its own mayor who rotated into and out of power annually. Politically, it was divided between those who supported August's absolutist and cosmopolitan cultural agenda (the court party) and those who resisted it (the city, or Estates, party). During most of Bach's tenure the councilor responsible for St. Thomas's Church, Gottfried Lange (1672–1748), was closely connected to the Dresden court. One of Bach's strongest champions, Lange was godfather for his first child born in Leipzig, Gottfried Heinrich (1724–63). Other councilors, however—notably Abraham Platz (1658–1728), who oversaw St. Nicholas's Church, and Jacob Born (1683–1758)—were outspoken Bach antagonists.

Cultural and Intellectual Institutions

The thriving commercial life, the international character and prestige of the trade fairs, the presence of a major university, and the wealth of its citizens effectively assured that Leipzig would support a significant cultural and intellectual life. With Johann Christoph Gottsched's founding of the German Society (*Deutsche Gesellschaft*) in 1727, Leipzig became a major literary center. Some citizens were active collectors. The merchant and town councilor Johann Christoph Richter (1689–1751) assembled a famous collection of minerals and fossils, the *Museum Richterianum*. The banker Gottfried Winckler (1731–95), a founder of the Gewandhaus concerts, also owned an impressive art collection containing works by such masters as Dürer, Holbein, Rembrandt, and Titian. Open to the public for a few hours each week, it was one of Leipzig's main attractions.

UNIVERSITY OF LEIPZIG. Founded in 1409, the University of Leipzig was at that time one of only two universities in electoral Saxony. Although its traditional rival had originally been Wittenberg, by the eighteenth century its leading competitor was the more progressive university recently founded in the Prussian-controlled city of **Halle**. The students from noble backgrounds typically studied law with the intention of entering the court bureaucracy. Those from humble backgrounds generally studied theology with the object of becoming pastors or schoolteachers. In Leipzig none of the university buildings that stood in Bach's time have survived.

Both Wilhelm Friedemann Bach and Carl Philipp Emanuel Bach enrolled as students at the university. Friedemann studied law, philosophy, and mathematics there from 1729 to 1733, when he left for Dresden to become organist at St. Sophia's Church. Philipp Emanuel studied law from 1731 to 1734. A small number of his compositions from this time have survived, notably keyboard pieces and trios, but also a cantata on the text *Ich bin vergnügt mit meinem Stande*. He continued his university studies in Frankfurt an der Oder until 1738, when he moved to Rheinsberg to join the court kapelle of the Prussian crown prince Frederick, later Frederick the Great.

OPERA. In 1693 the Dresden court kapellmeister Nikolaus Adam Strungk (1640–1700) founded a resident opera company in Leipzig. The performances were mostly in German, in deference to the middle-class audience, and took place during the three annual trade fairs in a newly built public opera house located on the Brühl. From ca. 1703 to 1705, the opera was directed by Telemann, making use of student instrumentalists who thus became unavailable for services at the main churches—to the considerable dismay of then-Thomaskantor Johann Kuhnau (1660–1722). Telemann continued to compose operas for Leipzig over the following fourteen years. In later decades, the fortunes of the company declined until it folded in 1720. Gottsched's hostility to opera presumably contributed to its downfall. The opera house became an orphanage in 1729; later a prison, it was finally demolished in the nineteenth century.

Between 1720 and 1744, there was essentially no musical theater in Leipzig. In 1744 the Italian opera troupe of Pietro Mingotti (1702–59) began to visit Leipzig, a practice that continued until 1751. The performances reportedly included castrati. Whether Bach ever attended them is not known. A new opera company and theater were finally established in 1766.

CONCERT ORGANIZATIONS. The *Grosses Concert* (Grand Concert), the precursor of the Leipzig Gewandhaus concerts, was called into life in 1743 by a group of Leipzig merchants. Early performances took place in the concert hall of the *Gasthaus zu den drey Schwanen* (Inn of the Three Swans), located on the Brühl. Although J. S. Bach had no known connection with it, his son Wilhelm Friedemann was a guest artist on several occasions. In 1781 the orchestra moved into a newly fashioned concert hall on the third floor of the old *Gewandhaus* (textile merchants' headquarters), a building dating back to 1498. It was named, accordingly, the Gewandhaus orchestra. This remained Leipzig's main concert venue until 1884, when a new concert hall was inaugurated. Both buildings no longer exist. A third Gewandhaus opened in 1981.

Leipzig's importance for the musical life of Germany even after Bach's death has been enormous. At present the city boasts museums commemorating Robert Schumann and Felix Mendelssohn, who lived and thrived there. The Grassi Museum not only houses an exceptional collection of musical instruments but also illuminates Leipzig's role as a center of piano manufacturing and music publishing throughout the nineteenth and twentieth centuries. The city has organized three itineraries that connect music-related sites: the *Leipziger Notenspur* and *Notenbogen*, each about 5 km/3 miles long and intended for walking, and the *Notenrad*, a bicycle path of ca. 40 km/25 miles length connecting musical sites in the outskirts of Leipzig. (www.notenspur-leipzig.de [G, E])

BACH IN LEIPZIG

Bach had misgivings about leaving Köthen. By 1723 he had served as a court musician for fifteen years—nine at Weimar (1708–17) as organist and concertmaster, followed by six at Köthen (1717–23). There, he served as court kapellmeister and had the obligation of pleasing a single individual: an appreciative ruler (initially, at least), Prince Leopold. In Leipzig, by contrast, he was a public servant answerable in varying degrees to several authorities who together constituted a formidable bureaucracy: the mayor (*Bürgermeister*) and members of the town council; the ecclesiastical consistory, pastor, and superintendent of St. Thomas's Church; the administration of the St. Thomas School (rector [headmaster] and conrector [assistant headmaster]); and, to a lesser degree, the university administration.

There was also the matter of rank. As kapellmeister in Köthen, Bach was the second-highest paid court official; as Thomaskantor in Leipzig he was the third in rank at the school, after the rector and conrector. His official annual salary was set at one hundred thalers ($9,600). Although his actual income, including additional fees and honoraria, amounted to about seven hundred thalers ($67,200), this was in fact exactly the same as the combined salaries of Bach (four hundred thalers) and his wife (three hundred thalers) had been in Köthen.

Finally, instead of a select ensemble of fine professional musicians, Bach's resources as Thomaskantor consisted primarily of the choirboys of the St. Thomas School, together with ten to fifteen instrumentalists recruited from among the university students and

41. Leipzig, St. Thomas's School and Church: Viewed from the Bose House in an engraving (1723) by Johann Gottfried Krügner the elder; the image depicts the school as it appeared before it was enlarged in 1732.

his private pupils. The instrumentalists also included professional town musicians, several of them artists of outstanding caliber.

Upon arriving in Leipzig in two coaches accompanied by four wagons of belongings (NBR, no. 102), Bach and his family of eight (Sebastian; his second wife, Anna Magdalena; five children; and his first wife's sister, Friedelena Margaretha) took up residence in a "newly renovated apartment" in the original St. Thomas School building. Built in 1553, it stood adjacent to the St. Thomas Church. The journey from Köthen had taken them along a route of some 70 km/45 miles, through the small towns of Prosigk, Gölzau, Radegast, Zörbig, and Landsberg until they reached Leipzig's Halle Gate.

As Thomaskantor or music master of the St. Thomas School, the elite boys school attached to the Thomas Church, Bach gave the pupils musical training and prepared them for the weekly performances at four Leipzig churches: St. Thomas's, St. Nicholas's, St. Peter's, and the New Church (*Thomaskirche, Nikolaikirche, Petrikirche, Neue Kirche*). During the eighteenth century, the St. Thomas School normally housed fifty-five resident pupils, called "alumni," who received stipends along with room and board in return for singing in the school choirs. Divided according to their abilities into four groups, they performed in the regular church services in the town's four principal churches.

Along with theology, music stood at the center of the school's curriculum. The kantor was expected to give twelve weekly classes, including Latin and the catechism. Like his predecessor Kuhnau, Bach managed to avoid teaching the Latin classes by hiring a substitute whom he paid from his own funds. Both Wilhelm Friedemann and Carl Philipp Emanuel were pupils at the Thomas School from the year of the family's arrival in Leipzig: Friedemann remained until 1729, Emanuel until 1731.

The focus of Bach's activity as the city's music director was concentrated above all on the two principal churches, St. Thomas's—and St. Nicholas's. In this capacity, the Thomaskantor also provided the music for municipal events such as the annual inauguration of the town council or the celebrations and occasional visits of members of the Saxon royal family. During the tenure of Bach's immediate predecessor, Johann Kuhnau (1660–1722), the Thomaskantor's responsibilities were extended to include St. Peter's, the New Church, and, for a time, the university church, as well.

The kantor himself conducted the most highly skilled group, the first *Kantorei*, consisting of the school's best singers. They were accompanied by eight professional instrumentalists on the municipal payroll: four *Stadtpfeifer* (literally, town pipers); the city's top-ranked musicians whose leader was the extraordinary trumpeter, Gottfried Reiche; three *Kunstgeiger* (trained violinists, also profession-als); and a journeyman. This ensemble was augmented as necessary by university students, who received honoraria. The instrumentalists performed the "con-certed," or "figural" music, that is, the cantata.

Throughout the first years of Bach's kantorate, the vast majority of the canta-tas were works of his own composition, set to mostly anonymous texts that had first been submitted to the city's church superintendent, Salomon Deyling, for his approval. They consisted of cantatas on the regular Sundays and feast days of the church year, Passion settings for the Good Friday Vespers, and a number of Latin works: notably Sanctus and Magnificat performances on some high holidays and Marian feasts. In his first two years as Thomaskantor Bach produced almost 90 new church compositions for the services, often at the rate of one per week— sometimes more. He also performed the music of others, a practice that increased substantially beginning in 1726 when he presented seventeen cantatas by his dis-tant cousin, the Meiningen kantor Johann Ludwig Bach (1677–1731).

The cantata performances alternated from week to week between St. Nicho-las's and St. Thomas's. For example, Bach's first cantata as Thomaskantor, *Die Elenden sollen essen*, BWV 75, was performed on May 30, 1723, the First Sunday after Trinity, in St. Nicholas's Church. The following Sunday, June 6th, the cantata *Die Himmel erzählen die Ehre Gottes*, BWV 76, was performed in St. Thomas's Church. While Bach was conducting the first chorus, the singers of the second chorus, under the direction of one of the student "prefects" (that is, an assistant chosen by Bach) performed a less-demanding work, normally a motet, in the other main church. The third and fourth choruses were deployed at the New Church and St. Peter's and led by student prefects, as well.

According to a famous memorandum submitted by Bach to the Leipzig town council on August 23, 1730, the first three choruses each contained at least twelve singers and preferably sixteen: three or four for each vocal range: soprano, alto, tenor, bass. The fourth chorus consisted of just eight singers: two for each vocal range (NBR, no. 151). Exactly what the memorandum and its numbers meant has been a matter of debate among Bach scholars for decades. According to the most recent research (Maul 2013), the first choir, the *Kantorei*, consisted of a nucleus of eight paid singers. To what extent they were augmented, that is, to what extent Bach was able to have twelve or sixteen singers available, cannot be determined. The very existence of the memorandum, however, indicates that by 1730 Bach was hardly able to assemble sufficient competent forces with appropriate funding to produce satisfactory performances. Over the course of the next two decades, Bach's situation in Leipzig deteriorated further.

By the early 1730s, Bach's production of new church cantatas had fallen precipitously. Instead, he largely repeated works composed earlier. During the years 1734 and 1735, Bach performed numerous cantatas by the **Gotha** court kapellmeister, Gottfried Heinrich Stölzel (1690–1749), rather than his own music. By the early 1740s, having already ceased to write new compositions for the church service, Bach even may have ceased to perform them. In a recently discovered document, a former alumnus and prefect of the St. Thomas School, Gottfried Benjamin Fleckeisen (1719–86), claims that for a period of "two entire years" during that decade—presumably 1744–46—he had assumed this task in the absence of the Thomaskantor.

This gradual and inexorable reduction—and perhaps eventual cessation—of Bach's official activities reflected the mutual hostility between the composer and his superiors at the Thomas School and his growing alienation. A series of "enlightened" reforms, begun at just about the same time that Bach assumed the position in 1723 but only implemented in 1733, reached a crisis point by 1736 in the so-called "prefects' dispute" (*Präfektenstreit*). The conflict erupted over the appointment of the first student prefect by the new rector of the Thomas School, Johann August Ernesti (1707–81). This "usurpation" by the rector of a privilege Bach considered to be his exclusive prerogative was symptomatic of the larger object of the reforms, namely, to diminish the historical role and importance of musical training and performance in the school curriculum in favor of more academic subjects. Bach, for his part, increasingly devoted his creative energies elsewhere: for example, to **Berlin** or the **Dresden** court.

42. Leipzig, Zimmermann's Coffee House: Engraving (ca. 1720) by Johann Georg Schreiber. The establishment was located at the elegant Katharinenstraße 14, the corner property left of the alley (i.e., Böttchergasse).

As Bach reduced his commitments to his official duties as Thomaskantor, he increased his participation in Leipzig's secular musical life. The most decisive step occurred in 1729 when, seizing an opportunity to gain access to competent musicians, he assumed the directorship of a talented student ensemble known as the Collegium

Musicum. There was more than one such ensemble in Leipzig; the most famous and important was the one created by Telemann around 1701. By the time Bach became the director, the group included professional players. Over the course of his Leipzig years, Bach led the ensemble from 1729 to 1737 and again from 1739 to 1741, performing some 250–300 pieces a year with the Collegium, amounting to a total of about 1,200 hours of concerts. The concerts took place at the coffee house and, during the summer months, in the coffee garden belonging to Gottfried Zimmermann (d. 1741). Admission was three groschen (ca. $12) and open to women (Stauffer 2008).

In his final years Bach devoted himself to private pursuits: the systematic organization and occasional publication of organ and keyboard music such as the *Klavierübung* Parts Three and Four (Goldberg Variations), putting the "Great Eighteen" organ chorales and Book Two of the *Well-Tempered Clavier* into final form, and attempting to complete two monumental works: the remaining portions of the B-minor Mass and the *Art of Fugue*.

Over thirty journeys undertaken by Bach during his Leipzig period can be documented, beginning with the organ and church consecration in nearby **Störmthal** in November 1723 and concluding with his legendary visit to Frederick the Great in **Potsdam** in May 1747. (The trips included multiple visits to Köthen, **Dresden**, **Weißenfels**, and **Berlin**. See the Appendix for a complete tabulation.)

LANDMARKS

Churches

Of the four churches under Bach's regular jurisdiction two have survived. Fortunately they are the most important: St. Thomas's and St. Nicholas's.

ST. THOMAS'S CHURCH (THOMASKIRCHE). In the eighteenth century, St. Thomas's Church, the city's second church in rank, was located near the wall at the western end of the old town. The building began with the construction of a new church as part of an Augustinian monastery in 1212. In its present state, it is the product of several periods of construction, renovation, and reconstruction; most portions, however, date from the late fifteenth century. The neo-Gothic western facade dates from the nineteenth century. The present three-aisle hall church has been described as consisting of "two interiors: the older choir—deep, narrow, and low—separated by gate and altar from the later nave—a six-bay hall church, almost square in plan, with nave and aisles of similar heights and widths" (Otto 2009).

In Bach's time, the aisles contained wooden galleries along the north and south sides as well as two musicians' galleries in the chancel area. The large organ, extensively renovated by Leipzig's principal organ builder, Johann Scheibe (1680–1748), in 1721–22, and again in 1730 and 1747, was located over the western entrance. A second, small organ, known as the "swallow's nest" organ, was built in 1489 and renovated several times thereafter. It was located from 1640 to 1741 in a balcony of its own above the triumphal arch leading to the chancel. The pews were arranged along the nave in rows facing one another rather than the chancel. Further improvements followed in later years. On a Leipzig visit in 1789, Mozart played the organ and heard a performance of Bach motets in the church. The rear gallery instrument was replaced in the nineteenth century; a completely new organ, by Gerald Woehl, was installed in a side gallery in 1998–2000.

Eleven of Bach's children born by Anna Magdalena were christened at the church's baptismal font (1614/15), made of alabaster and black and red marble. The walls are decorated with paintings of the superintendents and early St. Thomas pastors, including Christian Weiss, pastor and inspector of the St. Thomas School from 1714. Beginning in the late nineteenth century, the south wall of the nave was outfitted with painted glass windows of illustrious figures including Martin Luther and Bach. A window honoring Mendelssohn was installed in 1997 to commemorate the 150th anniversary of his death. The *Thomaner*, or boys choir of the church, regularly offer concerts on Fridays and Saturdays, in addition to singing in the Sunday service.

In the 1840s, the so-called "Mendelssohn Bach Memorial" was erected near the church. Robert Schumann and Felix Mendelssohn were instrumental in its creation. At its consecration in 1843, Mendelssohn conducted a concert in the Gewandhaus attended by Bach's last surviving descendant bearing the family name: the eighty-three-year-old Wilhelm Friedrich Ernst Bach (1759–1845), the son of Johann Christoph Friedrich Bach (1732–95), the "Bückeburg Bach."

Sixty-five years later, an over-life-size Bach statue was created by the Leipzig sculptor Carl Seffner (1861–1932) according to measurements based on the remains presumed to be Bach's that had recently been exhumed in the churchyard of St. John's Church. In 1949 the remains themselves were transferred to the church. In 1964 the tomb was permanently placed into the floor of the chancel, the plain bronze memorial plate reading simply: "Johann Sebastian Bach."

ST. NICHOLAS'S CHURCH (NIKOLAIKIRCHE). Leipzig's official municipal church, St. Nicholas's, is located to the east of the town square. Although the tower foundations were laid in the twelfth century, the present three-aisle,

43. Leipzig, St. Nicholas's Church (with "Peace Column"): The city's principal church was the site of Bach's debut as Thomaskantor in 1723 and of the first performance of the St. John Passion the following year.

square-shaped hall church mostly dates from the sixteenth century. St. Nicholas's was the venue of the city's church superintendent. Throughout Bach's tenure, the position was occupied by Superintendent Deyling, with whom Bach had a mutually respectful relationship. Bach's audition cantatas (BWV 22 and 23) as well as his inaugural cantata as Thomaskantor (BWV 75) were performed here. The annual ceremonies attending the installation of the town council, which included cantatas by Bach, took place here as well. The organ in use in Bach's time was largely rebuilt by Johann Scheibe and later by Zacharias Hildebrandt. It was replaced in the nineteenth century. The church's striking interior, with its distinctive interior columns in white, pink, and green crowned by fanciful capitals sprouting large palm fronds, dates from the late eighteenth century and

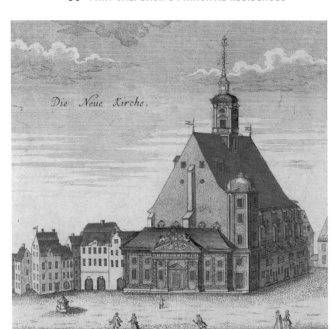

44. Leipzig, New Church: Hand-colored engraving (1749, Joachim Ernst Scheffler, *Scenographiae Lipsiacae*). The unusual architecture—the nave of the rectangular two-aisle Baroque hall church was bisected into two halves by massive pillars—resulted from a series of renovations.

represents a classicistic rethinking of Gothic interiors. During the 1980s, the church was the center of the so-called "Peaceful Revolution." A copy of an interior column, the "Column of Peace" (*Friedenssäule*) stands outdoors between the church and the old St. Nicholas School, which was once attended by Richard Wagner.

NEW CHURCH (NEUE KIRCHE). The city's third-ranked church in Bach's time, the New Church (1699), replaced the old Franciscan Barefoot Friar's Church (*Barfüsserkirche*) in the northwest end of the city. Beginning in 1704, the young law student Georg Philipp Telemann served for a year as organist and music director of the New Church; the position represented a threat at the time to the Thomaskantor Kuhnau. Rebuilt in neo-Gothic style in the late nineteenth century, when it was renamed St. Matthew's Church (*Matthäuskirche*), it was destroyed in 1943.

ST. PETER'S CHURCH (PETRIKIRCHE). Built in 1507 and rebuilt in 1710–12, the church stood on the Peterstrasse until it was demolished in 1886. Bach's responsibilities consisted only of providing the fourth chorus, the least competent pupils from the Thomas School, to participate in the singing of simple melody-only congregational hymns under the direction of a student prefect at the Sunday services.

In addition to the four churches that were his main responsibilities, Bach had connections with two other Leipzig churches.

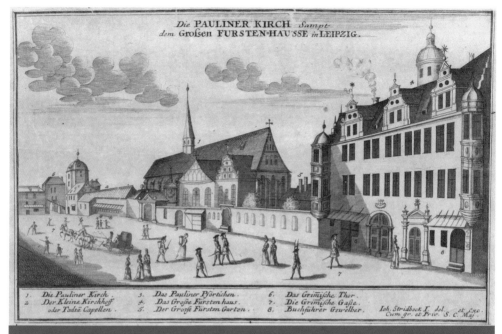

45. Leipzig, St. Paul's Church (University Church): Etching (ca. 1700) by Gabriel Bodenehr. Also visible: (far left) the Grimma Gate.

UNIVERSITY CHURCH/ST. PAUL'S CHURCH (UNIVERSITÄTSKIRCHE/ PAULINERKIRCHE). Located near the old wall at the eastern end of the city, just off the Grimmaische Strasse, the original church of St. Paul's dated from the 1240s. In 1543, some sixty years after its completion as a late Gothic hall church, it became the church for the university. The building survived World War II intact, but on May 30, 1968, exactly 245 years to the day after Bach made his official debut in Leipzig as Thomaskantor, it was dynamited by the Socialist regime. It has now been replaced by an "aula with vestry," a modern structure that imaginatively evokes the demolished edifice.

The new position of university music director was created in April 1723, that is, at about the same time that Bach was selected to be the Thomaskantor. Throughout his Leipzig tenure, Bach was permitted to provide music for the university's "Old Service" consisting of quarterly academic orations and for the high

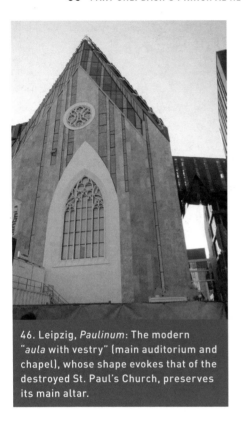

46. Leipzig, *Paulinum*: The modern *"aula* with vestry" (main auditorium and chapel), whose shape evokes that of the destroyed St. Paul's Church, preserves its main altar.

feasts (BDOK V, B 137a). He also composed music for a few special events held at the university, most notably the ode, *Laß Fürstin, laß noch einen Strahl*, BWV 198, which was performed in the University Church for the funeral of the Protestant Queen Christiane Eberhardine in 1727.

ST. JOHN'S CHURCH (JOHANNI-SKIRCHE). Attached to the Hospital of St. John and located outside the town walls in front of the Grimma Gate, St. John's Church opened ca. 1700. Bach and the pupils from the fourth chorus of the Thomas School were responsible for the music performed in the church on the three high feasts and for the burial services at the cemetery adjoining the church (*Johannisfriedhof*). The church was severely damaged during World War II, but its Baroque tower remained fully intact. Both were decisively demolished in 1963 by the Communist government. Its organ, however, which was built by Johann Scheibe in 1742 using elements from the dismantled "swallow's nest" organ of St. Thomas's and examined by Bach the following year, had been removed long before then. Its key-desk and organ bench are now displayed in the Bach Museum of the Bach Archive across town. Johann Sebastian and Anna Magdalena Bach were originally buried in the churchyard of St. John's Church—now a green space in front of the Grassi Museum. In 1894, their purported remains—which, according to legend, had been interred six steps from the south door—were exhumed and examined and subsequently buried in the Thomas Church.

Municipal Architecture

Since Leipzig was heavily bombed during World War II, most of the few "extant" buildings are in fact extensive restorations. Occasionally, only the facades were re-created, the interiors thoroughly modernized.

TOWN HALL (RATHAUS). The seat for the Leipzig municipal government and a masterpiece of German Renaissance secular architecture, the town hall was built in 1556/57 by Hieronymus Lotter (1497–1580). It was renovated in 1672 and rebuilt after World War II. It was here that Bach signed the employment contract for the Thomas kantorate. Professional municipal musicians—*Stadtpfeifer* and *Kunstgeiger*—performed music daily from its tower, a tradition with which the Thomaskantor had no connection. The Leipzig City Museum (*Museum für Stadtgeschichte*), housed in the town hall, displays one of the two famous oil portraits of Bach by the court and municipal painter, Elias Gottlob Haussmann (1695–1774). Painted in 1746, it is the earlier of the versions that have survived. Haussmann's portraits of the trumpet virtuoso Gottfried Reiche (1667–1734) and many town officials hang there as well.

47. Leipzig, Gottfried Reiche: Oil portrait (ca.1727) by Elias Gottlob Haussmann. Bach's principal trumpeter was the leader of the municipal musicians guild from 1719.

OLD WEIGHING STATION (ALTE WAAGE). The "Old Weighing Station," located at the corner of Katharinenstrasse and the town square, dates from 1555. The architect, once again, was presumably Hieronymous Lotter. Vendors from out of town had their wares weighed here and paid customs accordingly. Until 1861 the building included a tower (see p. 75). Destroyed in 1943, the facade of the weighing station, without the original tower, was reconstructed 1963–64. Bach is known to have used the tower on at least one occasion. On October 5, 1734, he performed the elaborately scored homage cantata, *Preise dein Glücke, gesegnetes Sachsen*, BWV 215, in the Leipzig town square, in the presence of the Saxon royalty. The occasion was the anniversary of the election of Elector Friedrich August II as King August III of Poland. According to the entry in the Leipzig town chronicle, "at about nine o-clock in the evening the university students offered their Majesties a serenade with trumpets and drums, which Capellmeister Bach had composed. Six hundred students carried wax tapers. . . . The procession made its way up to the King's residence [at the Apel house, see later in this chapter]. When the musicians had reached the weighing station, the trumpets and drums ascended it, while others took their places in another choir at the town hall" (NBR, no. 173).

The performance proved fatal for the great trumpeter. The town chronicler reported that on the following day Gottfried Reiche collapsed and died of a stroke on the street in front of his house, owing to "the great strenuousness of the trumpet part and the smoke of the tapers." He was sixty-seven years old.

OLD STOCK EXCHANGE (ALTE BÖRSE). Another major structure doubtless familiar to Bach was the old stock exchange (1678–87). The town's first large public structure in Baroque style, it was a meeting place for Leipzig's merchants.

48. Leipzig, "Old Stock Exchange": On the *Naschmarkt* (the former fruit and vegetable market), directly behind the town hall (visible at left). The symmetrical shape reflects Italian influence; the decorated facade is indebted to the Dutch. The lavish structure attests to the wealth and pride of Leipzig's merchant class.

Domestic Architecture

The town council had displayed its ambitions for the city by appointing out-standing architects skilled in making maximum use of the city's narrow plots. By the middle of the eighteenth century, Leipzig had the appearance of a thriving Baroque-style bourgeois metropolis. The elegant Katharinenstrasse and the Brühl, especially, featured a new style of multistory domestic house typically outfitted with two-story roofs, bay windows, statuary and gilt ornamentation. Commercial shops were accommodated in arcades at street level.

ROMANUS HOUSE. The luxurious residence on Katharinenstrasse once belonged to Franz Conrad Romanus (1679–1745), one of Leipzig's wealthiest bur-ghers and a former mayor. Dating from 1701–4, it was designed by Johann Gregor Fuchs (1650–1715), an outstanding architect who had worked in **Dresden** with Matthäus Daniel Pöppelmann (1662–1736). The richly decorated residence features an open cen-tral courtyard with a passage-way leading to both the Kathari-nenstraße and the Brühl fronts. Such a passage (*Durchgangshof*), a central court connected by corridors to two streets, was a hallmark of Leipzig Baroque architecture, as it facilitated the loading and unloading of wares. The mansion was later occupied by Romanus's daughter, the poet Christiane Marianne von Ziegler (1695–1760), an associate of Gottsched, an early feminist, and the librettist of nine church cantatas set to music by Bach.

APEL HOUSE. The man-sion belonged to the merchant and silk manufacturer Andreas Dietrich Apel (1662–1718). The architect, again, was J. G. Fuchs. The building was dubbed "the King's House," since members

49. Leipzig, Apel House (1705/6): Engraving (1720) by Martin Bernigeroth. Arguably Leipzig's most magnificent mansion stands on the town square. The inscription reads "Apel's house in which His Royal Majesty usually lodges." Townspeople, soldiers in formation, and a small band evidently await the king's arrival.

50. Leipzig, Bose House (late sixteenth century, expanded in 1711): Headquarters, since 1985, of the Leipzig Bach Archive.

of the royal Saxon family stayed here (as paying guests) whenever they visited Leipzig. These occasions often included performances of secular cantatas in their honor composed and conducted by Bach. Protestant Leipzig never allowed the Catholic king to build a personal residence within its borders.

BOSE HOUSE, BACH ARCHIVE, AND MUSEUM. This house, belonging to Georg Heinrich Bose (1682–1731), a manufacturer of gold- and silverware, stands at Thomaskirchhof 16, directly across the churchyard from the entrance to St. Thomas's. The Bach and Bose families were thus next-door neighbors and, in fact, good friends. Four of Bose's children were godparents for Bach's children. Anna Magdalena Bach was apparently especially close to Bose's daughter, Christiana Sibylla (1712–49), and Johann Sebastian may have performed in the mansion's music room.

The Bose House is the headquarters of the Leipzig Bach Archive, a scholarly research center containing the world's second-largest collection of original Bach sources (surpassed only by the Berlin State Library). In 2008–10 the building was extensively renovated and now houses, along with the archive, a modern Bach museum containing, among other significant holdings, the original key-desk that had belonged to the Scheibe organ from St. John's Church and a detailed scale model of the demolished St. Thomas School. A small concert hall on the top floor, the so-called "summer hall" (*Sommersaal*) features an oval-shaped musicians' gallery in the ceiling not unlike that of the *Himmelsburg* chapel in Weimar. Its central portion, painted to simulate the sky, can be opened via a clever mechanism dating to Bach's time, producing interesting acoustical effects.

In 2015 the Bach Archive acquired the later of the two original Haussmann portraits of J. S. Bach. Over the previous sixty years, this version of the work, dating from 1748, was in the possession of the American philanthropist and Bach connoisseur William H. Scheide (1914–2014). In far better condition than its twin, it presumably represents a truer likeness of the composer. With Scheide's bequest, both originals of this most iconic of Bach portraits are now accessible to the public in the most appropriate of venues, the city of Leipzig.

ZIMMERMANN'S COFFEE HOUSE. The venue for Bach's Collegium Musicum entertainments after 1723, the building was destroyed in World War II. Its former location is marked by a plaque.

PLEASURE GARDENS AND THE "LITTLE GOHLIS PALACE" (GOHLISER SCHLÖSSCHEN). Leipzig's bourgeois prosperity was displayed as well in numerous pleasure gardens located outside the town's old walls. Perhaps the most famous of the city's old pleasure gardens were those in French style belonging to members of the Bose family. By the 1730s, there were approximately 130 such garden parks in Leipzig, with pavilions and orangeries. Gottfried Zimmermann's coffee garden, located outside the Grimma Gate, hosted Bach's Collegium Musicum concerts during the summer months. The gardens eventually gave way to the expansion of Leipzig beyond its city walls. The walls themselves were replaced, beginning in the 1760s, by a fashionable promenade encircling the town. Their outline is still evident in the circular roadway (*Promenadenring*) around Leipzig's city center.

The "Little Gohlis Palace" (*Gohliser Schlösschen*) was built shortly after Bach's time by the Leipzig merchant Johann Caspar Richter (1708–1770) in the village of Gohlis (now part of Leipzig) to serve as his summer residence. With its formal park and orangeries it is a surviving example of such suburban gardens. It contains a festival hall adorned with wall paintings by Adam Friedrich Oeser (1717–1799), a leading Leipzig artist. His students included the art historian Johann Joachim Winckelmann, Goethe, and C. P. E. Bach's short-lived son, the painter Johann Sebastian Bach the Younger (1748–78). From 1950 to 1985, the palace housed the Bach Archive. It is now the site of special events, exhibitions, and concerts.

EPILOGUE: BACH'S RESIDENCE AT THE ST. THOMAS SCHOOL

The entrance to Bach's apartment in the original Thomas School building was situated in the south wing, on the left side of the building, as viewed from the church courtyard (*Thomaskirchhof*). The rector of the school, Johann Heinrich Ernesti (1652–1729), occupied the corresponding apartment on the right side. Ernesti had served in that position since 1684. Between the doors for the two apartments was the school entrance—a most convenient arrangement, since

51. Leipzig, St. Thomas's School: Photograph (before 1885) showing the building as it looked after its expansion in 1732. The plain western front of St. Thomas's Church (at left) received its current neo-Gothic facade and entry portal shortly after the photo was taken.

one of Bach's responsibilities as Thomaskantor was to serve one week a month as monitor of the dormitories.

Bach's apartment occupied three floors and contained approximately 2,000 square feet as well as basement and attic space. The music, composing, and main living rooms and the kitchen were located on the first floor. The second and third floors contained additional living space and bedrooms. In the years 1731–32, during the tenure of a new rector, the classicist, music lover, and Bach admirer Johann

Matthias Gesner (1691–1761), the building was thoroughly renovated and enlarged by the addition of two further stories after plans drafted by the leading Leipzig architect, Georg Werner (1682–1758).

The St. Thomas School building was further renovated in the nineteenth century but was completely razed in 1902. The site is now occupied by a new superintendent's building bearing a plaque that reads (in translation): "Until the year 1902 the old St. Thomas School stood on this site. Johann Sebastian Bach resided in it from 1723 to 1750." The original door to the cantor's apartment has survived and is now on display in the Bach Museum in Eisenach.

Literature: BDOK I; BDOK V; NBR; Stauffer 1993; Basso 1997; Siegele 1997; Leisinger 1998; Petzoldt 2000; Wolff 2000; Humbach et al. 2003; Hübner 2004; Hübner 2005; Langusch 2007; Leaver 2009; Schulze 2008; Stauffer 2008; Erickson 2009; Maul 2009; Otto 2009; Stauffer 2009; Wolff 2009; Organs; Glöckner 2012; Maul 2012; Maul 2013; Gardiner 2013; Maul 2015; Schulenberg 2014; Rathey 2016.

PART TWO

TOWNS CERTAINLY OR PRESUMABLY (*)
VISITED BY J. S. BACH

Altenburg and Rötha° (1739)

Altenburg

Located 48 km/30 miles south of Leipzig on the *via imperii* (an important north-south trade route), both the town and the palace of Altenburg were important outposts of imperial power during the Middle Ages, serving as centers for the expansion of Christianity into Slavic areas to the East. Emperor Frederick I Barbarossa (r. 1155–90) paid no fewer than seven visits to Altenburg, hence the city's nickname, "Barbarossa Town" (*Barbarossastadt*). The town's emblematic "red steeples" (*Rote Spitzen*), two red brick Romanesque church towers situated on a hill above the town, are the only surviving remains of the church of St. Mary's, part of a large collegiate convent initiated in 1165 by Barbarossa and consecrated in his presence in 1172. The church had been the largest and earliest sacred edifice made of brick to be found north of the Alps, betraying the influence of Northern Italian models.

A testimony to the town's former significance is the large market square with its Renaissance town hall and many attractive burgher houses. It was first mentioned in 1192.

Bach's connection with Altenburg rests entirely on the great organ for the court church St. George's by Tobias Heinrich Gottfried Trost (ca. 1680–1759). The instrument, built 1733–39 and still extant, generated great interest and admiration among musicians and fellow organ builders. During its construction, the **Gotha** court kapellmeister, Gottfried Heinrich Stölzel (1690–1749), paid a visit, as did both J. S. Bach and Johann Adolph Scheibe (1708–86) in 1739. Gottfried Silbermann, who was working on an organ at the time in nearby Ponitz (18 km/11 miles to the south), came to observe the work in progress, as well. Several of Trost's journeymen for the Altenburg project went on to become famous organ builders. One of them, Christian Ernst Friderici (1709–80), later opened a shop in **Gera**. Friderici was also a maker of stringed keyboard instruments, from whom Leopold Mozart (1719–87) purchased a two-manual harpsichord played by his son during his Salzburg years. One of Bach's students, Johann Ludwig Krebs (1713–80), served as the organist at the Altenburg court church from 1756 to his death.

Bach's visit to Altenburg is recorded in a court document dated September 7, 1739, before the official inspection of the instrument undertaken by Stölzel in late October. It reads as follows: "The well-known kapellmeister Bach, of Leipzig, was heard at the organ, and, in passing, judged that the organ's construction was very durable, and that the organ builder had succeeded in giving each stop its particular nature and proper sweetness" (BDOK II, no. 453). The exact nature of Bach's visit is not clear. Since two court letters to Duke Friedrich III of Saxony-Altenburg (r. 1732–72) refer to it, it may have had some semiofficial purpose. But there is no mention of any payment. At all events, a putative eye witness account, not published until 1798, reports that Bach also played the organ at a service, presumably on September 6, 1739, the Fifteenth Sunday after Trinity. According to the account, "Few are able to guide a congregation as old Bach could do, who once played the Credo chorale [*Wir glauben all an einen Gott*] on the large organ in Altenburg in D minor, but raised the congregation to E-flat minor for the second verse, and for the third verse up to E minor. But only a Bach could do this and only the organ in Altenburg. Not all of us are or have that" (BDOK V, no. C1005a, p. 259). To enable such modulations, the Altenburg organ clearly made use of some form of "well-tempered" tuning. In addition, the thirty-two-foot bass *Posaune* and the glockenspiel register, neither part of the original plan, were conceivably added to the organ on Bach's recommendation.

Landmarks

CASTLE AND COURT CHURCH (SCHLOSS AND SCHLOSSKIRCHE). The large Altenburg castle complex overlooking the town forms an almost circular, connected ensemble surrounding a large open court. Its beginnings can be traced to the tenth century. A stout Romanesque tower, the so-called "bottle," dates from the eleventh century. Three medieval towers, fortification walls, and a double-gate entrance belong to early phases of the complex.

The church is an integral part of the castle. In the years 1645–49, the late-Gothic church interior was redecorated and furnished in Baroque style evident as well in the organ case. Earlier remnants, aside from the highly filigreed star vaulting, include elaborately carved choir benches dating from 1500 and a fresco from ca. 1488 representing Christ before Pilate.

The Baroque palace forms a major part of the ensemble. Two side wings (the *Corps de Logis*) are connected to a third—the nineteenth-century festival hall (*Festsaalflügel*)—consisting of a sumptuous ballroom. The *Corps de Logis* contains a museum mostly devoted to the Wettin dynasty, which ruled Altenburg and surrounding regions from the fourteenth century on.

In the seventeenth century, the castle became the residence of the Saxony-Coburg-Altenburg line, precipitating a revitalization that accounts for the Baroque makeovers, including the building of the Trost organ. Almost life-size equestrian portraits of the dukes Friedrich II (d. 1732) and Friedrich III (d. 1772) are prominently displayed on the second-floor landing. The former, dating from 1732, is the work of Elias Gottlob Haussmann (1695–1774), the painter of the

52. Altenburg, Castle: With Court Church.

famous Bach portrait. One historic room—adjacent to the church and providing access to it—is dubbed the "Bach Hall" or "Church Hall" (*Bachsaal, Kirchensaal*). Now used for concerts, it is a late-nineteenth-century reinvention, in neo-Renaissance style, replacing a Baroque hall that had been consumed in a fire.

Other buildings were added, destroyed by fire, replaced, and repeatedly altered from the tenth century on. Some of the constituent Renaissance-style buildings are in fact nineteenth-century re-creations added in the aftermath of devastating fires. As late as 1992 the so-called "pages' quarters" (*Junkerei*) were rebuilt, five years after they had burned down. The castle's checkered and calamitous history has resulted in an exceptionally attractive architectural enclosure. A Neptune fountain, originally designed as a drinking trough for horses, stands in the center of the courtyard.

The castle also contains a *Skat* museum—a testimonial to the fact that the immensely popular German card game, *Skat*, was invented in Altenburg. The city is a center of playing card production to this day.

ST. BARTHOLOMEW'S CHURCH (BARTHOLOMÄUSKIRCHE). The city church of St. Bartholomew's was founded in the twelfth century. Its current structure dates mostly from 1459. Martin Luther repeatedly preached in this church. His friend and protector, Georg Spalatin (1484–1545), who engineered his escape to the Wartburg in Eisenach, is buried in St. Bartholomew's.

Bach's presumable route from Leipzig: Leipzig—Rötha—Altenburg.

Rötha•

Since Bach almost certainly passed through the town of Rötha (located some 19 km/12 miles south of Leipzig) and possibly overnighted there on his way to Altenburg, this trip would have presented him with a natural opportunity to visit the outstanding Silbermann organs in the Churches of St. George's and St. Mary's, the former instrument (1721) a collaboration of Gottfried Silbermann (1683–1753) and Zacharias Hildebrandt (1688–1757), the latter the work of Silbermann alone (1721–22).

Literature: Zürner 1753; BDOK II; BDOK V; Keil-Künzl 2001; Petzoldt 2000; Organs; Schrammek 1985; Badura-Skoda 2008.

Ammern• (1712)

Ammern, located 6 km/4 miles north of Mühlhausen, is now a part of the municipality of Unstruttal. Like other small villages in the vicinity, Ammern commissioned an organ from Johann Friedrich Wender (1655–1729). Wender built four new organs for Mühlhausen itself: one for the Brückenhof Church (but since relocated to the town of Dörna) and others for the churches of St. Peter's, St. Martin's, and St. George's. The latter three churches, all situated just outside the old city walls (but already part of Mühlhausen in Wender's time), still stand. Their organs unfortunately no longer survive.

The Wender instruments that played the most important roles in the life of J. S. Bach were the organ in the New Church in Arnstadt, examined in 1703 by Bach, who then became its first organist, and the renovated organ at St. Blasius's Church in Mühlhausen, for which Wender incorporated Bach's suggestions.

The organ for the St. Vitus Church in Ammern, built mainly between 1703 and 1706, was reexamined by Wender in 1710 at the church's request. Further documents reveal that in 1712 the parish made payments to the organ builder and to the organ builder's apprentice, and other payments for incidental expenses. In addition, a payment of three *schock* and four *groschen* was made "for testing the organ" to "H. N. N. Bachen," that is, *Herrn nomen nescio Bach* (Mr. Name Unknown Bach; facsimile Kröhner 1995, 88). In the absence of first names, one of two Bachs may have been meant: either Johann Friedrich Bach (1682–1730), the son of the Eisenach organist and "profound composer" Johann Christoph (1642–1703), or J. S. Bach himself. Sebastian Bach would have had to travel some 84 km/52 miles to Ammern from Weimar in order to examine the organ, whose beginnings he probably observed while he was organist in Mühlhausen. The fee, worth about $250, seems adequate, although no additional payments for travel expenditures are recorded. Bach's friendship with Wender, however, and his continued good relations with Mühlhausen after his departure suggest that he was the likely examiner of the Ammern organ.

The church of St. Vitus, dating from 1270, still stands. It is constructed as a *Chorturmkirche*, that is, one whose tower is situated above the chancel at the east end of the church, a Romanesque design not uncommon in Thuringia. A neo-Gothic gallery surrounds the base of the solid tower, which otherwise retains the character of the typical Thuringian fortress church (*Wehrkirche*). Some remnants of paintings are visible on the interior church walls, but nothing survives of the Wender organ.

Literature: Kröhner 1995; Kröhner 2015.

Bad Berka°

Bach's connection with Bad Berka, now a spa located 12 km/7 miles south of Weimar, is tenuous. A document from 1798 refers to the "Disposition of the organ in Berga [*sic*] which Mr. Sebastian Bach of Leipzig has made and which was built by the organ builder Trebs" (BDOK II, no. 515). Bach's proposed plan, in fact, was not followed, but rather a more modest one submitted by his former student, Johann Caspar Vogler (1696–1763), who in 1721 had succeeded him as Weimar court organist.

The Gothic St. Mary's Church in Bad Berka was damaged in 1608 in a major fire. The surviving ruined tower was weakened further in 1650 when Duke Wilhelm of Weimar (r. 1620–62) used it as a quarry for the building of the Wilhelmsburg palace in Weimar. In 1727 Duke Ernst August I (r. 1707–48) ordered the rebuilding of the church tower, crowning it with a weather vane in the shape of a stag as a tribute to the area surrounding Berka as a favorite hunting ground of the Weimar dukes. (The townspeople eventually responded in kind by placing a cross on the town hall.) The rebuilding of the church proper began in 1739 and was completed in 1743 with the installation of the organ.

The new organ was the work of the Weimar court organ builder Heinrich Nicolaus Trebs (1678–1748), his son Christian Wilhelm, and the journeyman Christian Immanuel Schweinefleisch (1721–71). Church accounts indicate that in 1740/41 Vogler received a payment of three *gulden*, four *groschen* "for the disposition of the new organ." Bach's plan was evidently too ambitious for the limited space. The present organ case is a modification of the original.

In 1739, between the rebuilding of the church tower and the new church itself, an enormous storehouse was erected in Berka for hunting paraphernalia

(*Jagdzeughaus*). The edifice was another extravagant testimonial to Ernst August's passion for the so-called "enclosed hunt," an activity that the local peasantry was obliged to support through compulsory service. The surviving building, now the town library and social center, contains a small permanent exhibit on the "enclosed hunt."

Berka, in the early nineteenth century, provided the setting for arguably Goethe's most profound encounter with the music of J. S. Bach. Shortly after sulfur springs were discovered in the town, Goethe, in his role as privy councilor to Archduke Carl August of Weimar (r. 1758–1828), supported the building of a bath complex. He befriended the town organist and bath inspector, one Heinrich Friedrich Schütz (1779–1829), who had studied with Bach's last pupil, Johann Christian Kittel (1732–1809). Serving in effect as Goethe's private pianist, Schütz played music "from Sebastian Bach up to Beethoven" (letter to Carl Friedrich Zelter, January 4, 1819). There is no indication, however, that Schütz had ever played the Berka organ for Goethe. Commemorative plaques on Schütz's house in Bad Berka memorialize both men.

Reminiscing about these experiences, Goethe set down his famous Bach aphorism in a letter to C. F. Zelter dated June 21, 1827: "I thought of the worthy organist of Berka; for it was there . . . that I first obtained some idea of your grand master. I said to myself, it is as if the eternal harmony were conversing within itself, as it may have done in the bosom of God just before the Creation of the world" (NBR, p. 499). These words were presumably inspired by Schütz's playing of the *Well-Tempered Clavier*.

In 1816 a major fire destroyed large parts of Bad Berka. Goethe engaged the duchy's eminent planning director, Clemens Wenzeslaus Coudray (1775–1845), to oversee the town's rebuilding. His major contribution was the spa and social meeting place now called "Coudray Haus," set in the large park designed according to Goethe's plans for the recreation of guests.

Literature: BDOK II; NBR; Häfner 2006.

Berlin (1719, 1741, 1745*, 1747, 1748?)

Berlin played a significant role in the lives of J. S. Bach and his two oldest sons. Wilhelm Friedemann spent much of the final decade of his life (1774–84) in the Prussian capital. Carl Philipp Emanuel spent approximately the first thirty years

(1738–68) of his professional career there in the service of its king, Frederick the Great.

In early 1719, J. S. Bach made his first known visit to Berlin. His mission was to acquire a harpsichord by the renowned royal builder Michael Mietke (d. 1719) for Prince Leopold and to oversee its transport back to the Köthen court, a journey of some 162 km/100 miles each way (BDOK II, no. 95). While in Berlin, Bach was introduced to Margrave Christian Ludwig of Brandenburg-Schwedt (1677–1734) who as the youngest son of Friedrich Wilhelm of Brandenburg, the Great Elector (r. 1640–88), was not in line for the throne. Like other members of the royal family, Christian Ludwig supported a small orchestra at his residence, the Berlin city palace (*Stadtschloss*). Bach famously dedicated his six Brandenburg concertos to him, sending him a meticulously copied autograph manuscript of the work in 1721. Bach's French dedication to the margrave, dated March 24, 1721, begins with a reference to their earlier encounter: "As I had a couple of years ago the pleasure of appearing before Your Royal Highness . . . and as in taking leave . . . Your Highness deigned to honor me with the command to send . . . some pieces of my composition . . . I have taken the liberty of rendering my most humble duty . . . with the present concertos." Most likely the solo harpsichord part in the Fifth Brandenburg Concerto—and the expansive, unprecedented virtuosic cadenza in the first movement, in particular—was conceived for the Mietke harpsichord and is a further testimonial to Bach's 1719 Berlin visit.

J. S. Bach's presumable route to Berlin from Köthen:
Köthen—Dessau—Wittenberg—Treuenbrietzen—Saarmund—Berlin.

No further trips to Berlin by Bach are documented until the 1740s. They are closely related to his son Carl Philipp Emanuel's role in the service of Frederick the Great (r. 1740–86). Upon becoming King of Prussia in the spring of 1740, Frederick had left his Arcadian residence at Rheinsberg and moved to Charlottenburg, eschewing both the Berlin city palace and the palace at **Potsdam**, the residence of his father, Friedrich Wilhelm I, the "soldier king" (r. 1713–40), and a garrison town harboring unpleasant memories for the new monarch.

Charlottenburg, now part of Berlin, is located 8 km/5 miles west of the city's center and provided Frederick the more pastoral, less formal environment he preferred. Newly in charge of Prussian finances, he was able to establish his court kapelle at full strength, consisting of some forty members with documented salaries.

Frederick set out immediately to expand and beautify Charlottenburg and to build a new opera house near the Berlin city palace. The architect Georg

Wenzeslaus von Knobelsdorff (1699–1753) was put in charge of these and all other architectural projects of the court. Despite his military engagements, which had begun in November 1740 with the first Silesian War, Frederick continued to maintain his large kapelle. Beginning in 1742, the ensemble was also responsible for the opera. Its members included the brothers Graun: Carl Heinrich (1704–59) as kapellmeister and Johann Gottlieb (1703–71) as concertmaster. It also featured the brothers Benda: Franz (1709–86) and Georg (1722–95). Hovering above them all, held high in Frederick's esteem, was Johann Joachim Quantz (1697–1773), Frederick's occasional flute teacher since 1728 and, from 1741 on, a permanent member of the court kapelle. As Frederick's musical confidante, teacher, and court composer, Quantz received a salary of two thousand thalers (ca. $192,000) and enjoyed the exclusive privilege of commenting on the king's playing (by exclaiming "bravo"—or not).

J. S. Bach's Later Berlin Visits

In late July or early August 1741, J. S. Bach took the ca. 200-km/124-mile journey north from Leipzig to visit his son in Berlin, staying through early August with a family friend, the physician and privy councilor Georg Ernst Stahl (1713–72), at his home on Unter den Linden, the city's elegant main street. The king was away at the time, engaged with the first Silesian War. On this occasion, Bach may have made or renewed his personal acquaintance with members of the court kapelle. Philipp Emanuel remarked in a letter to J. N. Forkel from January 1775, "In his last years he esteemed highly . . . Hasse, both Grauns, Telemann, Zelenka, Benda, and in general everything that was worthy of esteem in Berlin and **Dresden**. . . . [He] knew [them] personally" (NBR, no. 395). The visit, however, came to an abrupt end after Bach received two urgent letters from his cousin and amanuensis in Leipzig, Johann Elias Bach (1705–55), imploring him to return home at once, since Anna Magdalena, the composer's wife, was gravely ill (NBR, nos. 222–23). In the end, Anna Magdalena recovered her health. The cantata, *O holder Tag, erwünschte Zeit*, BWV 210, seems to have been composed for Stahl's impending wedding, which took place in St. Nicholas's Church on September 19, 1741, that is, after Bach had been summoned home. The conductor, in Bach's absence, was evidently his former pupil, Johann Friedrich Agricola (1720–74).

Emanuel's first child, Johann August, was baptized on December 10, 1745. J. S. Bach is listed among the godparents. Although his attendance is not documented, it would have been customary to indicate the name of a substitute, had the godfather not been present. No such name is recorded. A second grandson, Emanuel's third child Johann Sebastian Bach Jr., was baptized in Berlin on September 26, 1748. Once again, there is no record that J. S. Bach attended the ceremony.

Bach's next documented visit, in May 1747, in the company of Wilhelm Friedemann Bach, was his famous appearance at Frederick's court in **Potsdam**. After the Potsdam appearances Bach proceeded to Berlin to visit with Philipp Emanuel, who later reported to Forkel that he showed his father the new opera house. During the tour, Bach senior, upon seeing the dining room—presumably the large foyer now known as the Apollo Hall (*Apollosaal*)—deduced from the shape of its ceiling that it possessed an unusual acoustical feature that would enable people standing in opposite corners of the room to hear whispers inaudible to anyone elsewhere in the room (NBR no. 394).

J. S. Bach's presumable route to Berlin from Leipzig:
Leipzig—Bad Düben—Wittenberg—Treuenbrietzen—Saarmund—Berlin.

Landmarks

OPERA HOUSE (STAATSOPER). The opera house, now *Staatsoper Unter den Linden*, a masterpiece by Knobelsdorff, was Germany's first freestanding opera house and at the time the largest in Europe. It bears the inscription *Fridericus Rex*

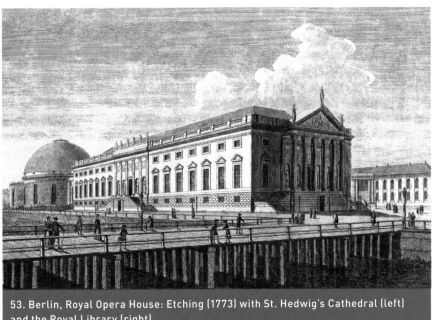

53. Berlin, Royal Opera House: Etching (1773) with St. Hedwig's Cathedral (left) and the Royal Library (right).

Apollini et Musis ("King Frederick [dedicates this] to Apollo and the Muses"). The edifice was to be a major component of the planned *Forum Fridericianum*, which was only partially realized. From its inauguration in 1742 until the outbreak of the Seven Years War (1756–63), when opera performances were suspended, the opera house was the central focus of Berlin court musical life during the December–February Carnival season.

ST. HEDWIG'S CATHEDRAL. Designed by Knobelsdorff and others and presented by Frederick to Berlin's Catholic community, the cathedral, built 1747–73 and modeled on the Pantheon in Rome, stands behind the opera house.

PALAIS PRINZ HEINRICH. Located directly across Unter den Linden from the opera house, the palace was built 1748–53 for Frederick's brother, Prince Heinrich (1726–1802). It now forms the core of the main building of Humboldt University.

THE ARMORY (ZEUGHAUS). The oldest building on Unter den Linden, built 1695–1706, the armory now houses the Museum for German History. A series of powerful stone "Masks of Dying Warriors," executed by the sculptor Andreas Schlüter (1664–1714, the "Michelangelo of the North"), adorns the arcades of the interior courtyard. Schlüter also created the equestrian statue of the Great Elector, now in front of Charlottenburg Palace.

CITY PALACE (STADTSCHLOSS). Schlüter was the main architect of the official residence of Prussian kings and later German emperors. Partially destroyed in World War II, the building, originally built from 1702 on, was completely razed in 1950 in an attempt to eradicate a major symbol of Prussian history and to make room for the Marx-Engels Square and the Palace of the Republic. In 2006–9, as part of a grand plan to restore the

54. Berlin, City Palace (model): Currently under reconstruction according to Schlüter's original design. Scheduled completion: 2019.

architectural ensemble of which the old city palace was a major component, the Palace of the Republic, in its turn, was demolished. Work is currently underway to re-create most of the exterior of the original palace. The structure's modernized interior will house the Humboldt Forum, a complex consisting of exhibits of non-European art, a scientific museum, and facilities for conferences and cultural events.

CHARLOTTENBURG PALACE. The palace is named for Sophie Charlotte (r. 1701–5), wife of Friedrich III, elector of Brandenburg (later King Friedrich I of Prussia (r. 1701–13). The Baroque-rococo style palace, on the outskirts of Berlin, was inaugurated in 1699, and later expanded by the architect Johann Friedrich Eosander (1669–1728).

Of signal importance to the Bach heritage in Berlin are two buildings from later centuries:

SINGAKADEMIE. When the composer Giacomo Meyerbeer (1791–1864) referred to Berlin in 1829 as the "Capital of Sebastian Bach," he may have had in mind the activities of the Berlin *Singakademie*, whose cultivation of Bach's sacred music culminated that year with Felix Mendelssohn's legendary performance of the St. Matthew Passion—the event that permanently established Bach's worldwide fame and position in the musical pantheon. The academy had been founded in 1791 by Carl Friedrich Christian Fasch (1736–1800). His successor was Carl Friedrich Zelter (1758–1832), best known as a close friend of Goethe's and a teacher of Mendelssohn's. The *Singakademie* acquired an enormous collection of musical manuscripts from the estate of C. P. E Bach, including some 500 manuscripts and original prints of music composed by members of the Bach family. In 1827 the *Singakademie* moved in to a newly built concert hall on Unter den Linden. The neoclassic building, designed by Karl Friedrich Schinkel (1781–1841), still survives and serves today as the Gorki Theater.

STATE LIBRARY (STAATSBIBLIOTHEK). The successor to the royal library and located at Unter den Linden 8, the State Library (1914) houses the world's largest collection of Bach manuscripts—80 percent of those surviving. The holdings of the *Singakademie*, which the royal library purchased in 1855, formed the basis of the collection. Many of the materials, which had disappeared after World War II, were discovered in Kiev in the summer of 1999. They were returned to the State Library in December 2001.

Churches

ST. NICHOLAS'S CHURCH (NIKOLAIKIRCHE). Occupying the center of the *Nikolaiviertel*, a small section of the city that gives an impression of the scale and ambience of medieval and Renaissance Berlin, St. Nicholas's is the oldest church in Berlin. Its fortresslike west front dates from 1230, the nave and west tower from 1380. A matching tower was added in the nineteenth century. The first Protestant church service in Brandenburg was held here. The composer Johann Crüger (1598–1662) was kantor from 1622 until his death; the poet Paul Gerhardt (1607–76) was pastor from 1657 to 1668. Crüger composed the melodies of the famous hymns "Jesu meine Freude" and "Nun danket alle Gott"; Gerhardt wrote the texts of "O Haupt voll Blut und Wunden," "Befiehl du deine Wege," and "Nun ruhen alle Wälder," among others repeatedly set to music by J. S. Bach. The church is now used as a satellite location of the Berlin City Museum (*Stadtmuseum*) and for concerts.

ST. MARY'S CHURCH (MARIENKIRCHE). Another thirteenth-century church, St. Mary's, now stands isolated in a large empty space surrounded by modern high-rise buildings near the Alexanderplatz Square. The organ was built by Joachim Wagner (1723). Its case is original, the current instrument a re-creation of the Wagner organ. The church, which is still in use, contains a Baroque altar and an alabaster pulpit by Andreas Schlüter. A rare fifteenth-century fresco depicting the Dance of Death extends along the entry wall for a length of about seventy feet. Whether J. S. Bach ever played on the organs of St. Mary's or St. Nicholas's is not known.

Literature: Homann; BDOK II; BDOK III; NBR; Helm 1960; Kadatz 1998; Hinrichsen 2000; Maul 2001; Wolff 2002; Oleskiewicz 2011; Organs; Schulenberg 2014.

Websites: www.stadtentwicklung.berlin.de/denkmal/denkmale_in_berlin/index_en.shtml (G, E)—especially the link "Unter den Linden"; www.staatsbibliothek-berlin.de/die -staatsbibliothek/die-gebaeude (G, E).

Celle° and Ebstorf° (1700/2)

Celle

The Obituary reports that during his student days in Lüneburg, where he was pupil at St. Michael's Latin School for about two years beginning around Easter time, 1700, Bach "had the opportunity to go and listen several times to a then famous kapelle kept by the duke of Celle, consisting for the most part of Frenchmen; thus he acquired a thorough grounding in the French taste, which, in those regions, was at the time something quite new" (NBR, p. 300, translation emended).

There can be little question that the source for this information was J. S. Bach himself. Doubts have been raised in recent years, however, as to whether the teenager actually traveled to Celle and whether he could ever have gained access, once there, to the ducal palace (Wolff 1985, Petzoldt 2000). Celle is located some 85 km/53 miles south of Lüneburg and represented a three-day journey, probably passing through the towns of Ebstorf and Uelzen.

Supporting the claim apparently implied in the Obituary (where the original German text is somewhat ambiguous) that Bach had heard the kapelle in Celle is the absence of any documentation attesting to a ducal visit to Lüneburg during Bach's time there. Moreover, had the duke paid such a visit to the most prosperous town in his realm, local musicians, sponsored by the city government, would have provided the appropriate music as part of the town's desire to display its wealth and resources. Such a display took place during a well-documented visit in 1666. The occasion was the formal inaugural homage (*Huldigung*) paid by Lüneburg to Duke Georg Wilhelm (r. 1665–1705). Accompanying the duke from Celle were the trumpeters and timpanists belonging to the military escort. No other musicians from the Celle court were included in the ducal entourage (Reinecke 1907). By the same token, in later years Bach had an opportunity to hear the Saxon court kapelle only when he was in **Dresden**, for when the elector visited Leipzig, the royal guest expected to be greeted by the town's own musicians.

Perhaps, then, the young Bach had in fact visited Celle during his Lüneburg years, after all. If so, he would most likely have been taken there by the Frenchman Thomas de la Selle (dates unknown). De la Selle played violin in the court kapelle but was also the dancing master at Lüneburg's *Ritterakademie*, the school for the sons of the nobility that shared space, some classes, and teachers with the St. Michael School. Given Bach's proficiency on the violin, de la Selle might have taken an interest in him and would certainly have gone to Celle by coach. The 1666 reports on the *Huldigung* reveal that the duke and his entourage stayed overnight in the ducal estate (*Amt*) Ebstorf before arriving in Lüneburg the next day. It seems reasonable to assume that Ebstorf was a stopover for de la Selle as well.

Celle was a ducal residence from 1378 until 1705, when the Celle line ended and the territories reverted to the house of Lüneburg-Brunswick (*Braunschweig*), also known as the House of Hanover. Georg Wilhelm's successor, Georg Ludwig (r. 1705–1727) was crowned King George I of Great Britain in 1714. Following the precedent set by the inaugural ceremonies forty years earlier, Georg Ludwig, traveling to Lüneburg from Hanover in 1706 to receive the town's homage, brought along no musicians other than the court trumpeters and timpanists.

55. Celle, Ducal Palace: Celle's oldest structure (begun in the thirteenth century) was extensively remodeled during the Renaissance and Baroque periods.

The period of Celle's musical prominence coincided with the reign of its last ruler, Duke Georg Wilhelm, who formed the court kapelle in 1666, one year after his accession. Until its dissolution in 1706, the kapelle was led by Philipp La Vigne (dates unknown). At its apogee it counted sixteen members (including three singers who also played violin). Jean-Baptiste Lully may have helped in the recruitment of musicians.

Like other German courts in the late seventeenth century, Celle showed a preference for French taste, an attitude greatly reinforced by the Duke's mistress and future wife Eleonore d'Olbreuse (1639–1722), a Huguenot from the low nobility. Eleonore brought French and Italian artisans to Celle. Both a French and an Italian garden were laid out, and, in the years 1670 to 1675, a court theater in the latest style was installed. It was part of the transformation and expansion of an earlier moated castle into an elegant four-wing Baroque palace. The theater, the oldest extant in Germany, is still used regularly for performances and concerts. It has been thoroughly restored to its late-eighteenth-century state, that is, a later stage than the one Bach might have seen. This includes a second balcony and floral decorations in gray on gray. Featured prominently above the stage is the British-Hanoverian coat of arms.

The large festival hall (*Festsaal*) of the castle has the stark, timbered look of a medieval hall, a remnant of the earlier castle. The new wings contain the theater, the *enfilade*—that is, the ducal suite of rooms—as well as two adjoining concert rooms in the southern wing that were the venue for concerts of the court kapelle. Items currently on view include three large gilded silver drinking vessels, which were presented to the ruler by his subjects on festive occasions like the Lüneburg inaugurations (*Huldigungen*).

In terms of artistic significance, however, the high point of the palace is the court chapel. Built in 1485 in late Gothic style, it is a rare example of a completely preserved Renaissance interior. The chapel walls are almost entirely covered with a sequence of paintings executed ca. 1565–67 by the Flemish master Marten de Vos

(1532–1603) and his workshop. The paintings extol the Protestant Reformation that had been introduced during the reign of Duke Ernst the Confessor (1497–1546), who had known Martin Luther personally. The pictorial program was part of an effort to glorify Protestantism and to denigrate Catholicism. The balconies are decorated with carved biblical figures and twenty-five music-making putti that offer a vivid representation of the musical instruments used at the time. It is conceivable that Bach heard a service with music in this small but magnificent church. All of these venues can be visited during a guided tour of the palace, now the Residence Museum (*Residenzmuseum*).

The Town Church (*Stadtkirche*), whose thirteenth-century interior was redecorated by Italian stucco artists during the same ducal period as the palace, continues to have twice-daily tower music.

Celle is one of the best-preserved Renaissance towns in Germany. The uniformly half-timbered houses, often intricately decorated with colored borders and inscriptions, make the town unique. The entire old town—including the palace and a magnificent Renaissance city hall—is a major tourist attraction. The town hall is considered a prime example of "Weser Renaissance," a style prevalent in North Germany.

Ebstorf●

Ebstorf, originally a Benedictine monastery, became a Protestant convent for noble ladies after the Reformation, when most of its landholdings were transferred to ducal ownership. The ducal estate Ebstorf (*Amt Ebstorf*), the eponymous village, and to a lesser degree the convent were obliged to house and feed the Celle court during hunting season and on other visits. According to oral tradition, a princely room (*Fürstenzimmer*) in the monastery's large dormitory was fitted out for Eleonore d'Olbreuse. The fall hunting season under Duke Georg Wilhelm lasted "almost a quarter of a year" (Dose 1994, 344) and included visits by foreign dignitaries and diplomats, as well as noble relatives. The duke arrived "with his household."

Would the entourage have included the court kapelle? It seems unlikely that the court would deprive itself of musical entertainment over a sojourn of two to three months. Bach, therefore, could possibly have heard the court kapelle not in Celle but in Ebstorf, considerably closer to Lüneburg: 26 km/16 miles to the south—a day's trip. The Obituary simply does not reveal precisely where Bach had heard the duke's kapelle: in Celle, Lüneburg, or somewhere else.

Ebstorf Monastery still functions as a Protestant women's convent. The late-fourteenth-century church includes a balcony for a nuns' choir. The complex consists of several large connected wings, including a so-called lords' residence (*Herrenhaus*), which accommodated the provost. In 1705, the director of the Lüneburg *Ritterakademie* was assigned the function of Ebstorf monastery commissar, an appointment attesting to the close links between St. Michael's monastery in Lüneburg and Ebstorf (Dose 1994, 39).

The monastery is famous for its unique "Ebstorf World Map" (*Ebstorfer Weltkarte*), measuring ca. 12 ft. × 12 ft., created by the nuns ca. 1300 and representing the world as it was imagined in the late Middle Ages. The map is a mixture of biblical history, geography, and mythology. Two wings of the cloister contain rare stained glass windows dating from the fourteenth century that present an iconographic cycle connecting Old and New Testament scenes.

Bach's possible route from Lüneburg:
Lüneburg—Melbeck—Velgen—Ebstorf.

Literature: *Homann; BDOK III; NBR; Reinecke 1907; Wolffheim 1910; Linnemann 1935; Fock 1950; Wolff 1986a; Dose 1994; Basso 1997; Petzoldt 2000; Marshall 2016; Gödecke.*

Website: *www.residenzmuseum.celle.de/Residenzmuseum/Geschichte/Schloss (G).*

Collmen (1735)

In late November 1735, Johann Sebastian Bach and the rector of the St. Thomas School, Johann August Ernesti (1707–81), attended a wedding in the town of Collmen, a small, scenic village of about forty houses (now administratively part of Colditz), located 52 km/32 miles southeast of Leipzig. The groom was their colleague, Abraham Kriegel (1691–1759), the school *tertius* (actually the fourth in rank in the school hierarchy, below the rector, conrector, and kantor), who married the local pastor's daughter.

Among other activities at the Thomas School, Kriegel taught the Latin classes that Bach was expected to instruct but had from the beginning of his tenure delegated to others for an annual payment of fifty thalers (ca. $4800).

The evidence for the trip to Collmen comes from a document submitted by Ernesti to the Leipzig town council, in which he rejects Bach's complaints regarding the filling of prefect positions for the school choirs—the notorious "prefects' dispute" (*Präfektenstreit*). In his memorandum, dated August 17, 1736, Ernesti mentions in passing: "When in the previous year, toward Advent, we rode home from Mr. Kriegel's wedding, he [Bach] asked me whether this Krause should join the prefects" (NBR, no. 186). The context of this feud reflects Ernesti's efforts at the Thomas School to reduce the power of the kantor in favor of the rector and to value academic ability over musical talent when admitting and promoting students. The prefects were senior students who conducted rehearsals and performances for the lesser church services under the supervision of the kantor. The battle was waged in a flurry of documents submitted to the town council over the course of two years. In the end, Bach appealed to the elector himself, Friedrich August II in **Dresden**, but never received a reply. The fateful coach ride shared by Bach and Ernesti presumably passed through the towns of Naunhof and Grimma.

The Collmen church, which can be traced to the thirteenth century, was extensively rebuilt in the early twentieth century. Its interior is currently decorated in art nouveau style. The tower, though renovated, appears much as it did when Bach would have seen it. He would also have heard two of its current three bells.

Literature: NBR; Petzoldt 2000.

Dornheim (1707)

Dornheim is a small village within walking distance of Arnstadt, about 5 km/3 miles to the east. There, on October 17, 1707, Bach married his second cousin, Maria Barbara Bach (1684–1720), in the old village church of St. Bartholomew. He had assumed his new position as organist in Mühlhausen in June of that year and come into an inheritance of 50 gulden (ca. $4,200, the equivalent of half his salary) from his uncle Tobias Lämmerhirt (1639–1707). In a word, the auspices were excellent for establishing a household and leaving his strained relationships in Arnstadt behind him. Seven months later, in June 1708, the officiating pastor, Lorenz Stauber (1660–1723), a recent widower, married Maria Barbara's aunt, Regina Wedemann (1660–1730). In so doing Stauber joined the Bach clan: his new wife was the youngest of five Wedemann sisters, the two oldest of whom had married the brothers Johann Christoph Bach (1642–1703), organist in Eisenach, and Johann Michael Bach (1648–94), organist in **Gehren** and Maria Barbara's father. According to an attractive hypothesis first suggested by Philipp Spitta (and endorsed by numerous writers since), Bach returned to Dornheim for Lorenz Stauber's wedding in order to perform the wedding cantata *Der Herr denket an uns*, BWV 196 (Spitta, 370). More recently, Mary Dalton Greer has plausibly suggested that Bach may in fact have composed the cantata for his own wedding (Greer 2008).

St. Bartholomew's Church (*Kirche St. Bartholomäus*)

The Dornheim church is tucked into a walled enclosure along with the manse and the cemetery and hence is not immediately visible from the street. A rough stone gatehouse provides the access to the charming, intimate wedding venue, one still in high demand. In 1710/11—that is, after Bach's wedding—the external covered staircase to the balcony was provided with the massive stone base seen today. Such exterior access for the organist was not uncommon. Typically built of wood, few examples remain. (See also **Weißensee**, Mühlhausen.)

In the interior, two panels now flanking the main altar date from the fifteenth century and belonged to the church in Bach's time—presumably as part of the altar before which Sebastian and Barbara took their vows.

56. Dornheim, St. Bartholomew's Church: Exterior. Tower base and west wall date from the twelfth century. The Romanesque church was expanded during the late fifteenth century to its current size.

In the late 1990s, a group of determined local citizens launched an ambitious and successful effort to restore the dilapidated and seemingly doomed church. The building stands as an example of the heroic work initiated by citizens in Thuringia and Saxony after the fall of the Berlin Wall. In 2007, following the restoration of the church and on the three-hundredth anniversary of the Bachs' wedding, the entire region took part in a reenactment of the event with the entourage proceeding on foot from Arnstadt to Dornheim, as it is believed was done in 1707. The celebration went one step further: scores of Bach family members, including the composer's "ancestors," marched in the procession.

57. Dornheim, St. Bartholomew's Church: Interior. The exuberant Baroque balconies, pulpit altar, and organ case date from 1723/24.

Literature: Spitta 1883; Petzoldt 2000; Dürr 2005; Greer 2008.

Websites: www.bach-in-dornheim.de (G; go to link "300 Jahre Bachhochzeit" and then link to "Bildergalerie" at the bottom of the page).

Dresden (1717, 1725, 1731, 1733, 1736, 1738, 1741)

On August 23, 1730, in his famous "Short But Most Necessary Draft for a Well-Appointed Church Music," addressed to the town council of Leipzig, Johann Sebastian Bach observed: "One need only go to Dresden and see how the musicians there are paid by His Royal Majesty. It cannot fail: since the musicians are relieved of all concern for their living, free of all grief; moreover, [since] each person has to master but a single instrument, [it simply follows] that something choice and excellent will be heard" (NBR, no. 151, translation emended).

58. Dresden, Town view: Oil painting (1748) by Bernardo Bellotto ("Canaletto"), showing (right) the Catholic Court Church (still under construction) and (left) the Protestant Church of Our Lady. The Augustus Bridge, designed by court architect Daniel Pöppelmann (1662–1736), traverses the Elbe River.

Forty-five years later, Carl Philipp Emanuel Bach reported to Johann Nikolaus Forkel in a letter of January 13, 1775, that his father "in his last years . . . in general esteemed highly everything that was worthy of esteem in **Berlin** and Dresden" (NBR, no. 395, p. 400).

Dresden, the capital of Saxony situated on the Elbe River near the Czech border, had indeed become one of Europe's leading cultural centers during the first half of the eighteenth century. The city owed this distinction to the patronage and ambition of the Saxon electors Friedrich August I ("August the Strong," r. 1694–1733) and his son, Friedrich August II (r. 1733–63). In particular, Dresden's exceptional musical establishment accounted for the outsized role the city played in the career of J. S. Bach even though he never lived there. By midcentury its population had reached ca. 35,000.

Although the population of Saxony was overwhelmingly Lutheran, both Dresden monarchs had converted to Catholicism in order to secure the Polish throne—the father in 1697, the son in 1712. The wife of August the Strong (and mother of Friedrich August II), Christiane Eberhardine (1671–1727), however, remained a devout Lutheran and lived in self-imposed exile. For this stance, she was especially revered in Leipzig. In marked contrast, Maria Josepha (1699–1757), wife of Friedrich August II and daughter of the Holy Roman emperor, Joseph I (r. 1705–11), was born a devout Catholic and remained so her entire life. She had married the prince-elector on August 20, 1719, seven years after his conversion—a nonnegotiable precondition for the marriage.

The Catholic faith of the royal family presented no obstacle to Bach's readiness to compose music in its honor. On February 19, 1734, in celebration of the coronation of Friedrich August II as King August III of Poland, Bach performed the *dramma per musica, Blast Lärmen, ihr Feinde, verstärket die Macht*, BWV 205a, in Leipzig in the Zimmermann coffee house. (The king, in Cracow at the time, was not in attendance.) This was one of the dozen cantatas that Bach is known to have composed and performed in Leipzig after May 1727 to celebrate the various birthdays, name days, and other auspicious events in the lives of the royal Saxon family.

Unlike August the Strong, whose taste ran to the French style, Friedrich August II favored the Italian *gusto*. In the course of a grand tour (1711–19) that took him to France and Italy, and above all, Venice, he recruited outstanding Italian instrumentalists and singers for the newly built opera. Chief among them were the violinist Francesco Maria Veracini (1690–1768) and the composer Antonio Lotti (1667–1740).

In contrast to their brilliance as patrons of the fine arts, father and son were considerably less successful in the arts of diplomacy and war. August the Strong, who had joined the Russian coalition led by Tsar Peter the Great against Sweden in the Great Northern War in 1700, was defeated in 1706 and temporarily lost the Polish crown. Friedrich August II's efforts during the War of the Polish Succession against France (1733–38) and later the War of Austrian Succession (1740–48), which entailed the First and Second Silesian Wars with Prussia (1740–42 and 1744–45, respectively), were similarly costly to Saxony. The Third Silesian War, 1756–63, better known as the Seven Years War, once again pitted Saxony against Prussia. It was at least as destructive as the first two Silesian conflicts.

Bach's Draft was written as his situation in Leipzig took a dramatic turn for the worse. Exactly three weeks earlier, on August 2, 1730, the town council discussed his alleged neglect of his teaching duties and absences without leave. One councilor noted, "the kantor was *incorrigibel*"—reaching to Latin for the appropriate word (NBR, no. 150a). Two days after Bach penned the document but presumably before the council had received it, his case was taken up again. This time Dr. Born reported that he had "spoken with the kantor, Bach, but he shows little inclination to work" (NBR, no. 150b).

In the ensuing years Bach intensified his efforts to strengthen his connections with the Saxon capital. These connections had begun at least thirteen years earlier, in the autumn of 1717, with possibly the most sensational triumph of his career. According to the Obituary, Bach had been invited to Dresden by the court concertmaster, Jean-Baptiste Volumier (1670–1728), to engage in a competition with the visiting French keyboard and organ virtuoso, Louis Marchand (1669–1732). Bach undertook the journey from Weimar to Dresden, a distance of about 202 km/125 miles (perhaps through the towns of Jena, **Gera**, **Zeitz**, Leipzig, and Meissen). Marchand failed to appear for the contest, which was to have taken place at the palace of Count Jakob Heinrich von Flemming (1667–1728), the Saxon Prime Minister in Dresden. In the words of the Obituary, "a large company of persons of high rank and of both sexes was assembled. . . . Bach, who thus remained sole master of the scene . . . exhibit[ed his] talents . . . to the astonishment of all present" (NBR, no. 306, p. 301). The particulars of this tale, which is related in a number of sources, are at times contradictory. There

59. Dresden, Palais Flemming: Colored engraving (ca. 1715). The lavish four-story Baroque structure, built in 1704, was located on the present Landhausstraße, close to the Church of Our Lady. The count purchased the mansion in 1714 and adorned it further. It was demolished in 1770.

is little doubt, however, that Marchand had been in Dresden at the time and that Bach in fact visited Dresden in the fall of 1717.

At this very time Bach's relations with his patron in Weimar, Duke Wilhelm Ernst (r. 1683–1728), were at least as fraught as they would be in August 1730 with his employers in Leipzig. Having been passed over in December 1716 for the position of Weimar court kapellmeister, Bach began to seek new employment. By August 1717, Prince Leopold had appointed him the new court kapellmeister at Köthen. Three months later, on November 6th, shortly after his return from Dresden, Bach was arrested and spent the following month in detention for "too stubbornly forcing the issue of his dismissal" (NBR, no. 68).

The year 1717 was also a milestone in the musical life of Dresden itself. In the words of a recent study, "the real beginning of the Dresden *Hofkapelle* . . . is seen around the year 1717" with the arrival of the recently recruited Italian musicians (Stockigt 2011, 23). Bach may have been present for the performance of Lotti's first Dresden opera, *Giove in Argo*, performed in the ballroom (*Redoutensaal*) on October 25th. By then the Royal Polish and Electoral Saxon Orchestra consisted of an outstanding international contingent of some 36 players, among them Johann Christoph Schmidt (1664–1728), principal kapellmeister (*Oberkapellmeister*); Johann David Heinichen (1683–1729), kapellmeister; and J. B. Volumier, violinist and concertmaster. Another member, chamber composer (*Cammer Componist*) and organist Christian Petzold (1677–1733) was also organist at St. Sophia's Church (*Sophienkirche*) and the composer of the popular minuets in G major and G minor, BWV Anh. 114–15, transmitted anonymously in the 1725 *Klavierbüchlein for Anna Magdalena Bach* and for many years thought to be a work of Bach's. Some of the Dresden players were lavishly paid, indeed. Schmidt, Heinichen, Volumier, and Veracini each received an annual salary of 1,200 thalers (ca. $115,000). By comparison, Bach's income at Weimar was 250 gulden (ca. $21,000.)

Other instrumentalists present in Dresden at the time included Pierre-Gabriel Buffardin (ca. 1690–1768), flutist; Jan Dismas Zelenka (1679–1745), contrabassist and composer—later responsible for church music; and, finally, the violinist Johann Georg Pisendel (1687–1755), whom Bach had met in Weimar in 1709 (and perhaps again in 1714 on Pisendel's return from Paris). Pisendel, who had studied with Vivaldi in Venice, was the composer of a challenging sonata for unaccompanied violin. Whether it predated or postdated Bach's famous compositions for unaccompanied violin is not known. After becoming concertmaster in 1728 upon Volumier's death, Pisendel reoriented the playing style and repertoire of the court capelle from the French to the Italian taste.

Bach surely made the acquaintance of many, if not all, of these extraordinary musicians on the occasion of the Marchand episode. He may also have met the flutist Johann Joachim Quantz (1699–1773), who had been in Dresden intermittently since 1716 but only joined the royal kapelle in 1727, remaining there until 1741. The great lutenist Sylvius Leopold Weiss (1686–1750) officially joined the kapelle in 1718 but may have been there the year before. He became a good friend of Bach's in later years, spending a month with him in Leipzig in 1739. Presumably all these artists were on hand for a performance of Lotti's *Teofane* in the newly built opera house in September 1719 after the return of the prince with his bride, the archduchess Maria Josepha.

Bach made at least six further visits to Dresden over the next quarter century, in the years 1725, 1731, 1733, 1736, 1738, and 1741. The ca. 115-km/71-mile journey from Leipzig to Dresden presumably represented three or four days of travel (possibly passing through Wurzen and Meissen). During Bach's Leipzig years the city of Dresden represented for him what the city of Prague represented for Mozart during his Vienna period: the place where the prophet, without honor at home, was appropriately appreciated. As C. P. E. Bach later recalled, "he was particularly honored in Berlin and Dresden" (NBR, p. 399).

Bach's first visit to Dresden from Leipzig took place on September 19–20, 1725, when he gave two recitals on the Silbermann organ in St. Sophia's Church with the participation of other musicians. As the Hamburg newspaper, *Relationscourier*, reported on September 27, 1725: "Dresden, 21 September 1725 . . . Mr. Bach . . . was very well received by the local virtuosos at the court and in the city since he is greatly admired by all of them for his musical skill and art. Yesterday and the day before, in the presence of the same, he performed for over an hour on the new organ in St. Sophia's Church preludes and various concertos" (NBR, no. 118). One of the programs may have included, as an organ concerto, the early version of the E-major keyboard concerto, BWV 1053, preserved in movements of cantatas BWV 169 and BWV 49, both dating from the fall of the following year (Wolff 2000, 318).

The lack of any securely documented performances of Bach's cantatas for the regular church services in Leipzig for some nine weeks in 1725, beginning after August 26th through October 28th, may be at least partially explained by Bach's Dresden visit, a sojourn perhaps extended (with or without permission) by several weeks and conceivably entailing excursions to nearby towns. Bach may have visited **Freiberg**, for example, located 38 km/23 miles southwest of Dresden, where Gottfried Silbermann (1683–1753) had his workshop. At all events, Bach was back in Leipzig in time to present the premiere of the Reformation Day cantata, *Gott der Herr ist Sonn und Schild*, BWV 79, on October 31st.

Bach's next known visit to Dresden, in September 1731, was once again to play recitals at St. Sophia's and at court. Bach no doubt took the opportunity on the night before his own performance on the 14th to attend the premiere of Johann Adolph Hasse's first opera in Dresden, *Cleofide*. Hasse (1699–1783) had arrived just two months earlier to assume the position of court kapellmeister, which had been vacant since J. D. Heinichen's death in 1729. He remained in Dresden until 1763. Arriving with him in July 1731 was his wife, the famed mezzo-soprano Faustina

Bordoni (1697–1781). According to C. P. E. Bach (in his letter of 1775 to Forkel), his father knew both Hasse and Zelenka personally. He doubtless met Hasse on this occasion, just as he had surely made the acquaintance of Zelenka in 1717.

Less than two years later, sometime before July 27, 1733, Bach was again in Dresden, this time to submit a petition to the monarch, requesting a court title. It is not known whether he performed on this occasion. The monarch was the recently crowned elector Friedrich August II, who succeeded to that position upon the death of his father on February 1st. As a demonstration of his qualifications in support of his request, Bach presented the manuscript of the Kyrie and Gloria sections of the Mass in B minor, BWV 232, in the form of a set of practical performance parts. In his petition, Bach announced that he was submitting "the present small work of that science which I have achieved in *musique*" and promised his "untiring zeal in the composition of music for the church as well as for the *orchestre*," that is, for the theater (NBR, no. 162; Marshall 1985).

Bach's letter, though addressed to "Your Royal Highness," in no other way indicates that the Mass was explicitly written in the elector's honor, to mark his accession to the electoral office, or with the expectation of an imminent performance in Dresden. If the work was performed there as part of the Catholic church service, the venue would probably have been the so-called "Court Church in the Theater" (*Hofkirche im Theater*), the court opera house that was located near the palace and had been renovated by August the Strong in 1708 to function as the Catholic court chapel. It served that purpose until the completion of the new Court Church (*Hofkirche*) in 1751. But the Mass could also have been performed as part of a Lutheran service in St. Sophia's Church (Stauffer 1997).

The style and scoring of the work strongly suggest that the *Missa*, or short Mass, may at the least have been written with Dresden in mind, since its form is modeled on that of the Neapolitan cantata Masses as cultivated by Zelenka and Hasse. In addition, the vocal writing in the "Laudamus te" seems to be a showpiece for Faustina, employing ornate coloratura passagework in a low tessitura of the kind for which she was famous. Similarly, the obbligato instrumental parts for solo violin, transverse flute, oboe d'amore, and horn in the "Laudamus te," "Domine Deus," "Qui sedes," and "Quoniam," respectively, seem designed to display the artistry of Pisendel, Buffardin, the oboist Johann Christian Richter, and one or the other of the horn-playing brothers Schindler (Johann Adam or Andreas).

Exactly when Bach arrived in Dresden is not clear. It is altogether likely that he accompanied his son Wilhelm Friedemann to his (successful) audition for the post of organist at St. Sophia's on June 22nd as the successor to the recently deceased Christian Petzold. (Friedemann held the position for thirteen years, leaving it in April 1746 to become organist and music director at the Market Church in **Halle**.) J. S. Bach was no doubt back in Leipzig by August 3, however, in time to conduct his cantata celebrating the new monarch's name day at Zimmermann's coffee garden. The work performed, the cantata, BWV Anh. 12, is lost.

———————————

As far as is known, Bach did not return to Dresden until November 1736, after having been notified that he had finally received the title of court composer he had requested three years earlier (NBR, no. 190). Count Hermann Carl von Keyserlingk (1696–1764), the Russian ambassador to the Dresden court since 1733, personally handed him the letter of appointment, which took effect November 19th. This occasion marks the first documented appearance in the biographical sources of this important Bach patron. It is not known how long they may have known each other by then.

On December 1, according to the *Dresdner Nachrichten*, "Bach made himself heard from 2 to 4 o'clock on the new organ in the Church of Our Lady (*Frauenkirche*), in the presence of the Russian Ambassador, von Keyserlingk, and many Persons of Rank, also a large attendance of other persons and artists, with particular admiration, wherefore also His Royal Majesty most graciously named the same, because of his great ability in composing, to be His Majesty's Composer" (NBR, no. 191). Also in the audience, no doubt, was the organist of St. Sophia's, Wilhelm Friedemann Bach. Years later Friedemann recalled a performance by his pupil "by the name of Goldberg" before the electress and others in the home of Count Keyserlingk (Falck 1913, 43–44). According to the famous anecdote related by Forkel, Keyserlingk had commissioned the Goldberg Variations from Bach, having once told him "that he should like to have some clavier pieces for his Goldberg . . . that he might be a little cheered up by them in his sleepless nights" (NBR, p. 464–65). Keyserlingk had reportedly been so impressed with the playing of the ten-year-old Johann Gottlieb Goldberg (1727–56) that he sent him to Leipzig at that time to study with J. S. Bach. Friedemann evidently took over the boy's instruction later on.

Information about Bach's two later journeys to the Saxon capital is meager. A poignant letter from the composer dated May 24, 1738, to **Sangerhausen** town council member Johann Friedrich Klemm (1706–67), in response to disconcerting news relating to his son Johann Gottfried Bernhard (1715–39), reveals in passing that Bach had just returned to Leipzig two days earlier from Dresden. Nothing is known about the purpose or duration of that visit. Bach's last known visit to

Dresden is documented in a series of letters written by his cousin and amanuensis, Johann Elias Bach (1705–55), to different recipients. They reveal that on November 17, 1741, the composer returned from Dresden and that during his stay there he had met with "His Excellency Count von Kayserling [*sic*] and his *domestics* . . . at the house of this great ambassador" (BDOK II, nos. 497–98, 502). The assumption of some connection between this meeting with Keyserlingk and the publication at that very time, the fall of 1741, of the Goldberg Variations, is irresistible but unverifiable.

60. Dresden, Our Lady's Church: Dresden's main Protestant church, begun 1722, consecrated in 1734, but only completed in 1743. Designed by George Bähr (1666–1738), the octagonal-shaped Baroque structure is capped by an enormous dome supported by free-standing pillars.

No further journeys of Bach to Dresden are documented. Since Wilhelm Friedemann was organist at St. Sophia's from 1733 to 1746, however, it is likely that Sebastian undertook private visits to the city during those thirteen years, accompanied perhaps by other members of his household: his wife, Anna Magdalena; Johann Elias; or one or the other of his sons. According to Forkel, in the years before Friedemann's appointment, Bach "often went thither to hear the opera. He generally took his eldest son with him," saying to the boy "'Friedemann, shan't we go again to hear the lovely Dresden ditties?" (NBR, p. 461).

Landmarks

During the reign of August, the Strong the court and the city of Dresden were virtually synonymous. August's love of art, architecture, entertainment, and pomp continues to manifest itself in the city's visual beauty, which has been largely restored after the devastating fire bombing of February 1945.

PALACE/RESIDENCE PALACE (SCHLOSS/RESIDENZSCHLOSS). The palace, a mostly Renaissance four-wing edifice, served as the official residence of the Saxon electors and later kings from 1485 to 1918. Based on a medieval castle, of which the base of the tall central watchman's tower (*Hausmannsturm*) is a remnant, it was transformed and expanded ca. 1530–91 into a princely residence.

61. Dresden, Palace Chapel: Engraving (1676) by David Conrad depicting Heinrich Schütz surrounded by court musicians.

62. Dresden, Palace Chapel: The "twined-rib" ceiling vaults were restored in 2013 on the basis of the Conrad engraving.

Its exterior walls were decorated in black and white sgraffito technique at that time. Today only the walls of the interior courtyard reproduce this treatment.

Of particular musical interest is the palace chapel (*Schlosskapelle*). Dating from 1551–53, it was the second Protestant structure built in Saxony, after the palace chapel in Torgau (see p. xxi). Heinrich Schütz (1585–1672) performed here during his years as Dresden court kapellmeister. The chapel's intricate ribbed vaulting was destroyed when it was secularized in 1737 and reused as part of the royal apartments. The chapel's 1662 altar, the work of the leading seventeenth-century Saxon architect Wolf Caspar von Klengel (1630–91), was removed to the Protestant St. Sophia's Church at that time.

Klengel also built the opera house (1664–67) that adjoined the palace, the so-called "Opera House at the Taschenberg" or "Klengel Opera House" (*Opernhaus am Taschenberg, Klengelsches Opernhaus*), which was connected to the palace by a passageway. In 1707–8, August the Strong had it reconfigured as the Catholic court church, called the "Court Church in the Theater" (*Hofkirche im Theater*). The venue served as a chapel until the consecration of the Court Church in 1751. The building then became an indoor tennis court (*Ballhaus*). It was demolished in the nineteenth century.

The reigns of August the Strong and his son represent the era of the Dresden Baroque. Following a fire in 1701, large portions of the palace, especially the interiors, were refashioned accordingly. The *Zwinger*, the Court Church, the Church of Our Lady, as well as numerous private mansions in the city and ducal palaces in the environs also date from this period. Beginning with the events commemorating the 800th anniversary of the Wettin dynasty in 1889, however, much of the palace exterior was remodeled in a neo-Renaissance style. The result has been a hybrid mixture of the original and the neo-Renaissance.

The palace houses various museums, among them the Green Vault (*Grünes Gewölbe*), an enormous collection of extravagant artistic artifacts initiated by August the Strong. Massively damaged during the Dresden bombing, reconstruction of the palace began in the 1960s and is only now approaching completion.

ZWINGER. The work was commissioned by August the Strong who initiated the ambitious building program after visiting Versailles during his grand

63. Dresden, *Zwinger*: Three-sided, rococo-style, nonresidential palace complex (ca. 1711–28), served as a permanent venue for extravagant indoor and outdoor court entertainments.

tour. Inaugurated in 1719 on the occasion of the marriage of the prince-elector, Friedrich-August II, the *Zwinger* contained an orangerie, fountains, an opera house (with a pit capable of holding over forty musicians), and a ballroom, as well as outdoor viewing platforms, pavilions, galleries, and a plethora of sculptures by Balthasar Permoser (1651–1732). J. S. Bach would have heard opera performances here on his Dresden visits. The central area of the complex measures 204 × 116 m/670 × 380 ft. A fourth side, in neo-Classical style, designed by Gottfried Semper (1803–79), the architect of the new Dresden opera house, was added in 1847–55. The new wing was built to house the world-famous Old Masters Painting Gallery (*Gemäldegalerie Alte Meister*).

CHURCH OF OUR LADY (FRAUENKIRCHE). The building is doubtless Germany's largest and most important Protestant church erected after the Thirty Years War. Conforming to the prescriptions of the architectural theorist Leonhard Christoph Sturm (1669–1719), its central layout enabled the congregation to assemble around the altar and pulpit; the organ was positioned above both. The three-manual organ, built by Gottfried Silbermann in 1732–36, was examined by Pisendel and others on November 22, 1736. The instrument was consecrated on November 25th, just six days before Bach's performance on December 1, which no doubt served as the inaugural concert. The Church of Our Lady was completely destroyed during the bombings of February 13–15, 1945. It was rebuilt from 1998–2005 according to the original plans using many of the original stones. Aside from a replica of the original case, however, the organ is of modern design (by Daniel Kern).

64. Dresden, Court Church (1738–51): Built during the reign of Friedrich August II according to a design by the Roman architect Gaetano Chiaveri (1689–1770). Left: palace and watchman's tower.

COURT CHURCH (HOFKIRCHE). The court church is located prominently between the palace and the Elbe as a freestanding building. It was intended as a Catholic counterpart to the Church

of Our Lady, completed just a few years earlier. The structure is characterized by a single
large tower in the center of the facade, and by
the pronounced difference in height between
the main nave and the side naves. Seventy-
eight over-life-size statues of saints, apostles,
and church fathers populate the balustrades
along the lower and upper roofs. The pulpit is
the work, once again, of Permoser. The crypt
houses the remains of members of the Wettin dynasty, including the heart of August the
Strong. The original organ of 1754, Gottfried
Silbermann's last work, was removed during
World War II and has been partially restored.

Bach spent his final years working on the
B-minor Mass, whose Kyrie and Gloria portions he had submitted in 1733 in support of
his petition for the title of Dresden court composer. Perhaps he intended to have the entire
work performed at the consecration of the
Court Church. The event took place on June
29, 1751, however, eleven months after his death
(Osthoff 1987).

ST. SOPHIA'S CHURCH (SOPHIEN-
KIRCHE). The church was completely
destroyed during World War II. Johann Sebas-
tian Bach gave organ recitals there in the years 1725 and 1731; Wilhelm Friedemann
Bach served as its organist from 1733 to 1746. With the demolition of the palace
chapel in 1737, church services for Protestant members of the court were moved
to St. Sophia's. The two-manual organ on which Bach and his son performed was
built 1718–20 by Gottfried Silbermann. Christian Petzold, organist of St. Sophia's
at the time, inaugurated the instrument in November 1720.

65. Dresden, St. Sophia's Church: Rendering (1850) by the Dresden landscape painter Christian Gottlob Hammer (1779–1864). Originally part of a Franciscan monastery, the two-aisle Gothic hall church dating from the fourteenth century was later renamed after the electress Sophia (1568–1622).

Literature: Homann; BDOK I; BDOK II; NBR; Falck 1913; Dadder 1923; Fitzpatrick 1970; Keller 1976; Marshall 1976; Loewenberg 1978; Schulze 1979; Marshall 1985; Osthoff 1987; Basso 1997; Stauffer 1997; Breig 1998; Petzoldt 2000; Wolff 2000; Delang 2007; Otto 2009; Stauffer 2009; Stockigt 2011; Organs; Wolff GMO, accessed November 15, 2014.

Erfurt (1716)

Capital of the modern German state of Thuringia, Erfurt is one of its best-preserved historic towns. Indeed, many of its buildings and neighborhoods would be familiar to Bach. During the Middle Ages, Erfurt was one of the most affluent cities in the German-speaking world. It was the largest city in Thuringia, its economic and cultural capital, and home to a prestigious university since 1392. The medieval east-west trade route, the *via regia*, led directly through Erfurt. The city's wealth was largely owing to a plant: the *Isatis tinctoria* (*Waid*, or dyer's woad), which was the source for blue dye before the discovery of indigo. A bishop's seat and the location of numerous monasteries, Erfurt was nominally subject to the Elector of Mainz from about 1000 on, although the town often asserted its own power. It remained bi-confessional after the Reformation. The city's fortunes waned during the seventeenth century: owing to an outbreak of the plague in the years 1682–84, its population fell by a third to ca. 11,000.

The Erfurt Bach Dynasty

The city's musical life, however, remained vibrant, owing in no small part to the presence of the Bach family. In fact, Johann Sebastian Bach's single securely documented visit to Erfurt, made in 1716, may be among the least of the town's distinctions in the history of the musical Bach family. Bach undertook the 24-km/15-mile journey west from Weimar to examine the new instrument in St. Augustine's Church begun by Georg Christoph Sterzing (ca. 1650–1717) and completed by the Erfurt builder Johann Georg Schröter (1683–ca. 1750). On July 31, 1716, Bach and the Arnstadt organ builder Johann Anton Weiser (1672–1750) submitted their positive report, pointing out that the instrument represented Schröter's first project as a master builder (NBR, no. 62).

This was surely not Bach's first or only visit to Erfurt. He almost certainly was there frequently during his youth, presumably attending the annual family reunions mentioned by Johann Nikolaus Forkel (1749–1818) in the opening chapter of his biography of the composer (NBR, p. 424). Bach may also have made the 58-km/36-mile journey east from Mühlhausen to attend a memorial service for his uncle, Tobias Lämmerhirt, who had died in August 1707. Bach's early masterpiece, the *Actus tragicus, Gottes Zeit ist die allerbeste Zeit*, BWV 106, may have been composed for this occasion. The appearance of the name "Salome" in the text of the wedding *Quodlibet*, BWV 524, a work written 1707/8, similarly hints that it was performed in Erfurt, where Bach's sister, Maria Salome (1677–1727) had been living since her marriage in 1700. The music theorist Jacob Adlung (1699–1762), organist of the Erfurt Preachers' Church (*Predigerkirche*) since January 1728, provided further evidence of a Bach trip to Erfurt when he reported decades later that Bach had once visited him there (BDOK III, no. 696). Adlung specified no year for the visit.

Although the extent of J. S. Bach's connections with Erfurt is uncertain, the town clearly played a leading role in the lives and careers of five generations of Bach musicians. That history began with the brothers Johann (1604–73) and Christoph (1613–61), the sons of Hans Bach (ca. 1550–1626).

66. Erfurt, St. Augustine's Church: Part of the Augustinian monastery. The octagonal bell tower and the monastery library date from the mid–fifteenth century. Martin Luther entered the monastery in July 1505 as a monk.

Among the most prominent members of the dynasty were: Christoph Bach, Johann Sebastian's grandfather; Christoph's sons Johann Ambrosius (1645–95, Sebastian's father), and his twin brother Johann Christoph (1645–93). After serving briefly as a town piper in Arnstadt, Ambrosius returned to Erfurt in 1661 as a violinist. In April 1668, he married Maria Elisabeth Lämmerhirt (1644–94), herself an Erfurt native. The wedding took place in the Merchants' Church (*Kaufmannskirche*). In October 1671, Ambrosius and his family moved to Eisenach. In 1684, after serving there for thirteen years, he requested permission to return to Erfurt, but his petition was denied. Had it been approved, Ambrosius's last child, Johann Sebastian, born March 21, 1685, would have been born not in Eisenach but in Erfurt, like his parents and siblings.

J. S. Bach's oldest brother, Johann Christoph (1671–1721), born in Erfurt four months before the family moved to Eisenach, returned to his birthplace in 1685 to study with Johann Pachelbel, organist of the Preachers' Church at the time. Sometime in 1688, he became organist of St. Thomas's Church in Erfurt but finally settled in Ohrdruf in 1690.

The Erfurt Bach dynasty effectively ended in the fifth generation with Johann Christoph Bach's grandson. Tobias Friedrich Bach (1723–1805) served as cantor and organist of the Franciscan Church (*Barfüsserkirche*) from 1762 until his death.

Landmarks

CHURCHES

Erfurt's old town had thirty-eight churches; twenty-seven survive. Four of them had significant connections to the Bach family.

ST. AUGUSTINE'S CHURCH (AUGUSTINERKIRCHE). The church and monastery complex were severely damaged during World War II. Along with major restoration work, a new monastery library was completed in 2010, replacing the original two-story building and complementing the so-called Ministry Library (*Ministerialbibliothek*) founded in 1646. It contains a theological collection of 60,000 volumes. Nothing remains today of the Sterzing/Schröter organ Bach had examined in 1716.

MERCHANTS' CHURCH (KAUFMANNSKIRCHE). The three-aisle basilica, framed by two towers, was consecrated in 1368. Luther preached here in 1522; a statue of the Reformer in front of the church commemorates the visit. J. S. Bach's parents were married in the Merchants' Church on April 8, 1668. In all, sixty-one Bach family members were baptized and twelve were married in this church. Its surviving artwork includes an outstanding ensemble consisting of carved altar, pulpit, and baptismal font created between 1598 and 1625. Also noteworthy are two portraits of local notables dating from ca. 1650 displayed in the side aisles. The background of one portrait contains a contemporary view of the city; the background of the other offers the oldest authentic representation of the Merchants' Church.

PREACHERS'/PREDIGER/DOMINICAN CHURCH (PREDIGERKIRCHE). The three-aisle basilica, Erfurt's principal Lutheran church and the official church of the town council, dates from the thirteenth and fourteenth centuries. The leading Erfurt organists of the seventeenth and eighteenth centuries, including members of the Bach family, held positions at the Preachers' Church, beginning with the patriarch Johann Bach who served from 1636 to 1673. Among his successors were Johann Pachelbel (organist 1678–90), Jacob Adlung (organist 1728–62), and Johann Christian Kittel, one of Sebastian's last pupils (organist 1762–1809). The organ, constructed 1572–79 by Heinrich Compenius (ca. 1530–1611), was continuously renovated by a series of builders, beginning in 1648 with Compenius's grandson Ludwig (ca. 1608–71). Of the original instrument only the case survives. The great theologian and mystic Meister Eckhart (1260–1328) was a prior at the Dominican monastery associated with the church.

BAREFOOT FRIARS'/FRANCISCAN CHURCH (BARFÜSSERKIRCHE). Dating from the early fourteenth century and once Erfurt's largest church, the Barefoot Friars' Church was severely damaged in a November 1944 bombing raid.

The surviving choir space of the ruin currently houses a museum, while part of the roofless nave forms an open-air stage for theatrical events. Tobias Friedrich Bach, grandson of J. S. Bach's brother and the last notable representative of the Erfurt Bach dynasty, was the kantor and organist at this church.

ST. MARY'S CATHEDRAL, SEVERUS'S CHURCH (DOM ST. MARIEN, SEVERIKIRCHE). Occupying a high promontory (the *Domberg*), two large Gothic churches only a few yards apart, form the city's architectural and artistic highpoint: the bishop's seat, the Cathedral of St. Mary's, and the parish church of St. Severus. They attest to the influence of the elector of Mainz in Erfurt. The churches lack any direct connections to the Bach family; still, J. S. Bach, no less than any other visitor, could not have failed to notice the imposing sight. The cathedral is richly adorned with paintings, stone and wood sculptures, and

67. Erfurt, St. Mary's Cathedral and St. Severus's Church: Dating from the thirteenth and fourteenth centuries, the cathedral (left) combines Romanesque and Gothic elements. The fourteenth-century Severus's Church is a more uniformly Gothic, five-aisle hall church; the high roof and east facade crowned by three pointed steeples date from 1495.

68. Erfurt, St. Severus's Church: Organ case designed by J. F. Wender. While large figures of angels seem to support the weight of the organ, smaller angels are depicted making music.

stained glass windows. Bach's friend and collaborator, the organ builder Johann Friedrich Wender (1655–1729), created the three-manual organ of St. Severus's Church in 1714. Wender is known to have personally designed his organ cases.

The two churches are complemented by a third edifice: the large Romanesque St. Peter's Church, once part of a Benedictine monastery. It stands on the grounds of the *Petersberg*, the citadel overlooking Erfurt, and provides a dramatic view of the entire city.

ST. MICHAEL'S CHURCH. Once the university church, it is located across from the *Collegium majus*, the original university building dating from the early sixteenth century. Martin Luther, during his student days, regularly attended Mass in this church.

FURTHER LANDMARKS

BACH FAMILY RESIDENCES. The street addresses Junkersand 1 and Junkersand 3 designate two houses once inhabited by early members of the Bach family. Bach's father, Ambrosius, lived in Junkersand 1, the house where Sebastian's oldest brother, Johann Christoph, was probably born in June 1671. Commemorative plaques are attached to the exteriors of both houses. Bach family residences were also located on the Shopkeepers' Bridge (*Krämerbrücke*), Rupprechtsgasse, and in the house "at the Green Shield" (*Zum grünen Schild*), on the corner of Kürschnergasse and Wenige Markt.

Along with the modest Bach residences, a number of elaborate Renaissance private houses survive in Erfurt. Also noteworthy is the large woad warehouse (*Waidspeicher*), dating from ca. 1550 and used today as a theater.

SHOPKEEPERS' BRIDGE (KRÄMERBRÜCKE). As emblematic of the city as the *Domberg* is the Shopkeepers' Bridge. It is Germany's only extant inhabited stone bridge, whose origins extend back to the late twelfth century.

OLD SYNAGOGUE. With origins dating back to at least 1096, the building constitutes the oldest surviving synagogue in Europe. It was secularized after a pogrom in 1349 and in the ensuing centuries served various commercial functions. In 2009, after extensive renovation work, the building opened as a Jewish museum. Its artifacts include medieval manuscripts along with an extensive gold and silver treasure (*Schatz von Erfurt*) discovered only in 1998. It may have been the personal wealth buried by a family fleeing the pogrom. The treasure includes an ancient Jewish wedding ring, one of just three of its kind in existence.

ANGERMUSEUM. Built in 1705–11 as part of the Mainz electoral administrative facilities, the palatial building is now an art museum. Among its holdings is the famous oil portrait attributed to the Weimar court painter, Johann Ernst

Rentsch the Elder (d. 1723), and purporting to depict J. S. Bach, ca. 1715, as Weimar concertmaster (BDOK IV, B6).

Literature: BDOK III; NBR; Schulze 1985; Brück 1996; Petzoldt 2000; Wolff 2000; Otto 2009; Knape 2011; Organs; Wolff GMO, accessed November 15, 2014.

Freiberg°

The wealth that silver mining brought to the Ore Mountains (*Erzgebirge*) region of Saxony manifests itself in Freiberg, the "City of Silver" (*Silberstadt*). At the center of the mining area and one of the most attractive and prosperous historic towns of Eastern Germany, Freiberg and the mining region have been proposed as a UNESCO World Heritage site.

Although a visit by Bach to Freiberg is not documented, he easily could have traveled there. The city is located just 38 km/24 miles southwest of Dresden, a short detour off the most direct route that he would have taken on any of his half-dozen trips from Leipzig to the Saxon capital between 1725 and 1741. A major attraction would doubtless have been five organs built by Gottfried Silbermann (1683–1753)—the three-manual instrument, dating from 1714, in the Cathedral of St. Mary, for example. Four of the organs have survived.

In 1711, Gottfried Silbermann opened a workshop in Freiberg and spent the remainder of his career there. In the following years, he built three major organs in **Dresden**: one for St. Sophia's Church (1720), where Wilhelm Friedemann Bach was organist from 1733 to 1746; one for the Church of Our Lady (1736), where J. S. Bach performed shortly after its consecration; and one for the Court Church (1754), completed after Silbermann's death by his nephew, Johann Daniel.

Silbermann's Freiberg residence, which still stands, may have been the venue where a conversation took place concerning the so-called "sun organ" in **Görlitz**. According to Johann Andreas Silbermann (1712–83), the son of Gottfried's older brother, Andreas (and hence a nephew of Gottfried's), "the old famous Mr. Bach of Leipzig did not judge this instrument unfairly when, in discussing it with my cousin, he called it a 'horse organ' because one has to be as strong as a horse to play it." The identity of the "cousin" is unclear. It may have been Johann Georg Silbermann who worked in Gottfried's shop (BDOK II, no. 486), or Gottfried himself (although Gottfried was Johann Andreas's uncle rather than his cousin).

Johann Andreas Silbermann related this anecdote in his travel diary after he had heard the "sun organ" in 1741 while on an organ tour through Germany.

The conversation, then, would have preceded by at least five years the first documented encounter between Bach and Gottfried Silbermann. That meeting took place in **Naumburg** in September 1746, when both men inspected the new organ in the Church of St. Wenceslas built by Silbermann's former student, Zacharias Hildebrandt.

Johann Friedrich Doles (1715–97), a former student of Bach's, provides another connection to Freiberg. Doles was kantor and music director there from 1744 until 1755, at which time he became Thomaskantor in Leipzig.

There is one further connection between Bach and Freiberg. In 1741, Bach became a stakeholder in a silver mine, the *Ursula-Erbstollen*, situated in Kleinvoigtsberg, 10 km/6 miles north of Freiberg. The estate inventory (NBR, no. 279) lists as the first entry one share out of 128 of this silver mine, valued at 60 thalers (ca. $5,750). The early stakeholder system was mostly a philanthropic undertaking. Owners of a share participated in the mine's profits. If, however, the mine did not yield a profit, shareholders were obliged to contribute monies to ensure its continued operation and thus save the miners' employment. By the end of his life, Bach had contributed some thirty thalers (ca. $2,880) to the mine, the equivalent of six months of a miner's wages. He never earned a profit from his share (Spree 2012/13).

Landmarks

CATHEDRAL OF ST. MARY (DOM ST. MARIEN). Freiberg cathedral is one of the most richly endowed churches of Saxony. Among its outstanding works of art is a late Romanesque "Golden Portal" (*Goldene Pforte*), dating from 1230. It is remarkably well preserved and the earliest complete sculptural portal in Germany. The portal's theological program recounts the salvation of man through Christ and the church. Biblical figures are located in the niches between the finely carved pillars, in the *tympanon*, and in the archivolts. In 1908, Kaiser Wilhelm II presented plaster-cast copies of the portal to the Germanic Museum (now one of the Harvard Art Museums) in Cambridge, Massachusetts, and to the Pushkin Museum in Moscow as a symbol of German greatness.

The cathedral's Gothic interior contains two extraordinary carved stone pulpits. The freestanding "tulip pulpit" (*Tulpenkanzel*) of ca. 1505–10 resembles in its delicacy an ivory carving. The "miners' pulpit" (*Bergmannskanzel*) of 1638 is attached to a pillar in more conventional fashion. While men in miners' garb seem to support the weight of the pulpit and the staircase, the donors, a mayor of Freiberg and his wife, are depicted kneeling on either side of a crucifix.

In addition to its large three-manual Silbermann organ, the cathedral houses a second Silbermann instrument: a one-manual organ originally installed in the

Church of St. John. It was transferred to the cathedral in 1939 and positioned on the left-hand balcony near the chancel. The cathedral's outstanding bells form a unique ensemble of two fundamentals and four chimes. Four of the six date from the fifteenth century.

Nine Saxon dukes are buried in the funeral chapel located in the chancel, hidden behind a rood screen. The vaulted ceiling area contains a representation of the Second Coming of Christ, executed 1585–94 in a combination of painting and sculpture. It is the work of Giovanni Maria Nosseni (1544–1620). On a ledge just below it stand thirty sculpted angels, all holding musical instruments. The mixed "heavenly" ensemble includes sacred, courtly, and folk instruments. Twenty-one of them were playable Renaissance instruments from the region. (Southern Saxony is still a center of instrument building.) Experts from Leipzig's Grassi Museum of Musical Instruments who examined the instruments during the 2002 restoration of the chapel discovered much about Renaissance instrument making and musical practice. Exact replicas of the Freiberg instruments made in the course of the study are now in the Grassi museum and used in performances by professional ensembles.

ST. PETER'S CHURCH (PETRIKIRCHE), ST. JAMES'S CHURCH (JAKOBIKIRCHE). Silbermann organs are preserved in two other Freiberg churches. St. Peter's, located at the town's highest point near the Upper Market Square (*Obermarkt*), has a large two-manual instrument dating from 1735. St. James's, a neo-Gothic successor to the original church, retains a small two-manual Silbermann organ from 1717.

Literature: BDOK II; NBR; Friedrich 2000; Organs; Spree 2012/13.

Websites: For the musical instruments of the Freiberg funeral chapel: www.mfm.uni-leipzig .de/dt/Forschung/ProjektFreiberg.php (G, E). To hear the bells of the cathedral: www.youtube .com/watch?v=Bo_CIrECIs4&feature=related.

Gehren°

Gehren, located 28 km/17 miles south of Arnstadt, was the birthplace of J. S. Bach's first wife, Maria Barbara (1684–1720). Her father, Johann Michael Bach (1648–1694), a native of Arnstadt, was organist and town scribe in Gehren from 1673 until his death. In the family Genealogy, Sebastian described his father-in-law as "like his brother, an able composer." The brother in question was Johann Christoph Bach (1642–1703), famously characterized in the same document as "a profound composer" (NBR, p. 288).

Bach would probably have met Johann Michael Bach during the first ten years of his life—perhaps in Eisenach, where his uncle (more precisely, first cousin, once removed), Johann Christoph, was organist at St. George's Church. According to Forkel, the extended Bach clan had annual family gatherings (NBR, p. 424). Therefore it is altogether possible that Bach had already known Maria Barbara and her parents since childhood. They were, after all, second cousins—their grandfathers were brothers.

In 1694, Maria Barbara Bach, like her future husband, lost her father at age ten. Her mother, Catharina (née Wedemann), was left with four unmarried daughters. When the widow died ten years later, in 1704, Maria Barbara, then twenty years old, left Gehren and, together with two older sisters, moved in with relatives in Arnstadt, where J. S. Bach had been an organist since the previous year. The pair evidently began courting at this time and married in the nearby town of **Dornheim** in October 1707, shortly after Bach had taken up a new position in Mühlhausen.

Although there is no documentary evidence that Bach ever visited Gehren, it is more than likely that he did so. An organ examination he had carried out in November 1706 in **Langewiesen**, located just 3 km/2 miles north of Gehren, would have provided a particularly favorable opportunity, especially since Bach and the Gehren organist, Johann Kister, were members of the same examination committee (BDOK II, no. 18).

The church where Johann Michael Bach served as organist no longer exists. It was replaced in 1834 by the current town church (*Stadtkirche*). An obelisk commemorating Michael and Maria Barbara stands nearby in the Michael-Bach-Strasse.

The castle of Gehren, an imposing three-story, four-wing building surrounded by a moat, functioned as a summer residence for the Schwarzburg-Sondershausen dynasty. Situated in the game-rich Thuringian forest, it also served as a hunting lodge. It was famous for its rococo stag hall boasting an impressive collection of antlers. Michael Bach would have played the organ there whenever the ducal family was in residence. The castle burned down in 1933. Only a massive Renaissance stone gate and a few looming ragged walls remain.

Literature: BDOK I; BDOK II; NBR; Petzoldt 2000.

Gera (1721, 1725)

Bach visited Gera, the capital of the county of Reuß-Gera located 68 km/42 miles south of Leipzig, at least twice. An archival entry documents his passage through the town in August 1721, on his return to Köthen after a guest performance in **Schleiz**, the residence of the ruling Reuß-Schleiz branch (BDOK II, no. 107). The purpose of this stay-over is not indicated.

Bach's second visit lasted from May 30 to June 6, 1725. During this time he examined and dedicated the organ of the town church, St. John's, and most likely played the organ in St. Salvator's Church as well. Both instruments were the work of Johann Georg Fincke the Elder (1680–1749): the St. John's just completed and the St. Salvator's built between 1720–22 and possibly the object of Bach's 1721 visit. On one or both of those occasions, Bach may also have performed at the Osterstein castle, the residence of Count Heinrich XVIII (1677–1735). Located just outside Gera, it, too, contained a Fincke organ, one dating from ca. 1719–21.

The examination and dedication of the St. John's Church organ probably took place on June 3, 1725, the First Sunday after Trinity. This was Bach's first examination of a major town organ since he became Thomaskantor. A bill reimbursing expenses indicates not only Bach's generous honorarium of 30 thalers (ca. $2,900) but also the presence of three guests—presumably Anna Magdalena Bach, and perhaps the fourteen-year-old Wilhelm Friedemann (BDOK V, nos. 189a–c; Maul 2004).

Bach's presumable travel route from Köthen (and Leipzig):
Köthen—Landsberg—Leipzig—Pegau—**Zeitz**—Gera.

Gera also has several connections with Heinrich Schütz (1585–1672). His maternal grandfather was once the mayor. His birthplace, Bad Köstritz, located 9 km/6 miles to the north, houses a Schütz museum in a former inn once belonging to his father and grandfather. In 1617, Heinrich Posthumus Reuß (r. 1595–1635), arguably Gera's most consequential ruler, engaged the composer to draft an organization plan for the town's musical institutions. Years later he commissioned Schütz's *Musicalische Exequien* (1636), intended for the count's own memorial service and set to texts he had himself chosen and that were also inscribed on his sarcophagus. Schütz's work is the first known funeral music in German.

Politically independent of Saxony, the county of Reuß-Gera was part of the Reuß territories of the younger line. Repeated partitions eventually created eight such counties, including Reuß-Schleiz. All are now part of the modern state of Thuringia. Gera was historically linked to Leipzig by close trading ties and appropriately excellent roads.

A catastrophic fire in 1780 destroyed nine-tenths of the town, including both churches, their organs, and the church archives. The older edifice, the Gothic church of St. John's, was not rebuilt; only the crypt containing the sarcophagi of the rulers survived.

Gera was severely damaged again during World War II. The only remnants of the old town are the market square just below St. Salvator's and a few adjoining streets. Osterstein Castle was destroyed completely. The surviving city hall (1576) resembles that of **Altenburg**. Both were designed by Nikolaus Gromann (ca. 1500–66), the Renaissance master builder also responsible for the Weimar city palace (*Stadschloss*), of which only the "bastille" survives.

ST. SALVATOR'S CHURCH (SALVATORKIRCHE). The church exterior appears much as it did in Bach's time except for the tower, which was completed later. After the fire of 1780, the church was rebuilt on the remnants of the old walls according to the original plan and consecrated in 1782. The elaborate double staircase leading to the entrance replaced houses consumed in the conflagration. The current interior, entirely in art nouveau style, dates from 1903.

Literature: Homann; BDOK II; BDOK V; Jung 1961; Wessely 1974/85; Krause-Graumnitz 1974/85; Petzoldt 2000; Organs; Maul 2004.

Websites: www.sankt-salvator-gera.de/kirche/sankt-salvator/baugeschichte/ (G); www.heinrich-posthumus.de/sarkophag.htm (G).

Görlitz

Bach's presence in Görlitz can be inferred from a report by Johann Andreas Silbermann (1712–83), Gottfried Silbermann's nephew. Johann Andreas visited Görlitz in 1741, at which time a Leipzig student of Bach's, David Nicolai (1702–64), demonstrated the famous "sun organ" (*Sonnenorgel*). "It has three manuals. . . . I pushed a few keys, but they were so hard and resistant and, moreover, had to be pressed down so far that I couldn't have played anything on it. The old famous Mr. Bach of Leipzig did not judge this instrument unfairly when, in discussing it with my cousin, he called it a "horse organ" (*PferdsOrgel*), because one has to be as strong as a horse to play it." (The cousin referred to was most likely a distant family member, Johann Georg Silbermann (1698–1749), who worked in Gottfried's shop in **Freiberg**. BDOK II, no. 486.)

In 1729 another student of Bach's, Johann Caspar Vogler (1696–1763), applied for the organist post in Görlitz, boasting: "I [have been] a pupil of the famous Mr. Bach, who . . . as he himself told me, has not yet been personally in Görlitz but whose reputation is perhaps known there. As regards virtue on the organ and speed of hands and feet, I come closest to him here in Saxony" (NBR, p. 320).

Vogler did not get the position because, according to the church records, he played too quickly. Assuming these accounts are credible, Bach visited Görlitz sometime between 1729 and 1741, presumably in connection with one of his Dresden visits. (Görlitz lies 109 km/68 miles east of Dresden, along a major trade and postal route passing through Bautzen.)

With an abundance of well-preserved Renaissance and Baroque houses, Görlitz is considered by many today to be Germany's most beautiful city. It appears in so many historical movies and TV series (among them the 2014 film *The Grand Budapest Hotel*), that it has been dubbed "Görliwood."

CHURCH OF ST. PETER AND PAUL. After a devastating fire in 1691 entirely destroyed the interior of the Gothic church (including two organs), it was redecorated in a flamboyant Baroque style that included the current white and

69. Görlitz, Church of St. Peter and Paul: The five-aisle Gothic hall church, built in the late fourteenth/early fifteenth century, sits atop a promontory overlooking the Neisse River (now the border between Germany and Poland). At left: the medieval *Waidhaus*, the oldest secular building in Görlitz.

malachite-green organ case. The new furnishings, donated by private citizens, attested to the town's wealth derived from its role as a major trading center on the *via regia* connecting Poland and Germany.

The father-son team of Eugenio and Adam Horatio Casparini (German-born despite their Italianized names) created the monumental "sun organ" in the Church of St. Peter and Paul between 1697 and 1703, upon returning to Germany after decades in Italy.

Literature: Homann; BDOK II; NBR; Winzeler 2010; Organs; Yearsley 2012.

Websites: www.youtube.com/watch?v=5jceKQ15HMM (demonstrates the organ in Vilnius, Lithuania, built by a later member of the family: Adam Gottlob Casparini, dating from 1776; one of very few surviving Casparini organs, it has been reproduced at the Eastman School of Music); www.vocativ.com/world/germany-world/görliwood-germanys-new-film-mecca/.

Gotha (1711, 1717)

Gotha is one of a sequence of three Thuringian towns on the ancient *via regia* that played significant roles in the lives of J. S. Bach and the Bach family. Proceeding from west to east, they are Eisenach, Gotha, and **Erfurt**, separated from one another in Bach's time by a day's travel. Although it is not documented, it is likely that Bach visited Gotha in his youth, perhaps en route from Eisenach to Erfurt where the Bach family had a substantial presence.

In recent years, our knowledge of Bach's connections with Gotha has dramatically increased. For example, the discovery of a court record has revealed that in 1711 "the court organist from Weimar" received a payment of 12 thalers (ca. $1,150)—a substantial sum attesting to Bach's considerable reputation by that time. The precise date and nature of the occasion are unknown. Bach presumably gave a recital, or possibly a series of organ and cembalo recitals, for the princely family.

Bach returned to Gotha, located 55 km/34 miles west of Weimar, six years later. On April 12, 1717, another payment of 12 thalers was made to "the *Concert-Meister* Bach," correctly reflecting his Weimar title at that time (BDOK V, B 81a). On the same day, the court printer was paid for the production of a Passion text booklet. The April 1717 payment to Bach, then, would seem to have been for a Passion performance that had taken place a few weeks before, on Good Friday, March 26th, in the castle church of Friedenstein Palace. As early as 1850, the biographer Carl Ludwig Hilgenfeldt (1806–after 1852) claimed that Bach had composed a Passion in the year 1717. Moreover, traces of a pre-Leipzig Passion setting have been discerned in movements belonging to a version of the St. John Passion, BWV 245, dating from 1725. All this evidence points to the one-time existence of a "Gotha" Passion.

The Passion performance no doubt represented an audition for the post of Gotha court kapellmeister. By early March 1717, preparations were underway to find a successor for the seriously ill incumbent, Christian Friedrich Witt (ca. 1660–1717), who in fact died on April 3, 1717. Bach had not received the expected promotion to that rank in Weimar just three months before and would have found the Gotha position most attractive. Over the following two years other musicians were considered, including Telemann, Reinhard Keiser, and Bach's predecessor in Köthen, Augustin Reinhard Stricker. After Telemann turned it down, the position was offered to Gottfried Heinrich Stölzel (1690–1749), at the time kapellmeister in **Gera**. Stölzel assumed the post in November 1719, retaining it until his death.

During his tenure Gotha became a major center of musical activity. The reigning duke for most of that time was the luxury-loving Duke Friedrich II of Saxony-Gotha-Altenburg (r. 1691–1732). Stölzel's successor as kapellmeister was Georg Benda (1722–95), who left the employ of Frederick the Great in Potsdam to accept the Gotha position, in which he served from 1750 to 1778. In the nineteenth century, the duchy of Saxony-Gotha-Altenburg was divided. Gotha was inherited by Duke Ernst I of Saxony-Coburg (r. 1806–44) and became part of the newly created duchy of Saxony-Coburg-Gotha (r. 1826–44). Ernst's son Albert (1819–61) was to be the future consort of Queen Victoria (r. 1837–1901).

Stölzel held a post that had been created by Duke Ernst I "the Pious" (1601–75), of Saxony-Gotha (from 1672 Saxony-Gotha-Altenburg). Ernst chose Gotha as his court in 1641, a year after the duchy of Saxony-Weimar had been divided among the three brothers of the ruling family, yielding the new duchies of Saxony-Gotha and Saxony-Eisenach.

FRIEDENSTEIN PALACE. Gotha's musical life began in 1646 with the creation of the court kapelle and the consecration of the court chapel, situated within the newly built castle, *Friedenstein* ("Rock of Peace"). Construction began in 1643, during the Thirty Years War. Its name repudiates that of the earlier castle, *Grimmenstein* ("Rock of Wrath"), and no doubt reflects the duke's desire for an end to the war. The palace currently houses archives, an important research library (with major holdings from the sixteenth through eighteenth centuries, including some 3,800 hymnals), scientific and historical museums, and period rooms. In 2010 they were combined under the rubric Baroque Universe Gotha (*Barockes Universum Gotha*). Many of the palace's elaborate parks and gardens from the early eighteenth century survive.

70. Gotha, Friedenstein Palace (1643–56): Residence of Duke Ernst I "the Pious." The enormous structure (325 × 455 ft.) is one of the earliest examples of German Baroque palace architecture.

71. Gotha, Court Chapel (consecrated 1646): An integral part of Friedenstein Palace and almost certainly the venue for a 1717 "Passion" performance by J. S. Bach.

The chapel is one of two sections of the palace that have retained their original functions. In 1692, an organ built by Severin Hohlbeck (d. 1700) was installed according to a specific Thuringian style: directly above the pulpit and altar. Only the original case survives. It was no doubt on this instrument that Bach had played during his visit of 1711. Of particular cultural interest is the court theater dating from 1681–87, also part of the palace complex. It bears the name of the great actor, Konrad Ekhof (1720–78), a friend of Goethe's and Lessing's, who in 1775 became director of the new court theater in Gotha. It was the first permanent theatrical company in Germany. The theater still uses the original Baroque sets and stage machinery from the 1770s. In 1775 Georg Benda introduced the genre of melodrama here with his *Ariadne auf Naxos*.

The earlier castle, *Grimmenstein*, was destroyed in 1567, but not before Hans Bach (ca. 1580–1626), the son of the family patriarch, Veit Bach, had apprenticed there with a town musician (*Stadtpfeifer*) who, according to the Genealogy, actually lived in the castle. Some years later, Caspar Bach (ca. 1575–after 1640), described in the Genealogy as Hans's brother, was the Gotha *Stadtpfeifer*.

Bach conceivably visited Gotha during his Leipzig period, too, which was a westward journey of some 175 km/108 miles. There is little doubt that he cultivated

professional and personal connections with kapellmeister Stölzel throughout that time and clearly
held Stölzel's music in high esteem. Sometime
after 1723, Wilhelm Friedemann Bach copied a
keyboard partita in G minor attributed to Stölzel
into his *Klavierbüchlein*, to which Sebastian added
a minuet, BWV 929. Around ten years later, Anna
Magdalena entered the famous song, "Bist du bei
mir," BWV 508, into her *Klavierbüchlein* of 1725.
The composition is now known to be an aria from
Stölzel's 1718 opera *Diomedes*.

Recent discoveries have revealed that many
church compositions by Stölzel were performed in
Leipzig during the 1730s. On Good Friday, April
23, 1734, his 1720 passion oratorio, *Die leidende und
am Creutz sterbende Liebe*, was performed in St.
Thomas's Church. For the 1735/36 liturgical year
either Bach, or perhaps a deputy, apparently performed an entire annual cycle of Stölzel's cantatas.
Earlier that decade, between 1732–35, an inde-
terminate number of Stölzel settings of cantatas
from another annual cycle also seem to have been
performed in Leipzig. Finally, around 1742, Bach prepared the aria "Bekennen will
ich seinen Namen," BWV 200. Long considered an original composition, it is in
fact Bach's arrangement of an aria from Stölzel's passion oratorio. The esteem was
evidently mutual: In 1747 Stölzel purchased a copy of Bach's *Musical Offering* for
the Gotha court kapelle.

72. Gotha, Town Hall: J. S. Bach's
ancestor, Caspar Bach, town
Stadtpfeifer from 1619. presumably
resided in the tower.

*Literature: BDOK V; Hilgenfeldt 1850; Krausse 1981; Ranft 1985; Beißwenger 1992; Baselt 1994;
Glöckner 1995; Dürr 2000; Glöckner 2002; Ahrens 2007; Pfau 2008; Schabalina 2008; Wollny
2008; Glöckner 2009; Siegmund 2011; Wolff GMO, accessed November 15, 2014.*

Halle (1713, 1714, 1716, 1719(?), 1740)

In December 1713, while employed as court organist in Weimar, Bach was
offered the prestigious position of organist at Halle's Market Church of Our Lady
(*Marktkirche unser lieben Frauen*), also known as the Church of Our Lady and
St. Mary's Church (*Liebfrauenkirche, Marienkirche*). Since the church had always

been considered one of the most important in central Germany, with a three-manual, sixty-five-stop organ then under construction that was almost twice the size of the *Himmelsburg* instrument at his disposal in Weimar, Bach was understandably intrigued by the prospect. The search for a successor to Friedrich Wilhelm Zachow (1663–1712), the deceased organist of the Market Church, had been initiated soon after his death sixteen months earlier. It turned out to be a long and convoluted process, however, owing mainly to the death of the Prussian king Friedrich I on February 25, 1713. The ensuing mourning period lasted six months, during which no church music, including organ recitals, could be performed. Four other candidates had applied for the position early on, but Bach's name is not mentioned in the archives until the autumn of 1713. He apparently had not formally applied but rather indicated interest, which led to his being actively recruited by the church board and invited to visit Halle, which is located about 140 km/87 miles from Weimar. (He presumably traveled via Jena, **Weißenfels**, **Naumburg**, and **Merseburg**.) During his sojourn, which took place during the first two weeks of December, Bach was put up in Halle's best inn, the Golden Ring. He "presented himself," perhaps assessing the ongoing organ construction, and then, seemingly to his surprise, was prevailed upon to stay on in order to compose and perform a cantata. The cantata, now lost, evidently was the setting of a text by the principal pastor, Johann Michael Heineccius (1674–1722). The performance presumably took place on December 10, 1713. Bach received the sum of 12 thalers ($1,150) for his trip and the cantata.

Bach apparently was offered the position almost immediately and accepted it verbally. Upon receiving the formal written contract (issued on January 11, 1714, but backdated to December 14, 1713; NBR, no. 48), he demurred, however. In the first of two surviving letters to August Becker (1668–1750), chairman of the church board (NBR, nos. 49–50), Bach asked for an increase in the proposed salary. He ultimately rejected the final offer and received a response accusing him of having unscrupulously used it as leverage to improve his situation in Weimar. Bach denied the accusation in a letter dated March 19, 1714. Hardly more than two weeks earlier, however, he had been promoted to the rank of concertmaster with a new salary of 250 thalers ($24,000). The total salary offered by Halle, including allowances for lodging and wood, was 171 thalers ($16,400).

The Halle church board appears to have harbored no lasting resentment. In April 1716, Bach was invited to examine the now-completed organ at the Market Church, built 1712–16 by Johann Christoph Contius (also Cuntzius, 1676–1722). The other examiners were Christian Friedrich Rolle (1681–1751), town kantor in Quedlinburg, and Johann Kuhnau (1660–1722), Bach's predecessor as

Thomaskantor in Leipzig. The occasion presumably marked the first meeting of Kuhnau and Bach. The detailed examination report, submitted on May 1, 1716, attested to the instrument's overall quality and adherence to the specifications (NBR, no. 59). The consecration of the organ took place on the same day. An elaborate banquet, whose menu has been preserved, followed two days later (NBR, no. 60).

Only the original case of the Contius organ has survived. The present instrument was built by Schuke Orgelbau in 1984. The church also contains an older, smaller organ, located above the altar. Built 1663–64 by Georg Reichel (ca. 1628–84, restored by the Schuke firm), it was used during lessons with Zachow by the young Halle native George Frideric Handel (1685–1759), who was baptized in the Market Church.

On two occasions in later years, Bach unsuccessfully attempted to meet Handel during the expatriate's visits to Halle. The first was in the summer of 1719, the second ten years later, when in mid-June 1729 Bach sent his son Wilhelm Friedemann to Halle to invite Handel to Leipzig—a distance of 45 km/28 miles. The meeting never took place.

After Bach's decision to remain in Weimar in 1714, the organist's position at the Market Church was filled by Gottfried Kirchhoff (1685–1746). Kirchoff, like Handel, was a student of Zachow's. Kirchhoff's successor was Wilhelm Friedemann Bach. Friedemann became music director and organist of the church in 1746 and held the post until 1764. A celebrated organ virtuoso, he was hired without the usual audition. In the following years he performed several of his father's cantatas, as well as his own, of which about two dozen survive. The Halle position was his last regular employment.

Landmarks

MARKET CHURCH OF OUR LADY/ST. MARY'S CHURCH (MARKT-KIRCHE UNSER LIEBEN FRAUEN/MARIENKIRCHE). The church's grandiose dimensions reflect Halle's importance as the favorite residence of its archiepiscopal administrator, Cardinal Albrecht von Brandenburg. The emphasis on Marian veneration was a response to the Reformation. By the time the building was completed, however, Lutheranism had been officially established in Halle. Luther preached in the half-finished church in 1545 and 1546.

In 1926 the New York-born German-American painter, Lyonel Feininger (1871–1956), was commissioned by the director of the *Kunstmuseum Moritzburg* to paint a view of Halle. Feininger eventually painted eleven, among them depictions

73. Halle, Market Church: Late-Gothic hall church. Its unique four towers resulted from connecting the towers of two earlier churches into a single large structure.

74. Halle, *Market Church with Arrow* (1930): Oil painting by Lyonel Feininger. The painting, along with Feininger's art in general, was condemned during the Nazi era as an example of "degenerate art" (*entartete Kunst*).

of the Market Church and the cathedral. These two paintings are exhibited in a gallery of the museum with a large window that provides a clear view of both churches. Throughout the town small plaques display reproductions of Feininger's versions of the particular views as seen from those locations.

CATHEDRAL (DOM) AND MORITZBURG. Halle's oldest church, dating from the thirteenth century, the cathedral was originally associated with the city's ecclesiastical rulers, the archbishops of Magdeburg. The distinctive Italianate roof gables were added in 1526. The seventeen-year-old Handel briefly served as organist at the cathedral (which despite its designation was by then already a reformed church) before leaving for Hamburg in 1703. The church is located near the New Residence (*Neue Residenz*) and the Moritzburg, both courtly residences and both now partially in ruins. Those of the Moritzburg have been transformed into the art museum, the *Kunstmuseum Moritzburg*.

ST. ULRICH'S CHURCH (ULRICHSKIRCHE) AND THE FRANCKE FOUNDATIONS (FRANCKESCHE STIFTUNGEN). A former monastery church located near the main square, the Gothic St. Ulrich's Church is now a concert hall. The Pietist theologian August Hermann Francke (1663–1727), founder of the so-called Francke Foundations, preached here from 1715 until his death. The foundations grew over fifty years from a small orphanage and school for the poor in 1695 to a large compound accommodating some 2500 people. It included schools, a pharmacy, and a bible printing shop. The simple buildings of the extended campus are now used by the university. They are located just outside the city walls in the neighborhood of Glaucha. When J. S. Bach visited the local kantor of Glaucha, Johann Georg Hille (d. 1744), during the Lenten season of 1740 (BDOK II, no. 477), he may have noticed the buildings of the Francke Foundations.

UNIVERSITY OF HALLE AND PIETISM. Francke and his teacher Philipp Spener (1635–1705) were leading figures in the development of Pietism, an introspective, individualistic form of Lutheranism often denigrated by the orthodox mainstream. Both Spener, known as the "Father of Pietism" and one of the founders of the University of Halle in 1694, and Francke had lived in orthodox Leipzig before moving to Halle, where they helped establish the new university as a center of Pietism. The *alma mater Halensis*, or Friedrich's University (*Friedrichs-Universität*), was later a center of early Enlightenment thought. It owed much to the influence of two of its early champions: the philosopher Christian Wolff (1679–1754) and the jurist Christian Thomasius (1655–1728).

WILHELM FRIEDEMANN BACH HOUSE. Friedemann Bach lived in the building located at Grosse Klausstrasse 12 from 1764 to 1770 during his Halle tenure. Since 2012 the structure has been designated the Wilhelm Friedemann Bach House. The small museum within contains panels and exhibits devoted to several composers associated with Halle, in addition to W. F. Bach.

HANDEL HOUSE MUSEUM. The official designation of the birthplace of G. F. Handel is "Handel City Halle" (*Händelstadt Halle*). He was born in the corner property located at Grosse Nikolaistrasse 5, a Renaissance-era building dating to 1558 acquired by Handel's father in 1666. A museum since 1937, it now serves as a performance venue as well.

Literature: Homann; BDOK II; NBR; Wollny 1994; Leaver 2009; Hübner 2011; Musketa-Barth 2012; Organs.

Website: www.stiftung-moritzburg.de/dauerausstellung/lyonel-feininger-empore (G; history of Feininger holdings).

Hamburg (1700–1702, 1720)

J. S. Bach in Hamburg

The Obituary reports that during his years as a pupil at the Lüneburg St. Michael's school (1700–1702) Bach visited Hamburg, about 58 km/36 miles away, several times to hear the famous organist at the St. Catherine's Church, Johann Adam Reinken (1623–1722). On foot, the journey would probably have taken Bach two days each way. In the home of his teacher Georg Böhm (1661–1733) in Lüneburg, Bach had made a copy, dated 1700, of Reinken's largest, most demanding composition, the Fantasia on "An Wasserflüssen Babylon," a powerful indication of the young musician's organistic ability at the age of fifteen.

It is possible that during his Lüneburg years Bach also heard the renowned Hamburg opera, including works by its principal composer, Reinhard Keiser (1674–1739), and others. The opera company existed from 1678 to 1738. The original house, the "Opera at the Goose Market" (*Oper am Gänsemarkt*), was demolished in 1763. Hamburg's modern opera house, the *Staatsoper*, built 1955, stands about one hundred meters away from the site of the original.

In November 1720, Bach undertook the 340-km/210-mile journey from Köthen (via Magdeburg) to Hamburg to compete for the vacant position of organist at the Church of St. James (*Jacobikirche*), a post once held by Matthias Weckmann (ca. 1619–74). The trip would have taken approximately twelve days. The four-manual organ dating from 1688–93 was built by Arp Schnitger (1648–1719). Curiously, it is not known whether Bach played the St. James instrument during this

75. Hamburg, Town view from the Elbe River: Colored engraving (1682) by Peter Schenk the Elder. Of the six major churches shown (left to right: St. Michael's, St. Nicholas's, St. Catherine's, St. Peter's, Cathedral, St. James's), all but the cathedral survive today.

sojourn. The organ underwent repairs in 1721 and may have been unplayable at the time of Bach's visit.

At all events, on Saturday, November 16th, Bach gave a memorable performance not in St. James's but in St. Catherine's Church, where Johann Adam Reinken was organist. The event, recently characterized as "perhaps the most famous recital in the instrument's long history" (Yearsley 2012), lasted two hours and, according to the Obituary, took place "before the Magistrate and many other distinguished persons of the town, to their general astonishment. The aged organist of this church, Johann Adam Reinken . . . listened to him with particular pleasure. Bach . . . performed extempore the chorale 'An Wasser-flüssen Babylon' . . . for almost half an hour" (NBR, p. 302). Whether one of the two Weimar versions of Bach's chorale prelude on the hymn, BWV 653a and b, bears any resemblance to the legendary 1720 Hamburg improvisation must remain a matter of conjecture. Since the theorist Johann

76. Hamburg, Principal Church of St. James: Three-aisle Gothic hall church, built 1350–1400, enlarged 1512.

Mattheson (1681–1764), music director of the Hamburg cathedral, later cited the theme and countersubject of the Fugue in G minor, BWV 542/2, in his *Grosse General-Baß-Schule* (1731; BDOK II, no. 302), it is likely that Bach had performed that work at his Hamburg recital, as well.

Bach's pupil Johann Friedrich Agricola (1720–74) reported decades afterward that "the late kapellmeister Bach in Leipzig gave assurance that the thirty-two-foot *Principal* and the pedal *Posaune* in the organ of St. Catherine's in Hamburg spoke evenly and quite audibly right down to the lowest C. But he also used to say that this *Principal* was the only one as good as that, of such size, that he had ever heard." As early as 1636, on the initiative of Reinken's predecessor and teacher,

Heinrich Scheidemann (ca. 1596–1663), the instrument became the world's first four-manual organ.

The official audition for the post of St. James's organist was held on November 28th. Bach, however, had been summoned back to Köthen on November 23rd, doubtless to prepare the annual birthday cantata on December 10th for Prince Leopold. Nonetheless, he was evidently regarded as the leading candidate, based on his earlier recital. The final decision, made on December 12th, was postponed to await Bach's response. At a meeting on December 19th, his letter (now lost) was read, in which he withdrew his name from consideration. According to local custom, appointees were expected to make a substantial monetary donation to the church—a gesture beyond Bach's means. A minor local organist, one Johann Joachim Heitmann (d. 1727), was named to the post in return for a donation of four thousand marks. Mattheson later reported that the renowned pastor of St. James's, Erdmann Neumeister (1671–1756), mocked the appointment decision in his Christmas sermon, remarking that "he was firmly convinced that even if one of the angels of Bethlehem should come down from Heaven, one who played divinely and wished to become organist of St. Jacobi, but had no money, he might just as well fly away again" (*Der musicalische Patriot*, 1728, NBR, no. 82).

In an earlier publication (*Critica Musica*, 1725, NBR, no. 319), Mattheson sarcastically mocked the opening choral exclamations of Bach's cantata, *Ich hatte viel Bekümmernis*, BWV 21. Along with source evidence, Mattheson's quotation strongly suggests that the cantata was performed in Hamburg in connection with Bach's visit, presumably as part of the audition process. Pastor Neumeister, widely credited as the creator of the late Baroque cantata text format, is presumably not the author of the libretto of BWV 21.

J. S. Bach's likely routes to Hamburg:
1. From Lüneburg: Lüneburg—Winsen an der Luhe—Bergedorf—Hamburg;
2. From Köthen: Köthen—Kalbe—Magdeburg; thence, either:
    a. Magdeburg—Gardeleben—Salzwedel—Lüneburg—Winsen an der Luhe—Hamburg; or, alternatively:
    b. Magdeburg—Stendal, followed by other minor towns along the eastern shore of the Elbe to Hamburg.

Landmarks

In the early eighteenth century the Hanseatic city of Hamburg was about three times the size of Leipzig with a population of some 75,000. After Vienna, it was the largest in the Holy Roman Empire. Devastated by fire in 1842, heavily bombed in World War II, and extensively rebuilt since, it has nonetheless retained

a skyline Bach would have recognized. Strict laws regulating the height of buildings downtown have ensured that the steeples of the five principal churches are
clearly visible. Three of the five have a Bach connection.

PRINCIPAL CHURCH OF ST. JAMES (HAUPTKIRCHE ST. JACOBI).
Although the church was destroyed in the bombing of June 18, 1944, its furnishings, including the pipes and wind chests of its famous Schnitger organ, had been
removed for safekeeping beforehand. From 1959 to 1963, the building was restored
to its historical form, with the addition of a modern steeple of reinforced concrete
covered in copper. After several unsatisfactory attempts in the 1960s, the organ
was successfully restored in 1993, moved to its original location on the west wall,
and rededicated. Incorporating 80 percent of the original pipework, it is now the
largest surviving Baroque organ of the North German type.

CHURCH OF ST. CATHERINE (KATHARINENKIRCHE). One of Ham-
burg's five principal churches, the foundation walls of the tower date from the
thirteenth century—making the church the second-oldest surviving structure in
Hamburg. The late-Gothic basilica was built between 1380–1425. Its Dutch-style
tower was added in 1657–59. The original organ was completed in 1520. It was
rebuilt numerous times over the ensuing centuries under the hands of a series of
organ builders, among them the Scherer family (1559–1629), Gottfried Fritzsche
(1630–31), and Friedrich Stellwagen (1644–47). The organ was mostly destroyed
in World War II, but a representative sampling of original pipes was saved. The
instrument has recently been reconstructed by the Flentrop firm on the basis of
the surviving pipes and contemporary documents. It was inaugurated in 2013 as a
"Bach organ," that is, one with a biographical connection to Bach and designed to
be optimal for the performance of his music.

ST. MICHAEL'S CHURCH (MICHAELISKIRCHE). The present Baroque
structure replaced a smaller edifice destroyed in 1750 by lightning. The new building mostly constructed between 1751 and 1786, is the most famous of Hamburg's
five principal churches; it serves today as the emblem of the city. The church was
consecrated in 1762, that is, before its completion in 1786. Carl Philipp Emanuel
Bach, along with members of his family, are buried in the crypt of the church, as
is Johann Mattheson. (C. P. E. Bach's predecessor and godfather, Georg Philipp
Telemann, was buried at the Church of the St. John's Monastery in the Hamburg
suburb of Eppendorf. The building is no longer extant.)

COMPOSERS' MILE (KOMPONISTENMEILE). An ongoing project located
near St. Michael's on Peterstrasse, a quiet pedestrian street lined by gabled brick
buildings, celebrates Hamburg's musical history. Dubbed the "Composers'
Mile," it will eventually contain several small museums dedicated to composers

associated with Hamburg. The Telemann, Brahms, and C. P. E. Bach museums are already open; museums devoted to Johann Adolph Hasse (born in nearby Bergedorf), Felix and Fanny Mendelssohn (both born in Hamburg), and Gustav Mahler (conductor of the *Stadttheater* from 1881–1897) are in various stages of completion. Within the hectic, ultramodern city of 1.8 million, the complex promises to provide a charming refuge of historic buildings, tastefully restored.

Literature: Lehmann 1709; Homann; BDOK II; NBR; Wenzel 1978; Buelow 1994; Wolff 2000; Maul-Wollny 2007; Stauffer 2009; Erickson 2009; Yearsley 2012; Organs; Wolff GMO, accessed November 15, 2014.

Heiligengrabe° (1747)

The link between Bach and Heiligengrabe rests entirely on a comment regarding the monastery's organ contained in a twentieth-century chronicle of the convent: "Johann Sebastian Bach played on this new instrument, too, when he visited the convent of Heiligengrabe during his visit to **Berlin** in 1747" (Kieckebusch 1949/2008, 244). The author provides no source for this assertion.

Located 122 km/76 miles northwest of Berlin, Heiligengrabe was not on the route back to Leipzig. On the contrary: such a visit on Bach's part would have constituted a substantial detour, passing through Neu Ruppin and Rheinsberg, towns later associated with the early career of C. P. E. Bach. But he may well have been curious to see and play the instrument if his Berlin itinerary took him through the village. The organ was built in 1725 by David Baumann (dates unknown), a craftsman known for his organs in the cathedral and palace of Schwerin. (The instrument has been restored within its original case.)

Once a monastery and then a Protestant convent for noble women, the institution stood under the special protection of the Prussian kings. The management of its extensive landholdings was overseen by a convent supervisor elected by the residents and confirmed by the king, who in turn paid out a fixed allowance in cash and in kind to each conventual. Recent authors have suggested that Bach might have been the beneficiary of such a payout in lieu of an honorarium, since, as far as is known, he was otherwise not paid or rewarded for his famous 1747 **Potsdam** performance before Frederick the Great. No records of such payments to outsiders or to the court seem to exist, although hospitality for visitors was expected and is in fact documented, especially visitors connected to the court. Christoph Trautmann speculates further that Heiligengrabe may have been a way station for Bach en route to Schwerin (located 99 km/61 miles further northwest), a visit nowhere documented. It is true, however, that Johann Gottfried Müthel (1728–88) had been appointed chamber musician and organist to the court of Schwerin in 1747. In 1750 his prince accorded Müthel a study sabbatical to become one of Bach's last students in Leipzig. Müthel lived in Bach's house until the kantor's death.

Following his performances in Potsdam, Bach visited Berlin on August 5th. By August 18th, he was back in Leipzig, where he took communion that day. A journey from Berlin to Heiligengrabe to Leipzig would have totaled about 425 km/264 miles and taken about 12–14 travel days. Including a visit to Schwerin within this time frame was altogether impossible. Conceivably, Bach visited Heiligengrabe (and Schwerin?) before his appearance at the Potsdam court. His whereabouts in the months before his arrival there are unknown, apart from his presumed participation in a wedding ceremony at St. Thomas's Church on April 9th. If he made the trip, he presumably went there in the company of his son, Wilhelm Friedemann, who is reported to have accompanied his father to Potsdam. Friedemann may have joined him in **Halle**, where he had been organist at the Market Church since April 1746. All such considerations belong entirely to the realm of speculation.

Convent

A visit to Heiligengrabe is quite worthwhile for the modern traveler. Founded in the late twelfth century as a Cistercian monastery, the large establishment is well preserved. It contains within its walls the convent church as well as the chapel dedicated to the "Holy Grave" (*Heiligengrabe*), which became a pilgrimage destination. Most of the buildings are executed in red brick, including the churches and the cloister. Later Baroque dwellings, the "ladies' houses" for the noble conventuals, are in half-timber and brick. In the mid–nineteenth century, the convent added a boarding school for orphaned or indigent young girls of noble families, who trained to become teachers. The school existed until 1945. Its illustrious alumnae include Friedelind Wagner (1918–91), granddaughter of Richard Wagner, who was sent to "Germany's most reactionary school" (her words) by her family to tame her rebelliousness, to no avail. She was at the school from 1932 to 1935, left Germany in 1939, and immigrated to the United States in 1940.

Today Heiligengrabe accommodates a small museum, a guesthouse, and meeting facilities used for retreats and seminars. A small group of resident conventuals continues to live there, dedicated to the religious life.

Literature: Kieckebusch 1949/2008; Trautmann 1983; Petzoldt 2000.

Karlsbad (1718, 1720)

As far as is known, J. S. Bach traveled outside the boundaries of modern Germany on only two occasions. Both times he was part of the entourage of Prince Leopold of Köthen, who visited the luxury spa of Karlsbad (Karlovy Vary) in northwest Bohemia, now part of the Czech Republic. The first journey took place from early May to late June 1718, the second from late May to early July 1720.

Founded by Emperor Karl IV (r. 1346–78) in 1370 at the confluence of the Teplá and Ohre Rivers and surrounded by three mountain ranges, Karlsbad became a popular resort for the nobility in the early eighteenth century after Karl VI (r. 1711–40) chose to spend his summer vacations there with his family. Though officially Catholic, the city tolerated guests of the various confessions. Nonetheless, Prince Leopold and other members of the Reformed Church presumably attended services in private. Besides the allegedly salutary hot mineral springs, the town's attractions included luxurious accommodations, extensive sanitary facilities, and entertainments ranging from billiards to concerts and grand banquets accompanied by *Tafelmusik* performed by some of the leading court musicians of Europe. Other musical performances enjoyed by the 200–300 noble guests presumably took place in the Saxon Hall (*Sächsischer Saal*), built in 1701 at the initiative of the Saxon elector.

In late December 1717, Bach arrived in Köthen and entered the service of Prince Leopold (1694–1728). Six months earlier, on June 23rd, the sickly twenty-two-year-old prince had returned from his first trip to Karlsbad, where he had gone to partake of the healing waters and to mingle with other members of the European nobility, among them the elector Friedrich August I of Saxony (August the Strong, r. 1697–1733) and the dukes of **Gotha** and **Zerbst**. The clientele was so illustrious that Leopold was listed in the guest register under the rubric "others."

During his visit of 1717, Friedrich August may have heard about Bach's performance of a Passion at Gotha the previous March, an event that may have helped precipitate the plan to stage a competition (ultimately aborted) in **Dresden** the following autumn between Bach and the French virtuoso Louis Marchand (Hübner 2006). Prince Leopold, for his part, had presumably been aware of the Weimar concertmaster since the wedding of his sister Eleonore Wilhelmine to Duke Ernst August of Weimar in January 1716 in **Nienburg**. At all events, on August 5, 1717, less than two months after he had returned to Köthen from Karlsbad, the prince officially appointed Bach as his new kapellmeister (BDOK II, no. 128).

The following year, Bach accompanied Prince Leopold on the trip south to Karlsbad, together with several other court musicians, including the

KARLSBAD 157

concertmaster Joseph Spiess (d. 1730) and the gambist Christian Ferdinand Abel (1682–1761). Departing on May 9, 1718, the group presumably passed through the towns of Radegast, Zörbig, Landsberg to Leipzig, thence perhaps via Borna, Penig, Chemnitz, Thum, Annaberg, Joachimsthal (Jáchymov), and Schlacken-werth (Ostrov), and finally to Karlsbad. A somewhat longer but better route from Leipzig passed through Zwickau, Plauen, and Oelsnitz. In any event, it was neces-sary to cross the Ore Mountains (*Erzgebirge*), the natural border between Saxony and Bohemia. According to contemporary travel guides, the entire journey would have covered a distance of some twenty-eight "imperial" miles (ca. 155 U.S. miles). (Modern maps put the distance Köthen-Karlsbad at ca. 275 km/170 miles.) A recent commentator, assuming a rate of ca. sixteen hours per day, suggests that the trip took just three-and-a-half to four days (Hübner 2006). The entourage returned on June 29th. The cost of the seven-week journey to the court treasury was over 3,000 thalers (ca. $288,000), which included the transportation of a harp-sichord across the mountain range.

Since Leopold's health continued to deteriorate, he returned to Karlsbad two years later, setting out around May 25, 1720. Besides Leopold and Bach, only two members of the group are mentioned by name: Leopold's physician and the court controller. The trip this time cost almost 4,400 thalers ($422,000). Bach no doubt renewed his acquaintance with musicians from the Dresden court on this occasion and very likely made the acquaintance of influential members of the Bohemian aristocracy, including Johann Adam Count Questenberg of Jaromerice (1678–1752) and Count Franz Anton von Sporck (1662–1738) of Lissa and Prague. Bach had dealings with both many years later.

Upon Bach's return to Köthen he was confronted with shattering news. In the words of the Obituary, "After thirteen years of blissful married life with his first wife, the misfortune overtook him . . . of finding her dead and buried, although he had left her hale and hearty on his departure. The news that she had been ill and died reached him only when he entered his own house" (NBR, no. 306). Maria Barbara Bach was buried on July 7, 1720, possibly just hours before her husband's arrival. She was not yet thirty-six years old.

Prince Leopold never returned to Karlsbad, nor did he ever regain his health. He died on November 19, 1728, nine days short of his thirty-fourth birthday.

Beginning in the 1730s, and especially in the aftermath of a devastating fire in 1759, virtually all of Karlsbad's older buildings were razed. Aside from the Black Eagle House (1705), the Petra house (1706–9), and the old castle tower, noth-ing remains in the town of the buildings that Bach would have seen. The only

77. Karlsbad, Town view: Copper onion domes of St. Mary Magdalene's Church (center), Mill Colonnade (right).

significant remaining Baroque edifice is the Church of St. Mary Magdalene, built 1732–36 by the noted Prague architect Kilian Ignaz Dientzenhofer (1689–1751). The historical core of the city today consists mostly of nineteenth-century and art nouveau structures, along with promenades, parks (including one named after Antonin Dvorak, a frequent guest), fountains, and colonnades scaling the high rock walls on either side of the Teplá and Ohre Rivers. Karlsbad remains a luxurious spa.

Eminent visitors to Karlsbad have included Tsar Peter the Great, Beethoven, Goethe (who visited the town thirteen times), Schiller, the musicians Hummel and Moscheles, the Polish poet Adam Mickiewicz, the Russian writers Turgenyev and Gogol, and Mozart's son Franz Xaver (1791–1844), who died in Karlsbad and was buried there.

Literature: BDOK II; NBR; Plichta 1981; Wolff 1981; Wolff 2000; Hübner 2006.

Kassel (1732)

When Bach visited Kassel for an organ examination in September 1732, he ventured as far westward as he ever had, into the Landgraviate of Hesse, a region he had probably never before visited. The 255-km/158-mile journey, which no doubt took at least a week and presumably passed through **Weißenfels**, **Erfurt**, **Gotha**, and Eisenach, would have provided him with an occasion to revisit many stations of his life.

Kassel at the time was the seat of a major princely court in a fortified medieval city. Accompanied by his wife, an unusual practice for him, Bach's arrival was noted in the local newspaper. The couple stayed in the inn "City of Stockholm" (*Stadt Stockholm*), named in honor of the local ruler Landgrave Frederick I (1676–1751), who was also king of Sweden (from 1720). Not only was a servant placed at the Bachs' exclusive disposal, payment records confirm that he and Anna Magdalena were also borne about town twenty-five times in a litter carried by two porters.

After the satisfactory conclusion of the examination (for which Bach's report is lost), the instrument was consecrated on September 28th in a festive service. Bach performed the "Dorian" Toccata and Fugue in D minor, BWV 538, on this occasion, according to an annotation in a copy of the work by the organist Michael Gotthard Fischer (1773–1829), a student of Bach's last student, Johann Christian Kittel (1732–1809). Another source reports that the twelve-year-old son of Landgrave Frederick was so impressed by Bach's rapid pedal technique that he took a ring from his finger and presented it to the inspiring virtuoso (NBR, no. 338). This episode presumably took place at the organ consecration service.

Since the princely residence in the city palace (*Stadtschloss*) boasted a large organ constructed at the same time as St. Martin's by the same builder, Hans Scherer the Younger, Bach's extravagant welcome in Kassel may well have entailed a visit to the palace, including its church and organ. The building burned down in 1809, during the reign of Napoleon's brother Jérôme.

The total fee and expenses for Bach's eight-day sojourn (September 22–29) amounted to 163 thalers (ca. $15,650).

Bach's presumable route from Leipzig via Eisenach (Brönner 1761): Leipzig—Weißenfels—**Naumburg**—Eckartsberga—Buttelstedt—Erfurt— Gotha—Eisenach—Creuzburg—Wanfried—Eschwege—Kassel.

(According to Lehmann 1709, the "most usual route" was Leipzig—Merseburg—Freyburg—Laucha—Bibra—Bachra—Kölleda— Weißensee—Bad Tennstedt—Langensalza—Mühlhausen—Wanfried— Eschwege—Kassel.)

78. Kassel, St. Martin's Church: The mid-fourteenth-century church was almost completely destroyed in World War II. The two new towers, like their nineteenth-century predecessors, have become a landmark of the city's skyline.

Landmarks

ST. MARTIN'S CHURCH (MARTINSKIRCHE). The Gothic Church of St. Martin's was Kassel's dominant edifice. Its original single steeple, dating from 1450, was replaced in the nineteenth century by two neo-Gothic towers. During the firebombing of Kassel on the night of October 22, 1943, the church, along with the entire old town, fell to ruins. Its rebuilding (1952–58) was a bold attempt to integrate whatever survived into a decidedly modern structure that is nonetheless evocative of its Gothic heritage.

The organ was built 1610–12 by the brothers Friedrich and Hans Scherer the Younger and had "finally been adapted to the fashion of today and brought to its perfection by the organ builder, Mr. Nicolaus Becker, of Mühlhausen" (BDOK II, no. 316).

HERCULES STATUE, WILHELMSHÖHE PALACE AND PARK. Bach would have seen and perhaps visited two of modern Kassel's most popular attractions: the "Hercules" statue and the "Giants' Castle." Both were initiated by the Italophile, Landgrave Karl I (r. 1675–1730). The "Hercules," a seventeen-foot-high copper statue based on the Farnese Hercules, was begun in 1701. It stands atop a high pyramid, which in turn sits on the "Giants' Castle" atop the *Karlsberg*, the highest mountain near Kassel. Visible from afar, the statue is also the point of origin for elaborate water cascades that descend for 250 meters.

The *Wilhelmshöhe* palace, begun in 1785, houses an art museum including a large collection of Rembrandts and ancient sculptures. In 2013, the surrounding *Bergpark Wilhelmshöhe* was declared a UNESCO World Cultural Heritage site.

KARLSAUE GARDEN AND ORANGERIE. The *Karlsaue* is a public garden in the floodplain of the Fulda River. A pedestrian staircase (*Gustav-Mahler-Treppe*) leading down to the river from the city's Bellevue promenade (*Schöne Aussicht*) commemorates Mahler's two-year engagement as conductor of the Kassel theater. The garden includes an elegant orangerie.

Literature: Lehmann 1709; Brönner 1761; BDOK II; NBR; Petzoldt 2000; BWV.

79. Kassel, Orangerie: The 140-meter-long, French-style orangerie (begun 1702) housed potted orange and lemon trees during the winter and, during the summer, served as a residence for the princely family and as a venue for formal balls.

Kleinzschocher (1742)

Located in Bach's time on the outskirts of Leipzig (but now a part of the city) the manorial estate of Kleinzschocher was the site of the premiere of Bach's Peasant Cantata (*Cantate en burlesque*, BWV 212) on August 30, 1742. The work was his last precisely datable cantata and evidently his last collaboration with his frequent librettist, Christian Friedrich Henrici, alias Picander (1700–64). The occasion was the inauguration of the estate's new lord and ruler, the baron Carl Heinrich von Dieskau (1706–82), whose family had owned the property (and others in the area) since 1664.

The event also marked von Dieskau's thirty-sixth birthday. The homage paid by the villagers was a common tradition (see also **Wiederau**) and included formal oaths of allegiance and fealty. The festivities at Kleinzschocher were capped at the end of the day with fireworks.

Both Bach and Picander had their own reasons to please the young baron. At the time von Dieskau was *directeur des plaisirs* at the **Dresden** court, to which Bach had been appointed as court composer in 1736. Although the Dresden position was an honorary post for Bach, von Dieskau was no doubt in a position to be a valuable ally: from 1747 he held the title of director of the royal kapelle and chamber music. Picander, for his part, had been appointed city, district, and country tax collector of beverage taxes and inspector of wines in 1740. In this role, he reported directly to Chamberlain (*Kammerherr*) von Dieskau, the supervisor of various tax administrations.

The Peasant Cantata, one of the rare examples of overt musical humor in Bach's oeuvre, is partially written in local dialect and features a rustic maid and her suitor as protagonists. The composition, however, was intended as an entertainment produced by professional forces—presumably dressed in peasant costume—for a sophisticated, courtly assembly, one amused by such fashionable invocations of rustic simplicity. The scoring—for soprano and bass, obbligato horn and flute, strings and continuo—is frequently limited to the three-part texture (violin, viola, bass) that was associated with popular music of the time.

The text is replete with allusions to local events and personages. Alternating between courtly and folk idioms, the music similarly incorporates references to popular songs. Although the pastor and the local tax collector are the butt of criticism, the new lord hears nothing but praise—not least for having protected his lads from the draft board. At the time of the performance, the honored couple had five daughters but no male heir, a situation that sufficiently explains the text of the soprano aria: *"Gib Schöne, viel Söhne von artger Gestalt, und zieh sie fein alt"*

80. Kleinzschocher, Manor House: Back side as viewed from the park (lithograph, ca. 1850, first published in Poenicke 1854). The church no longer stands; the small, half-timbered building between the church and the manor may be the tax collector's house.

("Give us, most beautiful lady, many sons of fine build and raise them to a good age"). An heir in fact was eventually born in 1745 but died at age two, leading to the end of the family line. (The renowned singer Dietrich Fischer-Dieskau (1925–2012) was a descendant of von Dieskau through his paternal grandmother.)

Landmarks

KLEINZSCHOCHER MANOR. Virtually nothing remains of the manor. The estate passed through several hands and was eventually acquired in 1848 by the Leipzig publisher Bernhard von Tauchnitz (1816–95), a pioneer in the development of the paperback book and the publisher of some five thousand volumes of English and American literature released in English for the continental market. The manor was bombed in 1945. Nothing survives but the entrance gate and the so-called "tax collector's house"(*Schösserhaus*), now a boarded-up ruin. The right-hand pillar of the original gate bears a plaque, affixed in 1962 and now barely legible, reporting that Bach's Peasant Cantata was performed here in 1742.

VILLA TAUCHNITZ. Adjacent to the manor and dating from the late nineteenth century, the Villa Tauchnitz is also in a dilapidated state. Numerous efforts to salvage these remnants have so far proved unsuccessful, despite their desirable setting in a larger, now public, park. The local road bears the name "Cantata Way" (*Kantatenweg*).

Literature: Neumann 1972; Schulze 1976; Petzoldt 2000; Dürr 2005; Schleuning 2014.

Langewiesen (1706)

On November 28, 1706, the First Sunday of Advent, Bach visited the small town of Langewiesen, located 28 km/17 miles south of Arnstadt in the foothills of the Thuringian Forest (*Thüringer Wald*) mountain range. His charge was to examine the new organ built by Johann Albrecht of Coburg (d. 1719) in the Church of Our Lady (*Liebfrauenkirche*). Bach carried out the examination together with Johann Kister (d. 1727), the organist from nearby **Gehren**. Neither Bach's report nor the original organ is extant. The event is confirmed, however, in the Langewiesen church records (BDOK II, no. 18).

Bach may have performed the chorale prelude "Wie schön leuchtet der Morgenstern," BWV 739, whose hymn tune is associated with the First Sunday of Advent in contemporary hymnals. One of Bach's earliest compositions, the imaginative use of manuals and pedal, specified in the composer's manuscript, make it an ideal test piece (Stinson 1985).

A few weeks earlier, on November 11th, Bach was formally rebuked—not for the first time—by the Arnstadt consistory. On this occasion, he was criticized for his refusal to make music with the local students and for having invited a young maiden into the choir loft (NBR, no. 21). Whether his participation in the Langewiesen organ examination was part of an effort to leave Arnstadt (where his situation had been deteriorating for over a year) and find new employment elsewhere cannot be known. On Easter Sunday, April 24, 1707, Bach auditioned for the organ post at St. Blasius's Church in the town of Mühlhausen. He was offered the position two months later and accepted it. On June 28th, exactly seven months after the organ examination in Langewiesen, he formally submitted his resignation in Arnstadt.

The historic area of Langewiesen, containing the church and city hall, stretches along the main street (Hauptstrasse), which harbors a large number of houses clad entirely in black slate—a rarity. The material, available locally, provides excellent insulation in this mountainous region. The variety and imaginative use of this rather severe material is worthy of note.

CHURCH OF OUR LADY (LIEBFRAUENKIRCHE). In 1675, after a city-wide fire, the church was rebuilt using the old foundation walls. The construction, however, was not completed until five years later. The organ would not be built for another twenty-five years; the church tower had to wait until 1715. The interior of the bright hall church is decorated in simple Baroque style following a white, green, and gold color scheme. The two levels of balconies and the pulpit-altar type are common features in Thuringian churches. The wooden barrel vault ceiling is plastered and painted blue with white star rosettes.

Literature: BDOK II; NBR; Stinson 1985; Petzoldt 2000; Organs.

Websites: www.360cities.net/image/langewiesen-stadtkirche-altar#265.18,-53.73,70.0 (E; provides 360-degree views of church interior).

Langula° (1707/8?)

The village of Langula, located ca. 9 km/5.5 miles southwest of Mühlhausen, was first associated with Bach by Philipp Spitta (1841–94). In his monumental biography of the composer, Spitta remarked that Bach "was not unmindful of the state of music in the immediate neighborhood, and he must have noticed that often more material of a better kind for the church was available there than in the town itself." He continued: "Among the surrounding villages Langula, however, has been distinguished from the beginning of the eighteenth century to the present time [ca. 1870] by having a succession of well-qualified kantors and an active feeling for music" (Spitta 1883: 343).

Spitta was clearly alluding here to a statement by Bach himself who, in requesting his dismissal from his Mühlhausen post after only a year of service, referred famously to the "hindrance" (Wiedrigkeit) that frustrated him there but also to "the church music that is growing up in almost every township, and often better than the harmony that is fashioned here" (NBR, no. 32).

Spitta also claimed to have "discovered in the 'Cantorei' (the cantor's house)," a Bach composition "apparently belonging to his Mühlhausen time. It is incomplete and is adorned with some certain and other apparent additions by later kantors of Langula; still it offers some genuine matter for the consideration of the historian" (Spitta 1883: 343f).

The cantata was known to Spitta only in two fragmentary sources, both now lost. One was a copy in the hand of the Langula kantor at the time, Herr Sachs. The opening chorus was missing; the text of the following duet, "Meine Seele soll Gott loben," serves as the work title in the BWV catalog, where it carries the number 223. In the meantime, a recently discovered manuscript of the entire composition in the British Library attributes it to Handel. Closer inspection indicates that the work is in fact almost certainly not by Bach or Handel (Marx 2004).

The Langula "Kantorei" is an L-shaped, half-timber house next to Langula's St. George's Church. The church nave is a mid-nineteenth-century replacement for a much older building, of which only the tower survives. The "Kantorei" today houses a museum of local history, a charming hodgepodge of furniture, utensils and tools, historic clothing, and memorabilia. It bears a plaque that reads, "In 1707 Johann Sebastian Bach stayed in this house."

Literature: NBR; Spitta 1883; BWV; Marx 2004; Meißner 2007.

Lübeck (1705–6)

In the autumn of 1705 Bach was granted a four-week leave of absence from his post in Arnstadt, where he had been employed as organist at the New Church for fifteen months. He arranged for his cousin Johann Ernst (1683–1739) to carry out his duties during his absence. Bach, however, did not return until sixteen weeks later, in early February 1706. When interrogated by the Arnstadt consistory as to where he had been so long, he replied that he had been to Lübeck, some 450 km/280 miles to the north, "in order to comprehend one thing and another about his art" (NBR, no. 20). As the Obituary proudly emphasizes, Bach made the journey on foot. Assuming a brisk pace of some 30 km/18.5 miles a day, it would have taken a hiker (or hitchhiker) at least fifteen days to complete the journey and another fifteen days to return, more than consuming the entire four weeks and leaving no time at all to spend at his destination. Bach, then, not only failed to inform his superiors of his destination, but also must have set out knowing full well that he would be overstaying his granted leave by a considerable margin.

The precise route Bach traveled from Arnstadt to Lübeck is not known. One possibility, suggested by an early-eighteenth-century map (issued sometime between 1710 and 1724 by Johann Baptist Homann), is that it passed through the towns of **Wechmar**, **Gotha** (or **Erfurt**), Langensalza, Mühlhausen, Duderstadt, Seesen, Goslar, Wolfenbüttel, Brunswick, **Celle**, Lüneburg, and **Hamburg**. (A detailed reconstruction of the last leg of the journey, from Lüneburg to Lübeck, suggesting that the route passed through the town of Mölln rather than Hamburg, appears in Snyder 1986.)

Lübeck, situated near the mouth of the Trave River before it empties into the Baltic Sea, was a prosperous, cosmopolitan trading city. Like Hamburg, it was part of the Hanseatic League and, since 1226, a Free Imperial City. Unlike Hamburg, its importance declined considerably and permanently after the discovery of the New World and the economic dislocations of the Thirty Years War. At the time of Bach's journey, it had a population of ca. 27,000, that is, it was about one-third the size of Hamburg and one-third larger than contemporary Leipzig (ca. 20,000).

The specific object of Bach's pilgrimage of sorts was no doubt to hear, see, and make the personal acquaintance of Dieterich Buxtehude (1637–1707), the preeminent organist and arguably the greatest German composer of his generation. Buxtehude was the organist of St. Mary's Church, traditionally the most important musical post in Lübeck and one he had occupied for almost thirty-eight years by the time of Bach's visit. Buxtehude had succeeded to the position in April 1668, five months after the death of Franz Tunder (1614–67). Three months later he married Tunder's daughter. It is not known whether the marriage had been a condition for obtaining the post. Buxtehude, for his part, laid down such a condition regarding his own successor. Whether Bach had contemplated marrying Buxtehude's daughter at the time of his Lübeck sojourn in order to be able to follow him as organist of St. Mary's or whether he was already betrothed by then, is unknown. At all events, Buxtehude died a little more than a year after Bach's visit, in May 1707. A month later, Johann Christian Schieferdecker (1679–1732) assumed the post and, in August, married Buxtehude's thirty-two-year-old daughter, Anna Margaretha. In the meantime, Bach left Arnstadt for Mühlhausen in June 1707 and married his cousin Maria Barbara Bach the following October.

It is possible that Bach not only heard Buxtehude perform but also played for him. He evidently acquired copies of many of Buxtehude's organ works along with other examples of the North German organ repertoire. Bach brought the manuscripts back to Thuringia and placed them at the disposal of his brother Johann Christoph in Ohrdruf, who in time made his own copies of them, incorporating them into the important anthologies known as the "Möller Manuscript" and

"Andreas Bach Book." While Johann Christoph's copies have survived, Sebastian's have not.

Bach's acquaintance with Buxtehude's music can be traced back to his boyhood. The earliest example of a musical manuscript in Bach's hand is a tablature copy of Buxtehude's elaborate chorale fantasia, *Nun freut euch, lieben Christen g'mein*, BuxWV 210. The copy has been dated to ca. 1698–99, that is, when Bach was about thirteen years old and living with his older brother in Ohrdruf. The experience of finally meeting and hearing the legendary master play in his own church on his own instrument seven years later must have had a profound effect on the twenty-year-old Johann Sebastian Bach.

The older master's influence on the young composer is evident in Bach's Toccata in C, BWV 564/1, a work indebted to Buxtehude's Praeludium in C, BuxWV 137. Bach's monumental Passacaglia in C minor, BWV 582/1, also shows signs of Buxtehude's influence

81. Lübeck, St. Mary's Church: Earliest example (ca. 1260–1350) of "brick Gothic" (*Backsteingotik*), a North German development in emulation of the French high-Gothic style using local materials. It features flying buttresses, ribbed vaults, clerestory, apsidal chapels, and two stately towers framing the facade.

and may have been composed not long after his return home from Lübeck. Along with Buxtehude's Ciacona in C minor, BuxWV 159, on a similar theme, Bach's masterpiece was copied into the Andreas Bach Book, as was Buxtehude's C-major Praeludium.

Bach's enthusiasm for the North German organs themselves, already familiar to him from his excursions to Hamburg during his student days in Lüneburg, was further renewed upon experiencing Buxtehude's instrument in St. Mary's Church. Some aspects of its disposition are mirrored in his recommendation for the new organ in St. Blasius's Church in Mühlhausen.

The precise timing of Bach's visit to Lübeck was surely not accidental. The foot-traveler was evidently willing to endure the expected inclement weather of the late fall in order to be present in Lübeck for the famous *Abendmusiken*, popular nonliturgical evening concerts at St. Mary's that had been established around 1646 by Franz Tunder. Under Buxtehude, the performances took place at the turn of the liturgical year, specifically, between 4 and 5 P.M. after the vespers service on the last two Sundays of the Trinity season and the Second, Third, and Fourth Advent Sundays. They were not a part of Buxtehude's official duties. In 1705, the concerts included special performances of two new Buxtehude composi- tions: *Castrum doloris*, BuxWV 134, and *Templum honoris*, BuxWV 135. Now lost, they were elaborate oratorios written to mourn the death of Leopold I and then to celebrate the accession of Joseph I as Holy Roman Emperor the previous May. Bach no doubt heard and possibly participated in the performances. Their lavish instrumentation and polychoral scoring, described in the surviving librettos, may have influenced the format of Bach's *Gott ist mein König*, BWV 71, written in Feb- ruary 1708 for the inauguration of the Mühlhausen town council.

Landmarks

ST. MARY'S CHURCH (MARIENKIRCHE). Hardly less impressive for Bach than hearing Buxtehude play on the St. Mary's organ was experiencing the building itself, the official church of the city council and probably the largest of its kind he would see during his lifetime. The interior contained six balconies near the organ, two of which were added by Buxtehude. Together they accommodated some forty singers and instrumentalists for his *Abendmusik* concerts.

The main organ, whose origins date to 1516–18, was frequently rebuilt and enlarged. As known to Buxtehude and Bach, the three-manual instrument (the norm, according to Mattheson, for large organs in Hanseatic cities) was mainly the work of Friedrich Stellwagen (d. ca. 1660) and carried out from 1637 to 1641. The church's small organ, located in a side chapel that contained a painting of *The Dance of Death* attributed to Bernt Notke (ca. 1435–1509), was accordingly known as the "*Totentanz*" organ. Originally built 1475–77, it, too, was frequently renovated. Following a rebuilding by Stellwagen in 1653–55, it was overhauled once again in 1701 in accordance with Buxtehude's instructions.

Bach would have heard both instruments as well as a rood screen organ, since all three were employed in Buxtehude's *Castrum doloris*. The organs were com- pletely destroyed in the bombing of Lübeck in March 1942, along with most of the church and Buxtehude's tomb. The church was rebuilt between 1947 and 1980, the main organ in 1968, the *Totentanz* organ in 1986. A plaque marks Buxtehude's burial place.

CATHEDRAL (DOM). The red brick Gothic hall church, begun in 1173 by Henry the Lion, duke of both Saxony and Bavaria, was built as the bishop's seat. At the time of Bach's visit it contained a new organ built in 1696 by Hans

Hantelmann (ca. 1655–1733) to a design by Arp Schnitger (1648–1719). The instrument was examined in 1699 by Buxtehude. Although the organ was replaced in 1893, the Schnitger key-desk has been preserved. The new instrument was destroyed during the 1942 bombing raid, which also severely damaged the church.

ST. JAMES'S CHURCH (JAKOBIKIRCHE). St. James's Church, consecrated in 1334 and one of Lübeck's main churches, completely survived World War II. As a seafarer's church, its interior is decorated with maritime motifs as well as large frescoes of saints and apostles dating from the fourteenth century. A three-nave hall church, it is made of the typical North German red brick. If Bach had occasion to visit, he would have discovered two important organs, both still extant. The smaller instrument was built by Stellwagen in 1636/37. The larger organ is an extraordinary Gothic instrument whose earliest parts date from the mid–fifteenth century. Its carved case dates from 1504. Renaissance elements were added in 1573, and Baroque additions followed in 1673. The composer Hugo Distler (1908–42) was the organist of St. James's from 1931 to 1937.

In 1987, Lübeck was designated a UNESCO World Heritage site in recognition of its unique qualities: a compact old town, surrounded by water, with five major Gothic churches and several monasteries. It boasts eighteen hundred listed historical buildings in all. Beginning in the thirteenth century, after a number of devastating fires, brick was proclaimed the only building material permitted. This practice helped preserve many medieval and Renaissance townhouses of both rich and poor.

When in Lübeck, Bach would also have seen the city's hallmark: the Holsten Gate (*Holstentor*). Nor could he have failed to notice the picturesque complex of buildings adjoining St. Mary's Church that constitutes the town hall (*Rathaus*). The structure was begun in the thirteenth century with accretions continuing into the nineteenth century. Similarly, Bach must have noticed the Hospital of the Holy Spirit (Heiligen-Geist-Hospital), built by the city's merchants in the fourteenth century and Europe's first secular institution of the kind,

Lübeck's most famous native son, Thomas Mann (1875–1955), used the patrician home of his grandmother on Mengstrasse 4 as the setting for *The Buddenbrooks*, a novel rich with the atmosphere and history of Lübeck. The house is now a museum, the *Buddenbrookhaus*, dedicated to the brothers Thomas and Heinrich Mann.

Literature: Homann; NBR; BuxWV; Snyder 1986; Hill 1987; Buelow 1994; Petzoldt 2000; Wolff 2000; Snyder 2006; Snyder 2007; Maul-Wollny 2007; Otto 2009; Yearsley 2012; Organs.

Merseburg* (1735?)

A bookkeeping entry dated February 7, 1735, once preserved in the archives of the Leipzig music publisher Breitkopf & Härtel but lost since World War II, reads, "For Kapellmeister Bach a Carmen for Merseburg" (BDOK II, no. 362). Assuming the document referred to the printing of the text (carmen = poem or song) for a work of his own composition, Bach would almost certainly have traveled to Merseburg, a town located only 29 km/18 miles from Leipzig, and performed it there himself. A likely occasion would have been the wedding on February 8, 1735, of the Merseburg court musician Johann Christoph Samuel Lipsius (b. 1695). A Leipzig University student from 1723 on, Lipsius had sung as a bass in Leipzig church music performances, for which he received payments from the town council in the years 1725–27. He may have been the bass soloist in Bach's cantatas *Ich will den Kreuzstab gerne tragen*, BWV 56, and *Ich habe genug*, BWV 82, as well as Jesus in the St. Matthew Passion performance of 1727. Lipsius may also have been the "singer from Merseburg" mentioned along with Bach as a participant in the February 1729 birthday celebrations in **Weißenfels** for Duke Christian (BDOK II, no. 254).

In any event, a Bach connection with Merseburg had been established at least as early as 1726, when the fifteen-year-old Wilhelm Friedemann went there to study the violin with Johann Gottlieb Graun (1703–71), who had been appointed "Capell-Director" to the court that same year. Friedemann remained there until 1727. A minor, "secundogeniture" duchy like those of **Weißenfels** and **Zeitz**, Merseburg had reconstituted a kapelle ca. 1712 under the rule of Duke Moritz Wilhelm (r. 1712–31), a passionate viola da gamba player, known popularly as the "fiddle duke" (*Geigenherzog*) owing to his collection of contrabasses (German *Bassgeigen*). An earlier kapelle had been dissolved in 1694 after forty-one years. The new one, which at its height employed 25 to 30 musicians, survived until the Merseburg line came to an end in 1738.

CATHEDRAL AND PALACE. Positioned on a cliff above the Saale River, the Merseburg cathedral forms the fourth wing of the palace complex. One side contained the ducal quarters, where Johann Gottlieb Graun would have performed with the court kapelle. While retaining Romanesque elements from its eleventh-century origins, the cathedral was transformed into a late Gothic hall church in 1510–17, when the nave was rebuilt. Decorated gables facing the courtyard side (a secular feature at odds with the cathedral's austere stonework) harmonize with the Renaissance wings of the palace. The cathedral's possessions include an altar by Lucas Cranach the Elder (1472–1553) and a manuscript from the ninth or tenth century containing the oldest known non-Christian German text: the *Merseburger Zaubersprüche*, pagan incantations written in Old High German.

The cathedral interior is dominated by an extravagant organ case dating from 1665. In 1714–16 Bach's friend, the Mühlhausen organ builder Johann Friedrich Wender (1656–1729), rebuilt the instrument, possibly in accordance with Bach's advice. Since 1855 the organ case has housed one of Germany's largest Romantic organs, built by Friedrich Ladegast (1818–1905). Franz Liszt's Prelude and Fugue on B-A-C-H was commissioned for its inauguration and eventually performed in Merseburg in May 1856.

Originally a medieval imperial palace (*Kaiserpfalz*) and a bishop's seat, the palace was the residence of the dukes of Saxony-Merseburg from 1657 to 1738. An administrative building since 1818, it now houses both a historic museum and the "Johann Joachim Quantz Music School." Quantz (1697–1773), orphaned by age ten, was raised and trained by relatives who were Merseburg town musicians. According to his autobiography he learned to play eleven instruments during his six-year apprenticeship; not one was the flute.

Literature: BDOK II; Nettl 1951; Schulze 1984b; Petzoldt 2000; Henzel 2005; Ruf 2011; Organs.

Naumburg (1746)

Between September 24 and 28, 1746, Bach traveled to Naumburg (68 km/42 miles southwest of Leipzig) to examine the new organ at the City Church of St. Wenceslas (*Wenzelskirche*). The instrument, a masterwork by Zacharias Hildebrandt (1688–1757), has survived. Bach was joined in the examination by Gottfried Silbermann (1683–1753), Hildebrandt's erstwhile teacher. Decades earlier the two organ builders had had a notorious altercation (see **Störmthal**). On friendly terms with both men, Bach may have played a role in reconciling the two—his efforts perhaps consummated in Naumburg. He almost certainly had a direct influence on the organ's disposition (Dähnert 1962). The examination report, signed on September 27, 1746, by the "Royal Polish and Electoral Saxon Court Composer" Bach and the "Royal Polish and Electoral Saxon Court and State Organ Builder" Silbermann, attests that "each and every part specified . . . in the contract . . . has been made with appropriate care." Indeed, "an extra bellows and a stop named *Unda Maris* have been provided over the contract." The *Unda Maris* (wave of the sea), an undulating register, was a novelty at the time. On the other hand, "it will be necessary [for] . . . Hildebrandt to go through the entire instrument once more, stop by stop, in order to achieve more evenness in the voicing as well as in the key and stop actions" (NBR, no. 236). This was Bach's last of seven surviving organ reports. Silbermann and Bach each received an honorarium of twenty-two thalers (over $2,000) for their service.

In September 1748, Johann Christoph Altnickol (1719–59), who from 1744 to 1746 had studied clavier and composition with Bach and had taken part in the Leipzig church services as an instrumentalist and bass singer, assumed the recently vacated organist position at St. Wenceslas's. Carl Philipp Emanuel Bach had unsuccessfully applied for the post in 1733. Altnickol remained in Naumburg until his death at age forty. Bach played a major role in the appointment, writing a glowing letter of recommendation for his former pupil, reliable copyist, and future son-in-law (NBR, no. 253). Six months later, on January 20, 1749, Altnickol married Bach's daughter, Elisabeth ("Lieschen") Juliana Friderica (1726–81), his only daughter to have wed.

After J. S Bach's death, the Altnickols took in Lieschen's older brother, the mentally handicapped Gottfried Heinrich (1724–63). After Lieschen returned to Leipzig following Altnickol's death, Gottfried Heinrich remained in Naumburg with other caretakers.

From 1029 until 1615 Naumburg had served as the seat of the bishopric Naumburg-Zeitz, which was dissolved in the wake of the Reformation. Situated along both the *via regia* and the Saale River, it had developed into a major trade center up to that point, its fairs rivaling those of Leipzig. Luxurious buildings from the Renaissance to Baroque periods attesting to the town's early wealth still stand in the market square.

During Bach's time, Naumburg was the secondary residence for the dukes of Saxony-Zeitz, one of the three "secundogeniture" duchies created in 1652 for the younger sons of the elector of Saxony, Johann Georg I (r. 1611–56). This duchy combined landholdings formerly belonging to the bishopric of Naumburg-Zeitz and encompassed both towns. Shortly after inheriting the new duchy in 1657, while the **Zeitz** palace was under construction, Duke Moritz (r. 1657–81) moved into the so-called "residence" on the Naumburg town square (today Markt 7). After moving to Zeitz in 1663, the duke maintained close connections with Naumburg, only nineteen miles away and the economic center of his realm. In 1701 his son and successor, Moritz Wilhelm (r. 1681–1718), built an opera house to compete with the Leipzig attractions. Both towns offered opera productions only during fair times. The Naumburg opera saw performances by J. D. Heinichen, J. F. Fasch, and G. H. Stölzel, among others—typically one per year until the opera house burned down in 1716. (The only surviving opera from this time, Heinichen's *Der glückliche Liebeswechsel oder Paris und Helena*, resurfaced in 2001 when the archive of the Berlin Singakademie was repatriated from Kiev to Berlin.)

Bach's presumed route from Leipzig: Leipzig—**Weißenfels**—Naumburg.

Landmarks

CITY CHURCH OF ST. WENCESLAS (WENZELSKIRCHE). The almost square form of this fifteenth-century parish church resulted from a decision not to build a full nave beyond the first two vaults. The altar and the organ are thus close to each other. Together with the pulpit, they add an exuberant Baroque layer to the otherwise simple, whitewashed Gothic interior. Hildebrandt's organ greatly benefits from the acoustics created by the church's squat shape. The church's tower served as the town watchtower, complete with a warder (*Hausmann*) as late as the 1970s. It houses an intact set of three bells dating from 1518—a rarity, considering the centuries of war and conflagration it has survived. The bells sound exactly as they did in Bach's time.

CATHEDRAL OF ST. PETER AND PAUL (DOM). Apart from its outstanding organ, St. Wenceslas's cannot rival the artistic importance of Naumburg's dominant structure, the famous Cathedral of St. Peter and Paul. Erected over an earlier cathedral, the large Romanesque edifice was built between 1186 and 1242, beginning with the chancel in the traditional eastern position; the unusual addition of a much larger western chancel in Gothic style (1243–ca. 1250), which houses the famous statues, was counterbalanced by

82. Naumburg, City Church of St. Wenceslas: The church overlooks the market square, which includes the ducal residence (left). At right: Naumburg's oldest secular building (1543), now the local tourist information bureau.

the expansion of the eastern chancel in high Gothic style (ca. 1330). The west-end chancel (added 1239–50) houses a major masterpiece of medieval stone sculpture: a group of twelve life-size figures created by the Master of Naumburg, an anonymous, French-trained sculptor who introduced western stylistic innovations to this eastern outpost of the Holy Roman Empire. Instead of traditional saints and biblical characters, the sculptures mostly portray identifiable individuals—founders and patrons of the cathedral. They are depicted in the psychologically penetrating and individualized thirteenth-century French Gothic style. A stone rood screen separating the chancel from the remainder of the church incorporates an equally powerful crucifixion scene along with a frieze depicting the life of Christ. All were carved by the same master.

Literature: NBR; Dähnert 1962; Petzoldt 2000; Wolff 2000; Wollny 2000; Hübner 2004; Messori 2010; Organs.

Websites: www.de.wikipedia.org/wiki/Opernhaus_vorm_Salztor (G); www.youtube.com/ watch?v=A6svAZefXig (audio of the St. Wenceslas Church bells).

Nienburg (an der Saale)* (1716)

Bach most likely met his future patron and employer, Prince Leopold of Anhalt-Köthen (r. 1716–1728), in the year 1716, while in the service of the dukes of Weimar. The occasion was the wedding of Leopold's older sister, Princess Eleonore Wilhelmine (1696–1726) with the Weimar coregent, Duke Ernst August of Weimar (r. 1707–48).

The festivities took place on January 24, 1716, in the town of Nienburg, located 22 km/13.5 miles northwest of Köthen at the residential palace of Leopold's widowed mother Gisela Agnes (1669–1740). Salomo Franck (1659–1725), court poet and Bach's principal Weimar librettist, provided the text for a wedding cantata. A court document records payment of forty-five florins and fifteen groschen "to the Secretary of the consistory Franck, . . . Concertmaster Bach . . . and the printer, for Carmina [songs] presented, April 4, 1716." The reference to Bach in the payment record strongly suggests that he set the text to music, now lost (BDOK II, no. 77). The text, however, may survive in Franck's *Heliconische Ehren-, Liebes-, und Trauer-Fackeln* (1718), which includes several congratulatory poems and the wedding text, *Diana, Amor, Apollo, Ilmene*.

Bach presumably accompanied the duke on the ca. 145-km/90-mile journey north from Weimar for the royal wedding, setting out immediately after the performance of his cantata, *Mein Gott, wie lang, ach lange*, BWV 155, on Sunday, January

19th. Such festivities typically lasted several days and offered many occasions for music-making. Prince Leopold was no doubt favorably impressed by Bach's offerings. Whether the other participating musicians were members of the Weimar court ensemble or Leopold's recently revived Köthen kapelle (or both) is unknown. In any event, by August 5, 1717, the prince had appointed Bach kapellmeister to the Köthen court, a post he was not able to assume until December of that year.

Bach's presumable route from Weimar:
Weimar—Jena—**Naumburg**—**Merseburg**—**Halle**—**Nienburg**.

The history of Nienburg is long and distinguished. As early as the eighth century, a castle there protected the eastern edge of the Carolingian empire. Between 930 and 950, a new castle (*Neue Burg* or *Nienburg*) was erected on a promontory strategically located at the confluence of the Saale and Bode rivers. This represented the crossroads of the north-south Halle-Magdeburg salt route and a major east-west trade and military artery. In 975, a group of Benedictine monks was sent to live in the castle with the mission of Christianizing the region's Slavic Sorb population. They expanded and modified the castle into a fortified monastery. In 1004 the monastery church was consecrated in the presence of King Heinrich II (r. 1002–24; later Holy Roman Emperor, r. 1014–24).

After the Reformation and the Peasants' War (1524–25), the monastery was transferred in 1563 to the princes of Anhalt-Köthen. It was converted into a residential palace for the dowager princesses ca. 1690, with the massive fortress-like church of St. Mary's and St. Cyprian's serving as the castle church. Almost nothing remains of the monastery/palace except for the church. It forms part of the "Romanesque Trail" (*Strasse der Romanik*), a network connecting numerous medieval cultural monuments in Saxony-Anhalt.

Literature: Zürner 1753; BDOK II; Terry 1933; Smend 1985; Hoppe 1997; Cobbers 2011.

Website: www.nienburg-saale.de/Historie/Benediktiner-Abtei/benediktiner-abtei.html (G).

Pomßen° (1727)

Located about 22 km/13.5 miles southeast of Leipzig, Pomßen is a village incorporated into the municipality of Parthenstein. Bach provided the music for a memorial service held there on February 6, 1727. His presence at the service is not documented, but it is reasonable to assume that he led the performance of two pieces: his cantata *Ich lasse dich nicht, du segnest mich denn*, BWV 157, set to a text by his frequent librettist Picander (Christian Friedrich Henrici), and another work, now lost. The cantata, transmitted only in posthumous, somewhat altered sources, features the unusual scoring of viola d'amore, oboe d'amore, flute, and basso continuo, an ensemble producing a mellow and subdued sound appropriate for the occasion.

The service honored the royal chamberlain Johann Christoph von Ponickau (1652–1726), who owned several estates in the region, including Pomßen. Christoph Gottlob Wecker (d. 1774), a member of the "Görner" Collegium Musicum in Leipzig and a participant in Bach's church music performances while he was a student at Leipzig University, saw to the publication of the cantata texts, the sermons, and the poems in a handsome format. Bach later recommended Wecker for posts in Chemnitz (NBR, no. 129) and Schweidnitz (BDOK II, no. 257). Wecker accepted the Schweidnitz position and held it until his death.

The memorial service took place in the Pomßen Church, a fortresslike thirteenth-century Romanesque church (*Wehrkirche*). The organ, the oldest extant organ in Saxony, is based on a Renaissance positive and was expanded and furnished with pedals by the brothers Georg and Gottfried Richter in 1670/71. In 2014, the instrument was renovated and made playable. The handsome organ case can be closed through wings displaying music-making angels rendered in grisaille on a yellow background. The same color scheme and decorative style embellishes the church's balconies and coffered ceiling, which is adorned with fifty-three panels depicting prophets, evangelists, and church fathers.

The Renaissance altar dating from ca. 1560 is a masterwork crafted in the Freiberg

83. Pomßen, Church: Interior. The church houses Saxony's oldest extant organ.

school. The donor and founder of the Pomßen dynasty, Hans von Ponickau (1536–73), is portrayed with his wife, eight sons, and four daughters. An exuberantly carved memorial epitaph in Baroque style contains painted medallions of Johann Christoph von Ponickau and his two wives. It is unlikely it would already have been in place at the time of the funeral service, held three months after von Ponickau's death.

A stone wall encloses the church and its cemetery. At the entrance gate there is a neck-iron of the kind used from the sixteenth to the early nineteenth century to shame and punish locals who violated laws and mores. The miscreants were locked into the device before the Sunday service, enabling all congregants to witness their humiliation. While the stark massive tower of the church forms a fitting backdrop to this relic of harsher times, various annexes to the building from the Renaissance and Baroque periods ameliorate its original austere appearance. One such addition is the private entrance to the von Ponickau family's balcony, a two-story enclosure from which the privileged clan would participate in the services.

Literature: Hofmann 1982; Günther 1995.

Website: www.orgelpomssen.de/cms/index.php?article_id=1 (G, E; includes history and photos of the church and organ).

Potsdam (1741(?), 1747)

Potsdam is renowned in Bach biography as the site of the historic encounter on May 7 and 8, 1747, between J. S. Bach and King Fredrick II the Great of Prussia (r. 1740–86), the celebrated event that precipitated the composition of *The Musical Offering*, BWV 1079.

When Frederick became king in the spring of 1740, he first moved to Charlottenburg, 8 km/5 miles west of Berlin, in order to avoid both the **Berlin** palace, where he had installed his unloved wife, Elisabeth Christine, and Potsdam, the erstwhile residence of his dreaded father, Friedrich Wilhelm I. As early as 1744, however, Frederick decided to remove himself further from Berlin by relocating to Potsdam, a town on the Havel River situated in a lake region 40 km/25 miles southwest of the Prussian capital. Potsdam was to be his main domicile for the rest of his life. He soon added a summer residence, Sanssouci, located just outside the town and inaugurated on May 1, 1747.

Charlottenburg was used henceforth for festivities and balls, while the Berlin palace became the site of official court and ceremonial business managed in part by the queen. As he had done in Charlottenburg, Frederick immediately arranged for the expansion and upgrading of the Potsdam palace and park under the aegis of his architect Georg Wenzeslaus von Knobelsdorff (1699–1753). The goal was to display the power and grandeur of Prussia, whose territory had just grown by a third owing to the recent annexation of Silesia in the War of the Austrian Succession (1742). Knobelsdorff's first assignment was to carve out a theater (*Komödien-*

84. Potsdam, "Sanssouci" music room: The small, one-story summer palace, inaugurated on May 1, 1747, sits atop a terraced former vineyard planted with exotic fruit trees; they are protected in the winter by specially designed glass doors.

saal) within the palace. Both the exterior and the interior of the palace were reconceived: the exterior in a Palladian classicistic style of sober grandeur and simplicity, the interior in exuberant "Fridician" rococo. The palace garden, which Frederick's father had converted into a field for military drills that he could observe from the palace, was made into a garden once again. The completed Potsdam palace was intended to be the equal of the foremost palaces in the German-speaking world: **Dresden**, Würzburg, and Vienna.

Whenever Frederick was not away on a military campaign and in residence, he devoted every evening to chamber music. Presented between 7 and 9 P.M., the programs consisted largely of flute concertos and sonatas by Quantz and Frederick himself, featuring the king as soloist. During the winter season, performances took place in the private rooms of Frederick's Potsdam city palace (*Stadtschloss*). From 1747 on, summer performances were held in Sanssouci.

Bach may have been in Potsdam years before his famous visit in 1747. A nineteenth-century copy of the Flute Sonata in E major, BWV 1035, claims that it was written "when the author was in Potsdam in the year 17— [*sic*], for the royal valet Fredersdorf." Michael Gabriel Fredersdorf (1708–58) was Frederick's chamberlain, confidante, and flute partner. Bach visited Berlin in late July and early August 1741 and may have made a trip to Potsdam at that time. The *galant* style of the E-major sonata suggests 1741 rather than 1747 as a more plausible date for the sonata.

At all events, J. S. Bach was accompanied on his legendary Potsdam trip of 1747 by his eldest son, Wilhelm Friedemann. Friedemann presumably arrived in Leipzig from **Halle**, where he was employed at the time, to join his father on the 160-km/99-mile journey. A report of the event appearing on the front page of the *Berlinische Nachrichten* and soon reprinted in newspapers elsewhere in Germany reads as follows: "One hears from Potsdam that last Sunday [May 7th] the famous Kapellmeister from Leipzig, Mr. Bach, arrived with the intention to have the plea-sure of hearing the excellent Royal music at that place. In the evening, at about the time when the regular chamber music in the Royal apartments usually begins, His Majesty was informed that Kapellmeister Bach had arrived at Potsdam and was waiting in His Majesty's antechamber. . . . His August Self immediately gave orders that Bach be admitted, and went, at his entrance, to the so-called *Forte* and *Piano*, condescending also to play, in His Most August Person and without any preparation, a theme for the Kapellmeister Bach, which he should execute in a fugue. This was done so happily by the aforementioned Kapellmeister that not only was His Majesty pleased to show his satisfaction thereat, but also all those present were seized with astonishment" (NBR, no. 239).

Friedemann later provided Bach's first biographer, Johann Nikolaus Forkel, with an account of the events that had led to the historic Potsdam appearance. As related by Forkel, "The reputation of the all-surpassing skill of Johann Sebastian was at this time so extended that the King often heard it mentioned and praised. . . . At first he distantly hinted to the son [Philipp Emanuel] his wish that his father would one day come to Potsdam. But by degrees he began to ask him directly why his father did not come. The son could not avoid acquainting his father with these expressions of the King's. . . . [Bach] at length, in 1747, prepared to take this journey" (NBR, p. 429). Forkel's narrative differs from the court report in several details. It suggests, for example, that Bach had asked the king for a fugue subject and indicates that the King had "invited Bach . . . to try his fortepianos, made by Silbermann, which stood in several rooms of the Palace [and which the king had begun to acquire the previous year]. The musicians went with him from room to room, and Bach was invited everywhere to try them and to play unpremeditated compositions." Curiously, neither Forkel, nor the newspaper accounts, nor C. P. E. Bach in his autobiographical sketch, make any mention of Emanuel's presence there.

Bach originally pledged to work out the fugue on the royal theme and have it printed, but the project grew beyond anything foreseen by either party. As early as July, Bach sent the king an engraved volume containing six canons, a *fuga canonica*, and a three-part ricercar on the royal theme. By September he issued the entire collection in print, having added a trio sonata for flute and violin, (the trio being a genre cultivated by his son Emanuel in Potsdam, at just this time), a six-part ricercar (which Frederick had requested but Bach had declined to improvise at the time), and three more canons. The ricercar's title was written as an acrostic *Regis Issu Cantio Et Reliqua Canonica Arte Resoluta* (By order of the king, the melody and other things resolved through canonic art).

The *Berlinische Nachrichten* also reported that Bach performed on the organ of the Church of the Holy Spirit (*Heiliggeistkirche*) in Potsdam on May 8th to a large crowd and great acclaim. The church no longer exists. According to Forkel, Bach had played on all the organs in Potsdam, which would have included the Garrison Church (*Garnisonkirche*) and St. Nicholas's Church (*Nikolaikirche*). Like the Church of the Holy Spirit, both are no longer extant. The Baroque-style St. Nicholas Church, in which Bach seems to have played, burned down in 1795. It was replaced in the 1830s by a radically different building vaguely reminiscent of the pantheon in Paris, designed by the leading Prussian architect Carl Friedrich Schinkel (1781–1841) and still extant.

Landmarks

CITY PALACE (STADTSCHLOSS). The Potsdam city palace, the site of J. S. Bach's celebrated encounter with Frederick the Great, stood at the old market place (*Alter Markt*) across from St. Nicholas's Church near the Havel River. Although the palace had burned down to the walls during a bombing raid in April 1945, the remnants were deemed 83 percent structurally solid. Nevertheless, in 1959 the East German government not only razed the entire building but removed all visual traces of it by rerouting major roads to cut across the area it had occupied. In recent years, the palace's exterior has been re-created, while the interior is completely modern. The new structure opened in 2014 and serves as the parliament building for the State of Brandenburg, whose capital is Potsdam. The nearby Baroque royal stables (*Marstall*), which escaped destruction, now house the Potsdam Film Museum, attesting to the major role played by the nearby town of Babelsberg in the history of the German film industry.

SANSSOUCI. The palace of Sanssouci (literally: "without care" or "carefree") and the large park surrounding it are unquestionably the aesthetic and cultural crown jewels of Potsdam. Here, Frederick tried to re-create the atmosphere of his Rheinsberg palace, but this time with royal splendor and grace. The palace was the venue for Frederick's private pursuits and the accommodation of invited friends, Voltaire among them. The king's suite includes a library, which, as he requested, is "just as in Rheinsberg," that is, a circular room with windows on three sides.

Throughout the summer, Frederick preferred to reside here. The city palace and Sanssouci reflected the "two lives" of Frederick, the scrupulous separation between official and private. Private correspondence was typically signed "Sans-souci," and official orders and documents "Potsdam." Everything necessary for the royal music making, however—sets of manuscripts and Silbermann fortepianos—were available at both venues.

Other historic sites in Potsdam include the new market place (*Neuer Markt*), and the Dutch Quarter (*Holländisches Viertel*), built 1737–42 to house Dutch artisans recruited to Potsdam.

Literature: *NBR; Marshall 1979; Kadatz 1998; Oleskiewicz 2011; Schulenberg 2014.*

Sangerhausen (1702, 1737?)

Sometime in the second half of 1702, the seventeen-year-old Bach success-fully auditioned for the organist position at the St. James's Church in the town of Sangerhausen. Located ca. 100 km/62 miles northwest of Leipzig, Sangerhausen at the time was part of the duchy of Saxony-Weißenfels. The reigning duke, Johann Georg (r. 1697–1712), overruled the selection committee and decreed that the appointment must go to a native son. His candidate was Johann Augustin Kobelius (1674–1731), a competent court musician who, in 1725, would succeed Johann Philipp Krieger (1649–1725) as **Weißenfels** court kapellmeister, a title later bestowed on Bach.

The circumstances surrounding Bach's 1702 Sangerhausen organ audition are known only from his own testimony contained in a letter dated November 18, 1736, to a member of the Sangerhausen town council, Johann Friedrich Klemm (1706–67). The letter's main purpose was to recommend Bach's third son, Johann Gottfried Bernhard (1715–1739), for the same organist's position (NBR, no. 189). In January 1737, Gottfried Bernhard passed the audition and was offered the post. He resigned as organist of St. Mary's Church in Mühlhausen and on April 4th was formally inducted in Sangerhausen, very likely in the presence of his father.

Bernhard Bach soon absconded from Sangerhausen, however, leaving behind a trail of debts (NBR, no. 203). His father had the humiliating duty of writing an apology to Councilor Klemm. His poignant letter, dated, May 24, 1738, survives (NBR, no. 203). By January 1739, Bernhard had enrolled at the University of Jena, where he died the following May at age 24.

Bach's presumable route from Leipzig:
Leipzig—**Merseburg**—Querfurt—Sangerhausen.

Landmarks

The Gothic St. James's Church dominates the large town square and is surrounded by attractive Renaissance and Baroque burghers' houses, the old town hall (1437), and the "New Palace" (*Neues Schloss*), a modest Renaissance building that served from 1712 on as a secondary residence for the dukes of Saxony-Weißenfels.

Although the chancel ceiling of the church is vaulted, the nave, owing to lack of funds, has just a flat wooden ceiling. The pillars and arches were decorated in the late seventeenth century, and adroitly positioned representations of human figures cover many of the unused arch supports. The painted wood pulpit (1593) is supported by the figure of St. Peter in the garb of a miner, a reference to Sangerhausen's early lucrative silver and copper mining industry.

85. Sangerhausen, St. James's Church, interior. Built between 1457 and 1542, the church appears today much as it did to Sebastian and his son, Johann Gottfried Bernhard Bach.

The glory of the church is its organ (1726–28). Bach may have helped the builder, Zacharias Hildebrandt (1688–1757), receive the Sangerhausen contract, drawing on his connections with the Weißenfels court and motivated by his concern for the livelihood of his friend, whose opportunities to build organs in Saxony were restricted in the aftermath of legal altercations with his former teacher, Gottfried Silbermann (1683–1753; see **Störmthal**). The handsome instrument, whose organ case is decorated with putti and music-making angels carved by Valentin Schwarzenberger (1692–1754), was inaugurated with a festive service on June 1, 1728, in the presence of the ducal couple and court. Music was provided by the Weißenfels kapelle.

ST. ULRICH'S CHURCH (ULRICHSKIRCHE). The duties of the Sangerhausen organist apparently included services at St. Ulrich's Church in addition to those at St. James's. A Romanesque building (ca. 1100), St. Ulrich's is a station on the "Romanesque Trail" (*Strasse der Romanik*) that connects major monuments of Romanesque architecture in Saxony-Anhalt, including **Nienburg** and **Naumburg**.

KLEMM RESIDENCE. The residence of Bach's correspondent, Johann Friedrich Klemm, built in 1679, still survives. Bach likely stayed there during his visit to Sangerhausen in the spring of 1737. Located at Kornmarkt 3, it bears a commemorative plaque along with the original owner's carved sign. Now a private home, it received an award recently in recognition of its outstanding restoration.

Literature: *Zürner 1753; NBR; Organs; Dähnert 1962; Petzoldt 2000.*

Website: *www.jacobigemeinde-sangerhausen.de (G; with history and images of the organ).*

Schleiz (1721)

During the summer of 1721, Bach visited Schleiz, the residence of the counts of Reuß-Schleiz, younger line. Court accounts dated August 7, 11, and 13, indicate that payments were made (1) to Bach as an honorarium, (2) to the Blue Angel Inn for his accommodations, and (3) to the postmaster for Bach's transport on to **Gera**. The purpose of Bach's visit is not indicated. The payments refer to Bach as the "Köthen Kapellmeister." This may imply a performance with the court kapelle rather than an organ recital or an organ examination. At all events, the distance from Köthen to Schleiz was rather long—ca. 155 km/96 miles to the south—representing a trip of at least five days. At the same time the honorarium of 6 gulden, 18 groschen (ca. $575) is relatively modest (Bach received 12 thalers [ca. $1,150] for earlier guest performances in **Halle** and **Gotha**). This suggests that the visit just may have taken place at Bach's own initiative. Like his trip to **Hamburg** in November 1720 and his dedication of the Brandenburg Concertos in March 1721 to the margrave, it may reveal his interest in leaving Köthen, in this case for an appointment at Schleiz. The position of kapellmeister was occupied at the time, however, and would not become vacant for another six years. All must remain conjectural.

Bach presumably performed in the court palace, a fairly simple building dating from 1689–1705 belonging to Heinrich XI, count of Reuß-Schleiz (1669–1726). Like its two predecessors, the palace burned down. Its successor, built after the 1837 fire on the ruined walls, was destroyed as well—this time in 1945 by bombs. Only the ruins of two round castle towers survive.

Bach's presumable travel route from Köthen:
Köthen—Zörbig—Leipzig—Pegau—**Zeitz**—**Gera**—Weida—Auma—Schleiz.

Landmarks

HILL CHURCH (BERGKIRCHE). Although virtually nothing related to Bach's Schleiz visit survives, the impressive Hill Church (*Bergkirche*) located just outside the town is of considerable historic interest. The extant building, a late-Gothic hall church, dating mostly from 1484–1507, was expanded after 1622 under Heinrich Posthumus Reuß (see **Gera**) and furnished with balconies, a carved and gilded Baroque altar and pulpit, and many private epitaphs by Schleiz burghers. The "heavenly meadow" decoration in the ceiling vaults, inspired by remnants of Gothic decoration, was added in the nineteenth century. The adjoining crypt was the resting place of the Reuss-Schleiz dynasty. Few churches in Bach Country are so richly endowed, well preserved, and restored, even though Napoleon's troops once used it as a stable.

The organ, built by Jacob Schedlich (1591–1669), takes the form of a wing altar. Only the case is original. When open, the organ pipes are surrounded by paintings depicting a heavenly concert; when closed, one views the burial of Jacob.

BURGK CASTLE (SCHLOSS BURGK). Burgk Castle, located 11 km/7 miles east of Schleiz, is set high above a loop of the Saale River. A fairy-tale castle with well-preserved features of the medieval fortress, it served as a summer residence and hunting lodge for the counts of Reuß-Burgk and Reuß-Greiz. Their lavishly furnished living quarters are on display, along with the court chapel organ built by Gottfried Silbermann (1743). Whether Bach visited the castle is unknown.

Literature: Homann; BDOK II; Petzoldt 2000; Weiß 2008.

Website: www.bergkirche-schleiz.de (G, includes minimal English text; click on "Bildergalerie").

Stöntzsch (1731, 1732)

The once-prosperous village of Stöntzsch no longer exists. It was completely leveled in 1963 by the Socialist Regime to make room for the brown-coal surface mining industry. In 1965, its population was incorporated into the nearby town of Pegau, located 26 km/16 miles south of Leipzig and part of the Leipzig administrative district. Only a memorial stone commemorates its onetime existence a few kilometers to the west of Pegau.

Bach visited Stöntzsch twice within three months in 1731–32 to examine the town church organ, which was being renovated by Johann Christoph Schmieder (dates unknown). Schmieder had been engaged to enlarge an earlier instrument of 1677–78 constructed by Georg Oehme (ca. 1646–1708). On his initial visit, which took place November 12, 1731, Bach evaluated the not-yet-complete organ and deemed the progress satisfactory. On his second visit, which occurred in February 1732, Bach was able to test and approve the finished instrument, enabling the church to pay Schmieder for his work. The church's archival records note that the organ case was decorated with "beautiful wood carvings and paintings" (BDOK II, no. 298).

Although the village of Stöntzsch no longer exists, the organ has survived. It was moved in 1964 to the town of Hohnstein, located in "Saxon Switzerland," near the Czech border, 46 km/28 miles east of Dresden.

Literature: BDOK II; Petzoldt 2000; Organs.

Störmthal (1723)

Less than six months after becoming Thomaskantor, Bach examined the new organ in the recently rebuilt church in the town of Störmthal, located ca. 15 km/9.5 miles southeast of Leipzig. The instrument was the first independent work of Zacharias Hildebrandt (1688–1757). The payment record of 400 thalers (ca. $38,400) provides an exhaustive list of the materials and labor that went into the finished organ. The document then declares: "which organ work, on November 2, 1723, was examined, played, acknowledged as sound and solid, and praised by the famous Princely Anhalt-Köthen Kapellmeister and Directore Musices, also Kantor at Leipzig, Mr. Johann Sebastian Bach" (BDOK II, no. 163). (The ordering of Bach's titles—Köthen kapellmeister, director of music, *also* kantor—is notable.)

From 1713 to 1722, Hildebrandt served as an apprentice, journeyman, and employee in the workshop of Gottfried Silbermann (1683–1753) in **Freiberg**.

Silbermann had obliged him to sign a contract at the outset of his apprenticeship stipulating that he would not build organs in Saxony and Alsatia "to the detriment" of Mr. Silbermann. Since Störmthal was in Saxony, Hildebrandt clearly violated the terms of the contract. Silbermann sued and obtained a ruling against his former apprentice. Apparently pleased with Hildebrandt's work, Bach helped Hildebrandt obtain commissions outside of Saxony (such as **Sangerhausen**). Bach remained a lifelong friend, and by 1746 may have brokered a reconciliation between the two organ builders (see **Naumburg**).

For the festivities on November 2, 1723, celebrating the renovation of the church and the completion of the organ—or perhaps on the preceding Sunday, October 31st (see Wollny 1997, 21)—Bach performed the cantata *Höchsterwünschtes Freudenfest*, BWV 194. The twelve-movement cantata makes use of movements from a lost secular cantata he had composed in Köthen (BWV 194a). Bach later performed BWV 194 as part of the regular Leipzig church service on Trinity Sunday, June 4, 1724. He performed it at least two more times, in 1726 and 1731, in slightly altered and possibly shortened form. The attractive movements for solo soprano conceivably were written for Anna Magdalena Bach and sung by her not only in Köthen, where she had been a salaried court singer since 1721, but in Störmthal, as well. She would not have sung them in the Leipzig church services, however.

STÖRMTHAL CHURCH. The renovation of the Störmthal hall church in 1722 involved expanding a smaller, crumbling, late-Gothic building, incorporating a few remnants of the original. The uniformly Baroque style is dominated by pink and dark gray painted marbling.

Two doors on either side of the altar form the entrance and exit for a Eucharist procession, a common tradition at the time. At the left door, decorated with ears of wheat and bearing the inscription "Take, eat, this

86. Störmthal, Church of the Cross: In 1723, Bach performed a cantata for the inauguration of the church and its organ.

is my body," congregants received the host. They then walked behind the pulpit altar and received the wine at the right door, similarly decorated with vines and grapes and inscribed "Drink ye all of it; for this is my blood."

The Hildebrandt organ, with just one manual and fourteen stops, survives essentially in its original state. Owing to its bright, robust, yet warm sound, and, above all, to its unique historical importance, the instrument is regularly played at concerts. Visitors to the church should inquire at the parsonage, located next to the church.

87. Störmthal, Church: Interior view showing the pulpit altar flanked by the doors of the Eucharist procession, as well as the unusual combination of lectern and baptismal font.

The village of Störmthal (now part of the township Großpösna), with a current population ca. 500, narrowly escaped obliteration. Plans drafted during the Socialist period called for the expansion of the local lignite surface mining industry and for the liquidation of the village in 2005. Accordingly, no further maintenance work in Störmthal was undertaken. After the fall of the regime in 1989, the village was gradually repaired and what had been vast mining excavations were transformed into recreational lakes (the Leipzig "new lakes district"). Störmthal today has a waterfront and is rapidly becoming an attractive destination for tourists, boaters, and weekenders.

Emblematic of the town's rebirth, the Blüthner piano firm, founded in 1853, relocated to Störmthal in 1996. There, it has resumed manufacturing its acclaimed grand pianos. (Let it be mentioned that The Beatles recorded "Let It Be" on a Blüthner.)

Literature: BDOK II; Dähnert 1962; Dürr 1995; Wollny 1997; Petzoldt 2000; Organs.

Website: www.youtube.com/watch?v=iolN9GmxWzY.

Taubach (1710)

Taubach, a village on the Ilm River surrounded in Bach's time by vineyards, is now incorporated into Weimar, located about 6 km/4 miles from the city center. On October 26, 1710, Bach examined the new organ in the recently built and consecrated (1705) Church of St. Ursula. The building completely replaced an earlier church but retained the tower from 1600. Bach was paid one thaler, sixteen groschen (ca. $160) for his services (BDOK II, no. 50a).

The Taubach organ examination was Bach's first documented encounter with the organ builder Heinrich Nikolaus Trebs (1678–1748), who soon thereafter moved to Weimar. In 1712/13, Trebs rebuilt the Weimar court organ under Bach's auspices, and in 1714, he became the official organ builder to the court. During Bach's Weimar years the Bach and Trebs families developed cordial relations. Bach (together with Johann Gottfried Walther) served as godfather to Trebs's first son in November 1713.

Bach's official organ report is lost, but in a letter of recommendation for Trebs in February 1711, he declares: "I assure the gracious reader that [Trebs] has applied his most praiseworthy industry to the work he has done in these parts, and I, as one appointed to inspect the same, have found both in the fulfillment of the contract and in subsequent work he has proven himself a reasonable and conscientious man, for he made us the lowest price and he afterwards performed the work agreed upon with the greatest industry" (NBR, no. 42).

ST. URSULA'S CHURCH (KIRCHE ST. URSULA). As early as 1820, the church building developed structural problems. It was demolished by midcentury and the present classicistic structure erected according to plans by the Weimar chief building director, Clemens Wenzeslaus Coudray (1775–1845). In the process, the Trebs organ was destroyed. The sturdy tower of 1600 was once again retained. The present church has a simple interior painted white, pink, and gray, with two balconies, a pulpit altar, and matching organ case. The stone exterior, with round-arch windows, is well matched to the older tower.

Literature: BDOK II; NBR; Petzoldt 2000; Organs.

Waltershausen*

Located in the heart of Thuringia ca. 26 km/16 miles southeast of Eisenach, Waltershausen possesses the region's largest Baroque organ. The instrument, boasting about 70 percent original pipes, is widely considered to be the "most authentic Bach organ." Dating from approximately 1724 to 1735, it was built by Tobias Heinrich Gottfried Trost (ca. 1680–1759) for the recently finished Town Church.

Although there is no record that Bach ever visited Waltershausen and its distance from Leipzig (ca. 185 km/114 miles) is substantial, it is easy to imagine that he would have paused there either on his trip to **Kassel** in September 1732 or his journey to Mühlhausen in June 1735 in order to experience firsthand the recently (or nearly) completed instrument. Trost subsequently built the organ for the Court Church (*Schloßkirche*) in **Altenburg**, an instrument Bach played and praised in September 1739.

Trost was originally contracted in 1722 to build a two-manual organ. After a visit that year to **Freiberg** to see the Silbermann organ in the cathedral, however, he evidently expanded his plans. His new design necessitated the lowering of the church's first balcony to accommodate the instrument's great height. An experimenter and innovator, Trost's bold ideas often led to cost overruns and friction with his employers. He seems to have left Waltershausen in 1730, well before the organ was completed. Further work continued until 1754/55.

TOWN CHURCH "BY THE HELP OF GOD" (STADTKIRCHE "ZUR GOTTESHILFE"). The building (erected 1719–23) is the oldest Baroque central-plan church, The exterior is designed as a short Greek cross, executed in warm, reddish local sandstone. The form embodies the ideals of Protestant church architecture by ensuring that all parishioners are close to the minister, who faces the entire congregation from the front of the sanctuary. It is a major precursor and perhaps the direct model for the Church of Our Lady (*Frauenkirche*) in **Dresden**. The altar, the pulpit, and the organ are stacked vertically to represent the integration of sacrament, word, and music. Three levels of balconies curve around the entire interior of the slightly elliptical church, interrupted only by the organ. A special court balcony is located at the rear. The ceiling, seemingly a cupola, is in fact a flat surface so fashioned as to depict the sky opening up to reveal the Trinity in glory.

Literature: Organs.

Websites: www.youtube.com/watch?v=dBm27P69Z98 (G; demonstration of individual registers and their combinations); www.organartmedia.com/trost (G, E; for electronic replication of the Waltershausen organ, click on "Demos" in top index line).

Wechmar°

"IN THE BEGINNING," according to Johann Sebastian Bach, "No. 1. Veit Bach, a white-bread baker in Hungary, had to flee Hungary in the sixteenth century on account of his Lutheran religion. . . . He moved to Germany; and, finding adequate security for the Lutheran religion in Thuringia, settled at Wechmar, near Gotha, and continued his baker's trade there. He found his greatest pleasure in a little cittern, which he took with him even into the mill and played upon while the grinding was going on. . . . And this was, as it were, the beginning of a musical inclination in his descendants" (NBR, no. 303). These are the opening words of the "Origin of the Musical Bach Family," the genealogy of the Bach dynasty as set down by Sebastian in the year 1735.

In compiling the Genealogy, Bach no doubt drew on an elaborate and long-standing family oral history. His engaging narrative remains an invaluable and often unique source of information for the early history of the musical Bach family. Whether Bach ever visited Wechmar cannot be documented, but it is altogether likely in light of his interest in the family history and the fact that the town is located in the heart of Thuringia, a short distance from places where he resided. It is just 43 km/26 miles east of Eisenach, for example, or 16 km/10 miles northwest of Arnstadt.

Family tradition apparently assumed that the Bach clan had its origins not in Germany but rather in Hungary, which at the time also encompassed the eastern portions of the Habsburg Empire, including Austria, the Czech Republic, and Slovakia. The Bach family name, however, can be traced back to the Wechmar region of Thuringia as early as 1372, suggesting that the family roots may have been in Germany after all.

The early history of the musical Bach dynasty is hopelessly murky owing not only to lacunae but also to pairs of individuals with the same name. The ambiguities cannot be resolved here. A plausible hypothesis, based on the few documented facts and the careers and identities of the direct line of J. S. Bach's forebears, begins with the assumption that Veit Bach's father, seeking his fortune, emigrated from Wechmar to Hungary, where Veit—Sebastian's great-great-grandfather—was born (ca. 1555), reputedly in Pressburg, now Bratislava, capital of Slovakia. Assuming the veracity of the Genealogy's assertion that the Lutheran Veit (or his father) was driven from Hungary owing to his faith, this may have been in reaction to the Counter-Reformation initiated by the new Holy Roman Emperor, Rudolf II, beginning in 1576. Sometime between 1580 and 1600 Veit and his family settled in Wechmar where he pursued the baker's trade, taking up residence near the town's upper mill. He remained there until his death in 1619.

A Wechmar document from ca. 1600 lists two Bachs by name, Veit and Hans Bach the "Musicus." They were neighbors and no doubt father and son. Hans (ca. 1580–1626), Sebastian's great-grandfather, may have been born in Hungary before the family settled in Wechmar. After initially working at

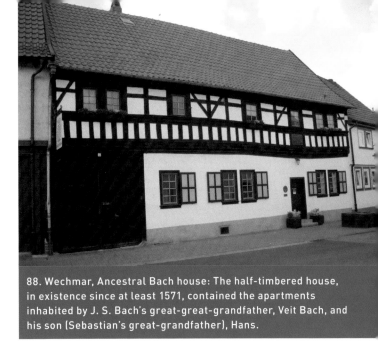

88. Wechmar, Ancestral Bach house: The half-timbered house, in existence since at least 1571, contained the apartments inhabited by J. S. Bach's great-great-grandfather, Veit Bach, and his son (Sebastian's great-grandfather), Hans.

the mill he became the first professional musician in the family, training as a town musician (*Stadtpfeifer*) in **Gotha**, then returning in 1603 to Wechmar, to the family residence in the upper bakery. His older brother Caspar (ca. 1575–ca. 1642/44) was a town musician in Gotha from ca. 1619–20, thereafter serving in the same capacity in Arnstadt (see Chapter 4, Figure 1).

Direct descendants of the Bach family took up residence in Wechmar once again in the year 2006. They live there to this day.

Landmarks

Located less than 10 km/6 miles south of Gotha, Wechmar has a combined population, with its legally conjoined village of Günthersleben, of less than 3,000. The town officially proclaims itself as the "Home of the founding fathers of the Bach musical family" (*Urväterheimat der Musikerfamilie Bach*) and maintains two Bach commemorative sites: the ancestral house, now a museum, and the upper mill.

ANCESTRAL BACH HOUSE, UPPER BAKERY (BACH-STAMMHAUS/ OBERBACKHAUS). The house, belonging to the baker Hein Eißer, contained, in addition to the baking oven, apartments in which Veit Bach, his son Hans, and their families took up residence beginning ca. 1600. The house was the birthplace of the brothers Johann (1604–73), Christoph (1613–61), and Heinrich (1615–92). Since 1994, it has functioned as a museum of the Bach family and of local history, with an emphasis on locally made musical instruments.

UPPER MILL (OBERMÜHLE). The mill, like the upper bakery, can be documented since 1571. It, too, belonged to Eißer and is assumed to be the mill where Veit Bach famously played the cittern. The structure was restored in 1999 as a mill museum and a commemorative monument to the Bach family.

CHURCH OF ST. VITUS (SANKT VITI KIRCHE). The neo-Romanesque church, with a circular interior reminiscent of the Pantheon and furnished in an elegant Biedermeier style, boasts the highest village church tower in Thuringia (68 meters/220 feet). The outsized edifice, built 1841–42, accommodates more than 1,000 congregants in a village population now numbering 2,800. It replaced the dilapidated Church of St. Vitus, which dated back to ca. 1450 and was named for Wechmar's patron saint (after whom Veit Bach was named).

Literature: NBR; Spitta 1884; Kreuch 2000; Petzoldt 2000; Wolff GMO, accessed November 15, 2014.

Weißenfels (1713, 1725, 1729, 1739)

The duchy of Saxony-Weißenfels existed for just ninety years: from 1656 to 1746. Along with the mini-duchies of Saxony-Merseburg and Saxony-Zeitz it was created through the last will of the elector of Saxony, Johann Georg I (r. 1611–56), who stipulated that his lands should be divided among his four sons with the largest portion, the electorship, and the capital of **Dresden** going to the first-born, and so-called "secundogeniture" duchies going to his three younger sons. Independent in certain respects but ultimately subordinate to Dresden, the territories reverted to Dresden whenever a line died out. All had done so within ninety years.

The town of Weißenfels is located on the Saale River, an important transportation route, ca. 68 km/42 miles northeast of Weimar (and ca. 42 km/26 miles southwest of Leipzig). With a population of ca. 2,000 inhabitants, it was the capital of the duchy from 1680 on—that is, after a suitable residence had been built by Duke Augustus (r. 1657–1680) for his son and his successors. The new palace, *Neu-Augustusburg*, was erected on the white cliff (*weißer Fels*), from which the town derived its name. The palace structure dwarfs the small town.

The ducal residence quickly acquired all the requisite institutions of a self-respecting Baroque prince:

- a palace, the *Neu-Augustusburg*, with park, orangerie, church, theater, picture gallery, armory, library, resident orchestra, and administrative quarters;

WEISSENFELS
Eine Hoch Fürſtl. Sæchſische
Reſſidenz in Meiſſen

Das Hochfürſtl:
Schlos.

89. Weißenfels, Town view: Colored engraving (1715) by Gabriel Bodenehr (1664–1758). The palace dwarfs the small town, located on the Saale River, an important transportation route.

- hunting lodges, one of which was the *Neuenburg* castle near the town of Freyburg an der Unstrut; another was the *Jägerhof* (see below);
- a secondary school, the *Gymnasium illustre Augusteum* (housed in the former St. Klaren monastery), to train the elite for administrative and military positions;
- residences for court officials, so-called *Kavaliershäuser*, and residences for the staff;
- a new city hall (*Rathaus*).

It is difficult to imagine the rich cultural life and lavish entertainments that thrived for a few decades. Hunts, balls, fireworks, sled parties, equestrian games, masques, birthday, and wedding celebrations were common events during the period. Bach had multiple contacts with Weißenfels, specifically with the court of Duke Christian (r. 1712–1736). The cultural efflorescence of Weißenfels went hand in hand with a general neglect and mismanagement of the duchy's economic well-being, however, which eventually led to its financial ruin. In 1719, the elector created a debt commission at the behest of the emperor, which henceforth administered the duchy's finances. The golden age was doomed.

Bach's first official engagement for Weißenfels was the composition of the Hunt Cantata, *Was mir behagt ist nur die muntre Jagd*, BWV 208, performed on the occasion of Duke Christian's thirty-first birthday, February 23, 1713. Christian had inherited the duchy in March 1712 upon the death of his brother, Johann Georg (r. 1697–1712).

Since the regular Weißenfels court kapellmeister, Johann Philipp Krieger (1649–1725), was a proper guest at the duke's table for the birthday banquet, someone else had to provide the *Tafelmusik*. Bach's former Weimar landlord, the singer Adam Immanuel Weldig (1667–1716), who had taken a court position in Weißenfels the previous month, may have brought Bach to the court's attention. The cantata was Bach's first known work making use of horns as well as the modern Italian operatic forms of recitative and da capo aria. It was performed under his direction.

Court records list the guests invited for the occasion and their expenses, among them "Mr. Johann Sebastian Bach, Court Organist in Weimar, board 16 groschen (ca. $64) daily" (BDOK II, no. 55). The cantata performance was preceded by birthday festivities that included battles between various animals brought in for the occasion (*Kampfjagen*). Such fights typically ended with a *coup de grâce* administered by the ruler.

Bach's connections with the Weißenfels court continued to flourish over the following decades. He attended at least two further birthday festivities for Duke Christian. In February 1725, he traveled from Leipzig to perform the Shepherd Cantata, *Entfliehet, verschwindet, entweichet, ihr Sorgen*, BWV 249a. The work marked the first known collaboration between Bach and his favorite poet, Christian Friedrich Henrici, alias "Picander" (1700–64). Only the printed text has survived. Bach wasted no time recycling the music of the arias with new texts (by an unknown librettist) in the earliest version of the Easter Oratorio, BWV 249, performed in Leipzig two months later on Easter Sunday, April 1, 1725.

On January 12, 1729, Duke Christian was welcomed on a visit to Leipzig with a performance of Bach's cantata, *O angenehme Melodei*, BWV 210a. Shortly thereafter, most likely during a visit to Weißenfels for the Duke's birthday the following month, Bach was appointed "Kapellmeister to the Prince of Saxony-Weißenfels," a title that he henceforth proudly affixed to his signature before that of "*Director Musices* of Leipzig and Kantor of the Thomas School." The honorific expired with Duke Christian's death in 1736.

In November 1739, Bach and his wife Anna Magdalena (1701–60) traveled to Weißenfels, evidently on family business. They presumably stopped there as well in September 1732 on their journey to **Kassel**, since the route from Leipzig passed through the town. A native of **Zeitz**, Anna Magdalena, had lived in Weißenfels from 1717/18, when her father, Johann Caspar Wilcke (ca. 1660–1731), became court and field trumpeter there, serving until his death. Weißenfels was in fact celebrated for its trumpet culture. Three of Anna Magdalena's sisters married Weißenfels court trumpeters; and her brother, Johann Casper the younger (1691–1766), was himself a court trumpeter, spending his career at the court of **Zerbst**.

In 1718, Anna Magdalena joined the Weißenfels court chapel as a soprano, perhaps having taken voice lessons with "Mme. Pauline"—Christiane Pauline Kellner (1664–1745), a prima donna whose salary was higher than that of the kapellmeister. In early 1721, Anna Magdalena was recruited by the court of Köthen, where she and J. S. Bach married the following December. Whether Bach had personally traveled to Weißenfels from Köthen sometime after 1718 to hear her sing and recruit her for Köthen, although likely, cannot be verified.

Bach's pride in his Weißenfels title reflected the town's importance at the time as a center of artistic and literary life. J. P. Krieger, who reigned as the court kapellmeister from 1680 to 1725, performed two to three German operas per year. This mirrored the Weißenfels dukes' leading role in the "Fruit-Bearing Society" (*Fruchtbringende Gesellschaft*), a society of mostly noble members dedicated to the refinement and promotion of the German language. Nonresident composers whose operas were performed in Weißenfels include Nikolaus Adam Strungk (1640–1700), the director of the Leipzig opera, and Georg Philipp Telemann (1681–1767); three native Weißenfelsers: Reinhard Keiser (1674–1739), principal composer of the **Hamburg** Opera; Johann Christian Schieferdecker (1679–1732), later Buxtehude's successor at St. Mary's Church in **Lübeck**; and Johann David Heinichen (1683–1729), later kapellmeister in **Dresden**.

The town's literary tradition was nourished further by the presence of the musician-writer Johann Beer (1655–1700), who was also the court concertmaster. Beer's numerous satirical novels shed light on the nature of a German Baroque musician's life from the village to the church to the court.

Weißenfels is equally significant in the history of the Lutheran church cantata. Beginning in 1700, Erdmann Neumeister (1671–1756), the pioneer of the so-called "new cantata," which made use of operatic recitative and aria forms (adopted by Bach in the Hunt Cantata), began to provide the Weißenfels court chapel with sacred poetry for the liturgical year. Krieger set the texts to music. From 1704 to 1706, Neumeister was deacon of the court chapel. By 1715, he had become pastor in Hamburg where he and J. S. Bach met in November 1720. It is also likely, finally, that Bach and his cousin Johann Gottfried Walther (1684–1748) first became acquainted with the music of Palestrina (1525–94) through Weißenfels sources (Melamed 2012). Palestrina's masses were collected and regularly performed there by Krieger, who had presumably studied this repertoire in Italy with his teacher Bernardo Pasquini (1637–1710).

Bach's presumable routes to Weißenfels:
From Weimar: Weimar—Jena—**Naumburg**—Weißenfels.
From Köthen: Köthen—**Halle**—**Merseburg**—Weißenfels.
From Leipzig: Leipzig—Weißenfels direct.

Landmarks

PALACE NEU-AUGUSTUSBURG. The entire palace complex, erected 1660–80, was designed by the architects Moritz Richter, senior and junior. The father was also the architect for the early Baroque palaces in **Gotha** and **Zeitz**, as well as

90. Weißenfels, Palace Court Chapel: View of the organ on the second balcony. Only the case of the instrument (1668–73) by Christian Förner survives.

for the no longer extant *Wilhelmsburg* palace in Weimar. With the exception of the court chapel, dedicated in 1682, most of the interiors have not survived.

COURT CHAPEL. An impressive monument of early Baroque Saxon church architecture, the court chapel gives a vivid idea of what the Weimar *Himmelsburg* chapel was like: a rectangular, narrow, exceptionally high space with organ high on the second balcony. The original pulpit altar, typical of Protestant church architecture, was replaced in 1749 when the church became Catholic. Dresden court sculptors designed the original altar; Italian artisans provided the heavy stucco work.

In the year 1693, the young George Frideric Handel's talent was discovered when he played on the chapel organ before Duke Johann Adolph I (r. 1680–97). (Handel's father, a resident in nearby Halle, was the duke's personal physician.) Bach's Toccata in F, BWV 540/1, may have been written for the Weißenfels chapel organ, since it is one of very few contemporary instruments whose pedal board extended upward to the required f'. No record of a performance there by Bach exists, however.

HUNTER'S LODGE (JÄGER-HOF). According to a contemporary report the performance of Bach's "Hunt" Cantata took place "after the hunt at the princely Hunter's Lodge" (*Jägerhof*), a building dating from 1301 with a varied history. It was acquired by Christian's predecessor, Johann Georg, enlarged, and made into a hunting establishment and the seat of the master of the hunt. Located just outside Weißenfels, it was surrounded by large enclosed grounds. For its inauguration in 1705, amid much pomp, a bear hunt was organized on the premises.

91. Weißenfels, Hunter's Lodge: Located at Nikolaistraße 51 and now a hotel. A plaque commemorates the performance here of Bach's "Hunt" Cantata under the composer's direction.

SCHÜTZ MUSEUM. J. S. Bach's greatest German musical predecessor, Heinrich Schütz (1585–1672), spent both his youth and old age in Weißenfels. In 1651, he acquired the house situated at Nikolaistraße 13 for his retirement. Now one of the most impressive museums dedicated to a musician and his time, the state-of-the-art interactive audio and visual displays survey the stations of Schütz's life and the musical developments of the era. A tour of Schütz's living quarters includes the small composing chamber (*Komponierstube*) located on the top floor that he used during the last twenty years of his life. Two small

92. Weißenfels, Heinrich Schütz Museum: The composer's stately residence was restored in 2012 to serve as a museum.

93. Weißenfels, Town Fountain: The fanciful sculpture (1989) by Bonifatius Stirnberg depicts the two eminent musicians associated with Weißenfels: Schütz and Bach.

but invaluable music fragments in Schütz' hand, discovered in the course of restoration, are displayed here.

TOWN FOUNTAIN (STADTBRUNNEN). Located on the Jüdenstrasse, the fountain is adorned with bronze figures representing various persons of Weißenfels' history. They include Heinrich Schütz seated at a harpsichord and J. S. Bach holding a horn, an obvious reference to the "Hunt" Cantata.

Literature: Homann; BDOK I; BDOK II; Dürr 1995; Fuchs 1997; Schulze 1997; Schulze 2000; Rampe 2002; Hübner 2004; Rose 2009; Klein 2010; Ruf 2011; Melamed 2012; Klein 2013; Schulze 2013; Rucker 2014.

Website: www.jaegerhof-wsf.de/cont/index.php/die-jaegerhofstory.html (G).

Weißensee (1735, 1737/38°)

On June 22, 1735, on his return to Leipzig from Mühlhausen, Bach examined the newly repaired organ in the Town Church of Weißensee executed by the builder Conrad Wilhelm Schäfer (BDOK V, B 365a). The composer apparently returned to Weißensee, located 62 km/38 miles east of Mühlhausen and ca. 145 km/90 miles west of Leipzig, once or twice thereafter. Although Bach's official organ examination report for the Weißensee organ does not survive, an account preserved in the archives of the town of Laucha reports that Schäfer's "large new work . . . was examined by the famous composer, Mr. Bach in Leipzig, and was shown approval through a great *Elogio* [praise]" (BDOK V, 425a).

It seems that Bach may have returned to Weißensee in December 1737 or July 1738, or both times, for one or two further organ examinations, apparently after additional repairs were carried out (BDOK B, 427a).

Bach's presumable routes to Weißensee:
From Mühlhausen: Mühlhausen—Bad Langensalza—Bad Tennstedt—Weißensee.
From Leipzig: Leipzig—**Merseburg**—Freyburg a.d. Unstrut—Kölleda—Leubingen—Weißensee.

Landmarks

CITY CHURCH OF ST. PETER AND PAUL (STADTKIRCHE ST. PETER UND PAUL). The church dates from the late twelfth century. Sometime after 1619, the original steeple was demolished and never replaced. A new bell tower, built in 1774, stands, oddly, in front of the church and contains two of the three original bells.

Two covered external staircases on either side of the nave (cf. **Dornheim**) provide access to the balconies and would have been climbed by Bach to reach the organ. Inside the edifice, he would have seen two levels of balconies with over one

94. Weißensee, Town Square: City Church of St. Peter and Paul (center) with bell tower; to the right, the oldest city hall in Thuringia.

hundred painted panels dating from the mid-1650s. The early-fifteenth-century winged altarpiece is a composite of two pre-Reformation altars, one stacked upon the other. The upper tier represents the Crowning of Christ; it originally depicted the crowning of Mary. After the Reformation, the main figure was transformed into Jesus by adding a beard. Of the original organ only the case survives.

TOWN SQUARE (MARKTPLATZ). The town square is dominated by a tur-reted city hall, with elements dating from ca. 1200. A bronze sculpture of the Min-nesinger Walther von der Vogelweide (ca. 1170–ca. 1230) forms a historical link to the nearby Runneburg castle.

ROUND CASTLE (RUNNEBURG). The castle, an important fortified hold-ing of the landgraves of Thuringia, was first mentioned in 1174. It is situated mid-way between the Wartburg in Eisenach and the Neuenburg near Freyburg—that is, between the western and eastern poles of medieval Thuringian power. Its cur-rent physical condition is much poorer than that of the other two castles.

Walther von der Vogelweide stayed in Weißensee as a guest of Landgrave Hermann I of Thuringia (r. 1190–1217), a great patron of poets. Here and in the Wartburg, Walther would have participated in song contests such as the one re-created in Wagner's *Tannhäuser*. Another Weißensee minstrel whose poems have survived is known as the "Düring," that is, "the Thuringian." His image in the fourteenth-century Manesse Codex (the major source of *Minnesang* poetry, also known as the "Great Heidelberg Songbook") depicts Düring defending a castle; the coat of arms on his shield resembles that of Weißensee.

Literature: *Homann; Zürner 1753; BDOK V; Braun 1999; Börner/Schubert 2005; Organs.*

Website: *www.digi.ub.uni-heidelberg.de/diglit/cpg848 (G, E; images of Minnesänger from the Manesse Codex).*

Wiederau (1737)

Wiederau, a small village located 23 km/14 miles south of Leipzig, is known to posterity because Bach composed a secular cantata bearing its name. The occasion for the composition was the installation of a new owner and ruler of the Wiederau country estate. The cantata, *Angenehmes Wiederau* (Pleasant Wiederau), BWV 30a, was one of only two known Bach "manor" cantatas (the other is the "Peasant" Cantata, BWV 212). The ruler was Count Johann Christian von Hennicke (1681–1752). From modest beginnings, Hennicke enjoyed a meteoric rise at the Saxon court in Dresden to the exalted rank of "privy councilor, state minister and vice president to his royal majesty." He was ennobled in 1728, made a baron in 1741, and made an imperial count in 1745. In July 1737, he purchased the estate of Wiederau for just under 19,000 thalers (ca. $1,825,000) and became lord of the manor. His installation ceremony on September 28, 1737, was a major event for the local population. Bach's cantata was performed as part of the festivities.

Bach had been appointed **Dresden** court composer less than a year earlier, on November 19, 1736, and may have made the acquaintance of the Dresden courtier and future lord of Wiederau in connection with that event. One of the sponsors of the Wiederau festivities was Bach's principal Leipzig librettist, Christian Friedrich Henrici, alias Picander (1700–64), who no doubt recruited the Thomaskantor to set his text to music. Another sponsor of the event was Johann Sigismund Beiche, who in 1732 had served as godfather for Bach's son, Johann Christoph Friedrich (later the "Bückeburg" Bach).

Angenehmes Wiederau is an elaborate, thirteen-movement work scored for four vocal soloists (representing allegorical figures) and chorus. They are accompanied by a large festive orchestra of trumpets, timpani, flutes, oboes, strings, and continuo that was typical of Bach's lavish ceremonial music written in the 1730s for Saxon dignitaries and royalty. He later refashioned most of the movements into a church cantata for St. John's Day, *Freue dich, erlöste Schar*, BWV 30, which was most likely first performed on June 24, 1738.

WIEDERAU ESTATE (LANDGUT WIEDERAU). The building sits on low, soft ground near the White Elster River, a location that necessitated an elaborate pile foundation to assure the structure's stability. Conjectures as to the identity of the unnamed architect have suggested

95. Wiederau, Hennicke Estate: The grand Baroque manor dates from 1697–1705. Bach's tribute cantata was most likely performed in the forecourt, with Count von Hennicke and his entourage seated on the entrance balcony.

both Johann Gregor Fuchs (1650–1715) and David Schatz (1668–1750), two leading Saxon architects of the time: Fuchs, the designer of the Romanus house in Leipzig, and Schatz, the architect of St. Salvator's Church in **Gera**. The interior (closed to the public) is adorned with illusionistic frescoes extending over two stories of the main hall, executed by the Italian artist Giovanni Francesco Marchini (1672–1745). The festive and elegant hall would likely have been too small for Bach's cantata performance, which presumably took place outdoors.

The manor was neglected during the Socialist period. Moreover, lignite mining conducted nearby lowered the water table, causing significant structural damage. The building was successfully secured during the years 1995–97, however, and in 2013 a private investor, the company Geiger Edelmetall, GmbH, began a thorough renovation of the property.

The same company has restored and currently occupies the nearby manor of Güldengossa, located about 20 km/12 miles from Wiederau. Bach may have known the Güldengossa manor since its owner, Johann Ernst Kregel von Sternbach (1652–1731), was a benefactor of the St. Thomas School. His son and namesake, Johann Ernst von Sternbach the younger (1686–1737), a jurist and town councilor, was godfather to Bach's short-lived son, Ernst Andreas Bach (born and died 1727). Both Kregels had voted in favor of the appointment of Bach as Thomaskantor.

Literature: BDOK II; Neumann 1972; Dürr 2005; Petzoldt 2000.

Zeitz°

Zeitz was the birthplace of Bach's second wife, Anna Magdalena née Wilcke (1701–60), the youngest daughter of the court trumpeter, Johann Caspar Wilcke (ca. 1660–1731). Although it is not documented, it is likely that Bach visited the town, which is located just 44 km/27 miles southwest of Leipzig and sits atop a hill at the crossroads of major north-south and east-west trade and postal routes. A suitable occasion for Bach to have visited Zeitz (via Pegau) would have been his collaboration with the Zeitz court kantor, Georg Christian Schemelli (ca. 1676–1762), producer of the "Schemelli Hymn Book" (*Schemelli Gesangbuch*, Leipzig, 1736), for which Bach provided figured basses.

Like **Weißenfels** and **Merseburg**, Zeitz is the capital of one of three "secundogeniture" duchies created in accordance with the last will of Elector Johann Georg I of Saxony (r. 1611–56) for the three younger brothers of the heir to the electoral throne in Dresden. Zeitz was bequeathed to his youngest son, Duke Moritz of Sachsen-Zeitz (r. 1657–1681).

Musical activity in Zeitz ebbed after Moritz's death in 1681 but was revived around 1700 during the reign of his son, Moritz Wilhelm (r. 1681–1718). In 1701, a palace hall was converted into an opera venue. At the same time, the duke had an opera house built at his secondary residence in **Naumburg**, which burned down, however, in 1716.

The duchy ceased to exist upon the death of Moritz Wilhelm in 1718. The kapelle was dissolved, and as a consequence Johann Caspar Wilcke moved his family to the nearby court of **Weißenfels**, where he served as court trumpeter, and his daughter, Anna Magdalena, became a professional singer.

PALACE (MORITZBURG), COURT CHURCH (SCHLOSSKAPELLE). The Moritzburg castle fronts the Elster River. Its official name, in fact, is "Moritzburg an der Elster" to distinguish it from Moritzburg near Dresden. The palace was built during the reign of Duke Moritz on the foundations and fortifications of a medieval castle that had been the seat of the bishops of Zeitz. The architect, Johann Moritz Richter (1610–67, see also **Weißenfels**), transformed the existing Gothic hall church into a Baroque court church, connecting the structure to the new palace. Baroque church furnishings were added, including two balconies with organs on either side of the altar. Moritz's musical advisor, Heinrich Schütz, had suggested the symmetrical layout to facilitate antiphonal singing on the model of St. Mark's in Venice.

The palace now serves as a multi-purpose museum: a survey of Zeitz court history is joined with an exhibit of furniture and artwork from the Renaissance to the Biedermeier (displayed in period rooms) and a collection of prams and strollers (reflecting Zeitz's importance as a center for that industry in the nineteenth and twentieth centuries). The large hall where the Baroque court kapelle performed is once again used for concerts. In the adjoining dining room, J. S. Bach's father-in-law, court trumpeter Johann Caspar Wilcke, would have announced meals and individual courses with fanfares, as was the custom at Baroque courts. The former opera venue on the top floor houses changing exhibits.

ANNA MAGDALENA BACH BIRTHPLACE. A plaque marking Anna Magdalena's birthplace is attached to the building now occupying the location of the original house, Messerschmiedegasse (now -strasse) 22. The street leads directly from the upper town (*Oberstadt*) down to the palace, which atypically is situated below the town.

Literature: Homann; Petzoldt 2000; Hübner 2004; Deye-Rittig 2010; Ruf 2011.

Zerbst* (1721, 1722)

Zerbst, along with Köthen, Dessau, and Bernburg, was one of the four Anhalt principalities created at the partition of Saxony-Anhalt in 1603. During Bach's Köthen and Leipzig periods, the prestige of the musical establishment at Zerbst under the direction of Johann Friedrich Fasch (1688–1758), was at least equal to Köthen's. The dynastic and geographic proximity of the two towns, separated by the Elbe River, suggests that Bach visited Zerbst during his Köthen years—perhaps several times. But no explicit documentary evidence to that effect survives. Zerbst court records do list, however, the payment in July/August 1722 of ten thalers (ca. $960) "to the Kapellmeister Back [*sic!*] of Köthen for a composition on our gracious prince's high birthday" (BDOK II, no. 114). Bach's usual fee elsewhere appears to have been twelve thalers. (See **Gotha**, **Halle**.)

Duke Johann August (r. 1718–42) celebrated his forty-fifth birthday on August 9, 1722, at a time when the kapellmeister post in Zerbst was vacant. In September 1722, Fasch was appointed court kapellmeister, remaining in Zerbst until his death. During the interim, the kapellmeister of the nearby Anhalt court of Köthen was apparently prevailed upon to jump into the breach (the composer possibly understanding the commission as a tacit invitation to apply for the temporarily

96. Zerbst, Palace: Photograph (1904). In August 1722, J. S. Bach presumably performed a cantata celebrating the forty-fifth birthday of Duke Johann August in the Dutch-influenced Baroque palace. With the exception of one ruined wing, the palace was mostly destroyed in April 1945.

vacant Zerbst position before Fasch's appointment the following month). Bach's music for the birthday cantata is lost. The text, possibly penned by the composition's initiator, the Zerbst vice-chancellor Georg Rudolph von Kayn (1678–1737), was discovered in 1999. It features two allegorical figures, Fama and Gloria, who, in the customary fashion, sing the praises of the prince in a series of recitatives and arias.

The performance of the birthday cantata would have taken place in the still-unfinished Zerbst palace. Its architect, Cornelis Ryckwaert (1652–93), also served the house of Brandenburg, with which the Anhalt princes, as Calvinists and neighbors, had close connections.

If Bach personally conducted the performance, which remains uncertain, he would have encountered among the musicians his brother-in-law, the Zerbst court trumpeter Johann Caspar Wilcke the Younger (1691–1766), the brother of Anna Magdalena, whom Bach had married just four months earlier. Assuming the performance took place on the very day of the duke's birthday (rather than at a later date), he would not have encountered the duke, who was not in Zerbst at the time.

Anna Magdalena Bach, for her part, had performed in Zerbst with her father, the Weißenfels court trumpeter, in 1720 or early 1721, that is, before her marriage to Sebastian. While her father was paid six thalers, she received twelve, possibly for singing on several occasions.

In later years, other works by Bach were apparently performed at Zerbst, most likely under the direction of Kapellmeister Fasch. Among them, in the year 1726, was the celebrated cantata *Ich hatte viel Bekümmernis*, BWV 21 (Wollny 2001).

Presumable route from Köthen to Zerbst: The two towns are 43 km/27 miles apart, but no direct post route between them existed during Bach's time. They were connected instead by a private transportation service, originating in **Halle** and continuing through Köthen—Aken—Elbe River ferry—Zerbst.

Landmarks

PALACE. The massive bombing of Zerbst in April 1945 destroyed much of the town. Of the palace, only the east wing survives, as a ruin. It was built from 1736 to 1744, that is, years after Bach's presumed Zerbst visit and years after the main portions of the palace were built (1696). The ruin gives a clear idea of the grandeur of the original edifice. The surrounding park still contains the former riding hall (built 1723- 32), now a municipal performance venue. The nearby bronze statue of Catherine the Great (1729–96) is a reminder that she was born Princess Sophie Auguste Friederike of Anhalt-Zerbst-Dornburg. She lived in Zerbst for two years before departing for Russia to marry the *tsarevich* in 1745. At that time, she changed her name to Katharina. In 1762, she ascended to the Russian throne.

THE CHURCH OF ST. BARTHOLOMEW (BARTHOLOMÄUSKIRCHE). Near the palace and also now a ruin, St. Bartholomew's functioned as the court church. Many of Fasch's cantatas would have been performed here. The surviving chancel and transept have been fashioned into an active church.

TRINITY CHURCH (TRINITATISKIRCHE). The Lutherans of Zerbst, like those of Köthen, were permitted to have their own church: the Baroque Trinity Church (1683–96), designed by Cornelis Ryckwaert, the same architect who designed the Zerbst palace.

ST. NICHOLAS'S CHURCH (NIKOLAIKIRCHE). Although large portions of the city walls remain, Zerbst otherwise still shows heavy war damage. The majestic St. Nicholas Church, the largest Gothic hall church in Anhalt (262 × 98 feet), is an impressive ruin (and likely will remain so). It is open to the sky but has a functioning bell tower that houses five bells mostly dating from the fifteenth century. One is the largest bell in Anhalt.

FRANCISCAN MONASTERY. After the Reformation, the former Franciscan monastery became the *Francisceum Gymnasium Illustre* (i.e., the Anhalt University). It was intended as the Calvinist counterpart to the Lutheran universities of Wittenberg and Leipzig. The cloisters and some buildings from 1470 survive. Now a school, the institution also houses the City Museum and the Historic Library, where the text of Bach's lost birthday cantata was discovered.

Literature: BDOK II; Reul 1999; Petzoldt 2000; Wollny 2001; Hübner 2004; Schulze 2004a; Schulze 2004b; Maul 2007; Reul 2011; Beißwenger 2012.

Websites: www.schloss-zerbst.de/ (G); www.youtube.com/watch?v=XCZGTkd-WcE (demonstrates bells of St. Nicholas Church).

Zschortau (1746)

The medieval Church of St. Nicholas in the village of Zschortau, located ca. 20 km/12 miles north of Leipzig, houses one of the best-preserved organs that Bach examined. In his report of August 7, 1746, he writes:

"I . . . have gone through the same [organ] piece by piece, tried it out, and carefully compared it with the contract placed before me . . . and I have found not only that the contract has been fulfilled in each and every part, and everything has been capably carefully and well built . . . there are nowhere any defects, but on the contrary the following stops, over and above the contract, have been found, and proved to be well made and good" (NBR, no. 235).

Among the five extra stops listed is a *Viola di Gamba* 8′. It is altogether possible that Bach had suggested adding this progressive and expensive register, for he had already desired a *violdigamba* register in his 1708 proposal for the organ for St. Blasius's Chuch in Mühlhausen. The builder of the Zschortau organ was Johann Scheibe (1680–1748), the father of Johann Adolph Scheibe (1708–76), who famously criticized Bach's music. Scheibe senior, a Zschortau native, had offered to add these registers *gratis* as a gift in honor of his birthplace. An additional payment of sixty thalers (ca. $5,760) was nevertheless authorized for the supernumerary stops.

A Leipzig citizen since 1705 and, as university organ builder, responsible for all the city's organs, Scheibe senior extensively rebuilt the organ of the Leipzig St. Paul's/University Church in 1717. Bach examined the instrument, then the largest in electoral Saxony, in December of that year. Scheibe also built the organ of St. John's Church, examined by Bach in 1743, and worked on the large organ of St. Thomas's. Since nothing of the Leipzig instruments survives (aside from the key-desk of the St. John's organ in the Leipzig Bach Museum), Zschortau's small, one-manual organ is all the more valuable in three notable respects: as a typical Thuringian Baroque instrument, as an instrument by a major builder, and as an instrument endorsed by Bach. Eighty percent of the pipework is original. The organ was restored in 2000.

ST. NICHOLAS'S CHURCH (KIRCHE ST. NICOLAI). The church tower, in the manner of a typical fortress church (*Wehrkirche*), has only a few small

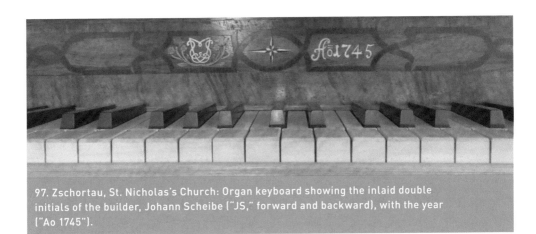

97. Zschortau, St. Nicholas's Church: Organ keyboard showing the inlaid double initials of the builder, Johann Scheibe ("JS," forward and backward), with the year ("Ao 1745").

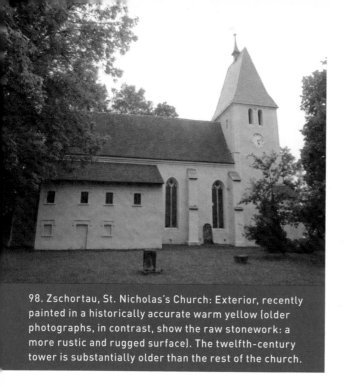

98. Zschortau, St. Nicholas's Church: Exterior, recently painted in a historically accurate warm yellow (older photographs, in contrast, show the raw stonework: a more rustic and rugged surface). The twelfth-century tower is substantially older than the rest of the church.

windows placed high up in the thick walls. (In the border regions of the Holy Roman Empire churches often functioned as refuges and defenses in times of war or attacks.) The massive wooden door itself is "fortified" by wrought-iron bars that end in elegant curves, softened by the addition of horseshoe shapes. Horseshoes are a reminder that St. Nicholas is the patron saint of travelers and merchants.

A Romanesque arch leads into the interior, which is smaller than the massive tower would lead one to expect. Its Gothic vaults are traced in red color against the white masonry. A superb double-wing altar, dating from 1517 and combining carved and painted panel views, fills the small chancel. As is typical for pre-Reformation iconographical programs, saints outnumber biblical figures. The altar was already present in Bach's time.

The west balcony and adjoining galleries built in 1870 house "Bach's" organ in its recently restored organ case (see book cover image). As in many small churches, the wood is painted to suggest marble, with intense, almost gaudy, tones of grayish blue and rust, and florid veining organized into gilt-edged panels and insets suggesting marble intarsia.

(To visit the church it is necessary to inquire at the parsonage, located diagonally across from the church. It is the second-oldest building in the town. Pfarrgasse 1, 04519 Rackwitz OT Zschortau, Tel. 34202–92200, email: kirchspiel .zschortau@gmx.de.)

Literature: NBR; Theobald 1986; Petzoldt 2000; Butler 2011; Butler 2013; Organs.

APPENDIX

BACH'S TRAVELS: AN OVERVIEW

With the exception of the move from Eisenach to Ohrdruf in March 1695, following the death of his parents, no travels by Johann Sebastian Bach during his childhood years in Eisenach (1685–95) and Ohrdruf (1695–1700) are known. His next documented journey was in March 1700 to the north German city of Lüneburg, where he was a student at the Latin School of St. Michael's Monastery for the next two years.

The following tabulation by month and year lists all of Bach's known and presumed* travels, over seventy in all, beginning with his Lüneburg years. Details are provided in the entries for each town.

From Lüneburg (1700–1702)
Dates uncertain (Obituary: "now and again"): Hamburg
Dates uncertain: Celle* and/or Ebstorf*
Between July and September/October 1702: Sangerhausen
December 1702: Weimar

From Weimar (1702–3)
July 1703: Arnstadt
August 1703: Arnstadt

From Arnstadt (1703–7)
October/November 1705 to early February 1706: Lübeck
November 1706: Langewiesen
April, June 1707: Mühlhausen

From Mühlhausen (1707–8)
1707: Langula*
October 1707: Dornheim
July 1708: Weimar

Beginning with Bach's employment at the court of Weimar in 1707 and throughout his Köthen and Leipzig periods, the number of his documented and presumed travels substantially increases.

From Weimar (1708–17)
February 1709: Mühlhausen*
February 1710: Mühlhausen*
October 1710: Taubach
1711: Gotha
1712: Ammern*
February 1713: Weißenfels
September 1713: Ohrdruf
December 1713: Halle
January 1716: Nienburg*
April 1716: Halle
July 1716: Erfurt
March 1717: Gotha
Autumn 1717: Dresden
December 1717: Leipzig
December 1717: Köthen

From Köthen (1717–23)
May–June 1718: Karlsbad
March 1719: Berlin
Summer 1719: Halle
May–July 1720: Karlsbad
November 1720: Hamburg
Between 1718 and spring 1721: Weißenfels*
August 1721: Schleiz
August 1721: Gera
August 1722: Zerbst*
February, May (twice) 1723: Leipzig

From Leipzig (1723–50)
November 1723: Störmthal
Before July 1724: Köthen
February 1725: Weißenfels
May–June 1725: Gera

September 1725: Dresden
November 1725 (or 1726?): Köthen
December 1725: Köthen
January 1728: Köthen
February 1727: Pomßen*
February 1729: Weißenfels
March 1729: three-week absence from Leipzig
March 1729: Köthen
September 1731: Dresden
November 1731: Stöntzsch
February 1732: Stöntzsch
September 1732: Kassel
July 1733: Dresden
February 1735: Merseburg*
June 1735: Mühlhausen
June 1735: Weißensee
November 1735: Collmen
July 1736: Dresden
May 1737: Sangerhausen
September 1737: Wiederau
December 1737 (?): Weißensee
May 1738: Dresden
September 1739: Altenburg
November 1739: Weißenfels
Lent 1740: Halle/Glaucha
August 1741: Berlin
November 1741: Dresden
August 1742: Kleinzschocher
December 1745: Berlin*
August 1746: Zschortau
September 1746: Naumburg
(April?) 1747: Heiligengrabe*
May 1747: Potsdam
May 1747: Berlin

There is every reason to think that Bach took many more trips than the written records unambiguously attest to. Enigmatic archival notations, available opportunities, or mere proximity, suggest that the composer may well have paid (undocumented) visits to:

> Gehren (near Langewiesen) in 1706,
> Ammern (near Mühlhausen) in 1707/8,
> Wechmar (near Arnstadt) sometime during the years 1703 to 1707,
> Bad Berka (near Weimar) during his Weimar period, 1708 to 1717,
> Rötha (near Leipzig) perhaps en route to Altenburg in 1739,
> Freiberg (near Dresden) perhaps as part of one of his six trips to or from the Saxon capital between 1725 and 1741,
> Waltershausen perhaps en route to Kassel in September 1732 or to Mühlhausen in June 1735.

During the last decade of his life in particular Bach seems to have been away from Leipzig for considerable stretches of time. In a letter of May 16, 1744, to the mayor of Salzwedel, Bach reported that he was away from Leipzig for five weeks, that is, between March 29 and May 13, 1744 (BDOK V A 45d, p. 271). His whereabouts during that period are unknown. Moreover, a former Thomas pupil and prefect, Gottfried Benjamin Fleckeisen, reported in a letter of application from 1751 that for "two entire years" he "had to" direct the services in the St. Thomas and St. Nicholas Churches "in place of the kapellmeister" Bach. One can well imagine that the kapellmeister made a number of trips during that period as well.

Presumed Way Stations

Although Bach's exact itineraries are nowhere documented, it seems desirable to record the names of the towns that he is likely to have passed through (perhaps overnighted in), when traveling to distant destinations. The following compilation, inevitably conjectural, lists some sixty towns that, apart from the inclusion of their names in the route reconstructions provided for individual entries, are not discussed in the main text. Future archival research will perhaps uncover positive evidence confirming Bach's presence in one or the other.

Station	Journey	Year
Aken	Köthen—Zerbst	1722?
Annaberg	Köthen—Karlsbad	1718, 1720
Auma	Köthen—Schleiz	1721
Bachra	Leipzig—Kassel	1732
Bad Düben	Leipzig—Berlin	1741, 1747

Station	*Journey*	*Year*
Bad Tennstedt	Leipzig—Kassel	1732
	Mühlhausen—Weißensee	1735
Bautzen	Dresden—Görlitz	1729/41
Bergedorf	Lüneburg—Hamburg	1700/2
Bibra	Leipzig—Kassel	1732
Borna	Köthen—Karlsbad	1718, 1720
Brunswick	Arnstadt—Lübeck	1705/6
Chemnitz	Köthen—Karlsbad	1718, 1720
Creuzburg	Leipzig—Kassel	1732
Dessau	Köthen—Berlin	1719
Duderstadt	Arnstadt—Lübeck	1705/6
Eckartsberga	Leipzig—Kassel	1732
	Leipzig—Mühlhausen	1735
Eschwege	Leipzig—Kassel	1732
Freyburg/Unstrut	Leipzig—Weißensee	1737/38
Gardeleben	Köthen—Hamburg	1720
Gölzau	Köthen—Leipzig	1723
Goslar	Arnstadt—Lübeck	1705/6
Grimma	Leipzig—Collmen	1735
Jena	Weimar—Weißenfels	1713
	Weimar—Halle	1713
	Weimar—Nienburg	1716
	Weimar—Dresden	1717
Joachimsthal	Köthen—Karlsbad	1718, 1720
Kalbe	Köthen—Hamburg	1720
Kölleda	Leipzig—Weißensee	1737/38
Landsberg	Köthen—Karlsbad	1718, 1720
	Köthen—Gera	1721
Langensalza	Arnstadt—Lübeck	1705/6
	Mühlhausen—Leipzig	1735
Laucha	Leipzig—Kassel	1732
Leubingen	Leipzig—Weißensee	1737/38
Magdeburg	Köthen—Hamburg	1720
Meissen	Leipzig—Dresden	1725ff
Melbeck	Lüneburg—Ebstorf	1700/2
Mölln	Arnstadt—Lübeck	1705/6
Naunhof	Leipzig—Collmen	1735

Station	Journey	Year
Neu Ruppin	Berlin—Heiligengrabe	1747?
Oelsnitz	Köthen—Karlsbad	1718, 1720
Pegau	Köthen/Leipzig—Gera	1721, 1725
	Leipzig—Schleiz	1721
	Leipzig—Zeitz	
Penig	Köthen—Karlsbad	1718, 1720
Plauen	Köthen—Karlsbad	1718, 1720
Prosigk	Köthen—Leipzig	1723
Querfurt	Leipzig—Sangerhausen	1737
Radegast	Köthen—Karlsbad	1718, 1720
Rheinsberg	Berlin—Heiligengrabe	1747?
Rötha	Leipzig—Altenburg	1739
Saarmund	Köthen—Berlin	1719
	Leipzig—Berlin	1741, 1747
Salzwedel	Köthen—Hamburg	1720
Schlackenwerth	Köthen—Karlsbad	1718, 1720
Seesen	Arnstadt—Lübeck	1705/6
Stendal	Köthen—Hamburg	1720
Thum	Köthen—Karlsbad	1718, 1720
Treuenbrietzen	Köthen—Berlin	1719
	Leipzig—Berlin	1741, 1747
Uelzen	Lüneburg—Celle	1700/2?
Velgen	Lüneburg—Ebstorf	1700/2
Wanfried	Leipzig—Kassel	1732
Weida	Köthen—Schleiz	1721
Winsen an der Luhe	Lüneburg—Hamburg	1700/2
Wittenberg	Köthen—Berlin	1719
	Leipzig—Berlin	1741, 1747
Wolfenbüttel	Arnstadt—Lübeck	1705/6
Wurzen	Leipzig—Dresden	1725ff
Zörbig	Köthen—Karlsbad	1718, 1720
	Köthen—Schleiz	1721
Zwickau	Köthen—Karlsbad	1718, 1720

BIBLIOGRAPHY

Abbreviations

BDOK   *Bach-Dokumente.* 8 vols. Kassel: Bärenreiter, 1963–2010.

BDOK I   *Schriftstücke von der Hand Johann Sebastian Bachs,* ed. Werner Neumann
           and Hans-Joachim Schulze. Kassel: Bärenreiter, 1963 and 1982.

BDOK II   *Fremdschriftliche und gedruckte Dokumente zur Lebensgeschichte Johann
           Sebastian Bachs 1685–1750,* ed. Werner Neumann and Hans-Joachim Schulze.
           Kassel: Bärenreiter, 1969.

BDOK III   *Dokumente zum Nachwirken Johann Sebastian Bachs,* ed. Hans-Joachim
           Schulze. Kassel: Bärenreiter, 1984.

BDOK IV   *Bilddokumente zur Lebensgeschichte Johann Sebastian Bachs,* ed. Werner
           Neumann. Kassel: Bärenreiter, 1979.

BDOK V   *Dokumente zu Leben, Werk, Nachwirken Johann Sebastian Bachs 1685–1800,*
           ed. Hans-Joachim Schulze and Andreas Glöckner. Kassel: Bärenreiter, 2007.

BJ   *Bach-Jahrbuch,* ed. Alfred Dürr and Werner Neumann (1953–74); Hans-
           Joachim Schulze and Christoph Wolff (1975–2004); Peter Wollny (since 2005).
           Leipzig: Neue Bachgesellschaft.

BL   *Das Bach-Lexikon,* ed. Michael Heinemann. Laaber: Laaber-Verlag, 2000.

BuxWV   *Thematisch-systematisches Verzeichnis der musikalischen Werke von Dietrich
           Buxtehude: Buxtehude-Werke-Verzeichnis (BuxWV),* 2nd enlarged ed., ed.
           Georg Karstädt. Wiesbaden: Breitkopf & Härtel, 1985.

BWV   *Thematisch-systematisches Verzeichnis der musikalischen Werke von Johann
           Sebastian Bach* [Bach-Werke-Verzeichnis, BWV], 2nd ed., ed. Wolfgang
           Schmieder. Wiesbaden: Breitkopf & Härtel, 1990.

CBH   *Cöthener Bach-Hefte.*

Courts   *Music at German Courts, 1715–1760: Changing Artistic Priorities,* ed. Samantha
           Owens, Barbara M. Reul, and Janice B. Stockigt. Woodbridge: The Boydell
           Press, 2011.

JRBI   *Bach. Journal of the Riemenschneider Bach Institute.* Berea, Ohio.

LBE   *Music and Society: The Late Baroque Era: From the 1680s to 1740,* ed. George J.
           Buelow. *Music and Society.* Englewood Cliffs, N.J.: Prentice Hall, 1994.

NBR	*The New Bach Reader: A Life of Johann Sebastian Bach in Letters and Documents*, ed. Hans T. David and Arthur Mendel. Revised and enlarged, Christoph Wolff. New York: Norton, 1998.
Organs	Wolff, Christoph, and Markus Zepf. *The Organs of J. S. Bach: A Handbook*, trans. Lynn Edward Butler. Urbana: University of Illinois Press, 2012.
Routledge	*The Routledge Research Companion to Johann Sebastian Bach*, ed. Robin A. Leaver. New York and Abingdon: Routledge, 2016.
WBC1	*The World of the Bach Cantatas. [1] Johann Sebastian Bach's Early Sacred Cantatas*, ed. Christoph Wolff. New York: Norton, 1997.
WBK2	*Die Welt der Bach-Kantaten. Band 2: Johann Sebastian Bachs weltliche Kantaten*, ed. Christoph Wolff. Weimar, Kassel: J. B. Metzler/Bärenreiter, 1997.
WBK3	*Die Welt der Bach-Kantaten. Band 3: Johann Sebastian Bachs Leipziger-Kirchenkantaten*, ed. Christoph Wolff. Weimar, Kassel: J. B. Metzler/ Bärenreiter, 1999.
WJSB	*The Worlds of Johann Sebastian Bach*, ed. Raymond Erickson. New York: Amadeus Press, 2009.

Literature

Ahrens, Christian. 2007. Neue Quellen zu J. S. Bachs Beziehungen nach Gotha. BJ 93: 45–60.

Badstübner, Ernst. 2007. *Eisenach: St. Georgen und St. Nikolai*, 6th ed. Regensburg: Verlag Schnell & Steiner.

Badura-Skoda, Eva, and Paul Badura-Skoda. 2008. *Interpreting Mozart: The Performance of His Piano Pieces and Other Compositions*, 2nd ed. New York: Routledge.

Baselt, Bernd. 1994. Brandenburg-Prussia and the Central German Courts. LBE: 230–53.

Basso, Alberto. 1997. Opera und "Dramma per musica." WBK 2: 49–63.

Beißwenger, Kirsten. 1992. *Johann Sebastian Bachs Notenbibliothek. Catalogus Musicus XIII.* Kassel: Bärenreiter.

———. 2012. Weltliche Kantaten. In *Bachs Kantaten: Das Handbuch, Teilband I/2*, ed. Reinmar Emans and Sven Hiemke, 203–77. Laaber: Laaber-Verlag.

Billeter, Bernhard. 2007. Wann sind Johann Sebastian Bachs Choralfughetten (BWV 696–699 und 701–704) und die sogenannten "Arnstädter Gemeinde-Choräle" (BWV 726, 715, 722, 732, 729, und 738) entstanden? BJ 93: 213–21.

Blaut, Stephan, and Hans-Joachim Schulze. 2008. "Wo Gott der Herr nicht bei uns hält" BWV 1128—Quellenkundliche und stilistische Überlegungen. BJ 94: 11–32.

Börner, Walter, and Karl H. Schubert. 2005. Zu Johann Sebastian Bachs Aufenthalt in Weißensee (Thüringen). BJ 91: 287–89.

Botwinick, Sara. 2004. From Ohrdruf to Mühlhausen: A Subversive Reading of Bach's Relationship to Authority. JRBI 35: 1–59.

Braun, Werner. 1999. Ein unbekanntes Orgelbau-Attestat von Johann Sebastian Bach. BJ 85: 19–33.

Breig, Werner. 1998. Bach und Marchand in Dresden. Eine überlieferungskritische Studie. BJ 84: 7–18.

Brönner, Heinrich Ludwig. 1761. *Carte pour Servir de Suite à la Partie Meridionale du Landgraviat de Hesse-Cassel avec les pays voisins de la Thüringe.* Frankfurt am Main.

Brück, Helga. 1996. Die Erfurter Bach-Familien von 1635 bis 1805. BJ 82: 101–31.

Buelow, George J. 1994. Hamburg and Lübeck. LBE: 190–215.

Butler, Lynn Edwards. 2008. Johann Christoph Bach und die von Georg Christoph Stertzing erbaute große Orgel der Georgenkirche in Eisenach. BJ 94: 229–69.

———. 2011. Bach, Johann Scheibe und die Orgeln in Zschortau und Stötteritz—Vier neue Quellen. BJ: 265–68.

———. 2013. Four Sources Relating to Bach, Organ-Builder Johann Scheibe, and the Organs in Zschortau and Stötteritz. JRBI 44/2: 1–5.

Cobbers, Arnt. 2011. *Auf den Spuren von Johann Sebastian Bach.* Berlin: Jaron Verlag.

Cowdery, William Warren. 1989. The Early Vocal Works of Johann Sebastian Bach. Studies in Style, Scoring, and Chronology. PhD diss., Cornell University.

Dadder, Ernst. 1923. Johann Gottlieb Goldberg. BJ 20: 57–71.

Dähnert, Ulrich. 1962. *Der Orgel- und Instrumentenbauer Zacharias Hildebrandt.* Leipzig: Breitkopf & Härtel.

Delang, Kerstin. 2007. Couperin—Pisendel—Bach. Überlegungen zur Echtheit und Datierung des Trios BWV 587 anhand eines Quellenfundes in der Sächsischen Landesbibliothek—Staats- und Universitätsbibliothek Dresden. BJ 93: 197–204.

Deye, Detlef, and Roland Rittig, eds. 2010. *Musikkultur in Zeitz. Schriften des Museums Schloß Moritzburg Zeitz.* Halle: Mitteldeutscher Verlag.

Dirksen, Peter. 2003. Ein verschollenes Weimarer Kammermusikwerk Johann Sebastian Bachs? Zur Vorgeschichte der Sonate e-Moll für Orgel (BWV 528). BJ 89: 7–36.

Dose, Hanna. 1994. *Evangelischer Klosteralltag. Leben in Lüneburger Frauenkonventen 1590 bis 1710 untersucht am Beispiel Ebstorf, Veröffentlichungen der Historischen Kommission für Niedersachsen und Bremen.* Hannover: Verlag Hahnsche Buchhandlung.

Dürr, Alfred. 2000. *Johann Sebastian Bach's St John Passion: Genesis, Transmission, and Meaning*, trans. Alfred Clayton. Oxford: Oxford University Press.

———. 2005.*The Cantatas of J. S. Bach with Their Librettos in German-English Parallel Text.* Rev., trans. Richard D. P. Jones. Oxford: Oxford University Press.

Eisenach. 2011. *Bachhaus Eisenach*, 5th rev. ed. Regensburg: Verlag Schnell & Steiner.

Erickson, Raymond. 2009. Introduction: The Legacies of J. S. Bach. WJSB: 1–64.

Ernst, H. Peter. 1987. Joh. Seb. Bachs Wirken am ehemaligen Mühlhäuser Augustinerinnenkloster und das Schicksal seiner Wender-Ogel. BJ 73: 75–83.

Falck, Martin. 1913. *Wilhelm Friedemann Bach: Sein Leben und seine Werke.* Repr., Lindau: Kahnt, 1956.

Fitzpatrick, Horace. 1970. *The Horn and Horn-Playing and the Austro-Bohemian Tradition from 1680 to 1830.* London: Oxford University Press.

Fock, Gustav. 1950. *Der junge Bach in Lüneburg.* Hamburg: Verlag Merseburger.

Friedel, Alwin. 2007. *Arnstadt—Bachstadt. Zwei Vorträge.* Arnstadt: Kultur- und Heimatverein Arnstadt.

Friedrich, Verena. 2000. *Der Dom zu Freiberg.* Passau: Kunstverlag Peda.

Fuchs, Torsten. 1997. *Studien zur Musikpflege in der Stadt Weißenfels und am Hofe der Herzöge von Sachsen-Weißenfels.* Lucca: LIM Editrice.

Gardiner, John Eliot. 2013. *Bach: Music in the Castle of Heaven.* New York: Knopf.

Glöckner, Andreas. 1988. Gründe für Johann Sebastian Bachs Weggang von Weimar. In *Bach-Händel-Schütz-Ehrung 1985 der Deutschen Demokratischen Republik. Bericht über die Wissenschaftliche Konferenz zum V. Internationalen Bachfest der Neuen Bachgesellschaft,* ed. Winfried Hoffmann und Armin Schneiderheinze, 137–43. Leipzig: VEB Deutscher Verlag für Musik.

———. 1995. Neue Spuren zu Bachs "Weimarer" Passion. LBBF 1: 33–46.

———. 1997. Stages of Bach's Life and Activities. WBC 1: 49–76.

———. 2002. Neues zum Thema Bach und die Oper seiner Zeit. BJ 88: 172–74.

———. 2009. Ein weiterer Kantatenjahrgang Gottfried Heinrich Stölzels in Bachs Aufführungsrepertoire? BJ 95: 95–115.

———. 2012. Figuralaufführungen in der Leipziger Johanniskirche zur Zeit Johann Sebastian Bachs. BJ 98: 163–80.

Gödecke, Silke. n.d. *Residenzstadt Celle: Fachwerkjuwel an der Aller.* Lübeck: Schöning Verlag.

Gränitz, Frauke. 2007. *Landverkehrswege als Faktoren der Entwicklung der Kulturlandschaft und des Straßenwesens im Kurfürstentum Sachsen von 1648 bis 1800. Der Beispielstraßenzug Leipzig—Deutscheinsiedel.* PhD diss., University of Chemnitz.

Greer, Mary Dalton. 2008. From the House of Aaron to the House of Johann Sebastian: Old Testament Roots for the Bach Family Tree. In *About Bach,* ed. Gregory G. Butler, George B. Stauffer, and Mary Dalton Greer, 15–32. Urbana: University of Illinois Press.

Günther, Klaus. 1995. *Wehrkirche Pomßen.* Beucha: Sax-Verlag.

Häfner, Ludwig. 2006. Neue Erkenntnisse zur "Berkaer Bach-Orgel." BJ 92: 291–93.

Helm, Ernest Eugene. 1960. *Music at the Court of Frederick the Great.* Norman: University of Oklahoma Press.

Henzel, Christoph. 2005. Zur Merseburger Hofmusik unter Herzog Moritz Wilhelm. In *Mitteldeutschland im musikalischen Glanz seiner Residenzen—Sachsen, Böhmen und Schlesien als Musiklandschaften im 16. und 17. Jahrhundert,* ed. Peter Wollny, 95–105. Beeskow: ortus-musikverlag.

Hilgenfeldt, Carl Ludwig. 1850. *Johann Sebastian Bach's Leben, Wirken und Werke.* Leipzig: Breitkopf & Härtel. Repr., Hilversum: Frits A. M. Knuf, 1965.

Hill, Robert. 1987. *The "Möller Manuscript" and the "Andreas Bach Book": Two Keyboard Anthologies from the Circle of the Young Johann Sebastian Bach.* PhD diss., Harvard University.

Hinrichsen, Hans-Joachim. 2000. Berlin. BL: 106–7.

Hofmann, Klaus. 1982. Bachs Kantate "Ich lasse dich nicht, du segnest mich denn" BWV 157. Überlegungen zu Entstehung, Datierung und Bestimmung. BJ 68: 51–80.

Homann, Johann Baptist. n.d. *Postarum seu Veredariorum Stationes per Germaniam et Provincias Adiacentes. Neu vermehrte PostCharte durch gantz Teutschland . . . Verbesserte Auflage.* Nuremberg, n.d. (ca. 1720?).

Hoppe, Günther. 1985. Das Leopold-Porträt in der Bachgedenkstätte und andere Bildnisse vom Köthener Mäzen. CBH 3: 29–46.

———. 1997. Musikalisches Leben am Köthener Hof. WBK 2: 65–82.

———. 2000. Bach Memorial at Köthen Castle: A Little Guide through the Exhibition. CBH 9.

Hübner, Maria. 2004. *Anna Magdalena Bach: Ein Leben in Dokumenten und Bildern.* Leipzig: Evangelische Verlagsanstalt.

———. 2005. *Bach Unterwegs: Die Reisen J. S. Bachs. Kabinettausstellung im Bach-Museum Leipzig vom 7. April bis 23. August 2005.* Leipzig: Bach-Archiv.

———. 2006. Neues zu Johann Sebastian Bachs Reisen nach Karlsbad. BJ 92: 93–107.

———. 2011. Wilhelm Friedemann Bachs Wohnungen in Halle—Einige Ergänzungen. BJ 97: 103–16.

Humbach, Rainer, Michael Imhof, and Susan Gildersleeve. 2003. *Reisewege zu Bach: Ein Führer zu den Wirkungsstätten des Johann Sebastian Bach (1685–1750).* Petersberg: Michael Imhof Verlag.

Jauernig, Reinhold. 1950. Johann Sebastian Bach in Weimar: Neue Forschungsergebnisse aus Weimarer Quellen. In *Johann Sebastian Bach in Thüringen: Festgabe zum Gedenkjahr 1950,* ed. Heinrich Besseler and Günter Kraft, 49–105. Weimar: Thüringer Volksverlag.

Jeschke, Joachim. 2006. *Die kursächsischen Postmeilensäulen in der Stadt und im Amt Torgau.* Torgau: Torgauer Geschichtsverein e.V.

Jung, Hans Rudolf. 1961. Ein neuaufgefundenes Gutachten von Heinrich Schütz aus dem Jahre 1617. *Archiv für Musikwissenschaft* 18: 241–47.

Kadatz, Hans-Joachim. 1998. *Georg Wenzeslaus von Knobelsdorff,* 3rd ed. Leipzig: E. A. Seemann Verlag.

Kaiser, Rainer. 1994. Johann Sebastian Bach als Schüler einer "deutschen Schule" in Eisenach? BJ 80: 177–84.

Keil, Günter, and Uta Künzl. 2001. *Schloß Altenburg, Thüringen. (Schnell, Kunstführer No. 1901),* 2nd rev. ed. Munich: Verlag Schnell & Steiner.

Keller, Harald. 1976. Architektur und Bildende Künste. In *Johann Sebastian Bach: Zeit, Leben, Wirken,* ed. Barbara Schwendosius and Wolfgang Dömling, 37–50. Kassel: Bärenreiter.

Kieckebusch, Werner von. 1949/2008. *Chronik des Klosters zum Heiligengrabe von der Reformation bis zur Mitte des 20. Jahrhunderts.* Typescript 1949. Berlin: Lukas Verlag.

Klein, Otto. 2010. *Barockes Weißenfels: Grüne Stadt an der Saale.* Weißenfels: arps Verlag.

———. 2013. *Werden und Vergehen des Musenhofes Weißenfels.* Weißenfels: arps Verlag.

Knape, Wolfgang. 2011. *Erfurt: Der Stadtführer,* 5th rev. ed. Wernigerode: Schmidt-Buch-Verlag.

Koch, Ernst. 2006. "Jakobs Kirche"—Erkundungen im gottesdienstlichen Arbeitsfeld Johann Sebastian Bachs in Weimar. BJ 92: 37–64.

Krause-Graumnitz, Heinz. 1974–1985. Heinrich Schütz' schöpferische Gestaltung der zyklischen Großform dargestellt an seinen "Musikalischen Exequien" des Jahres 1636.

In *Heinrich Schütz in seiner Zeit*, ed. Walter Blankenburg (*Wege der Forschung, Band 614*), 344–57. Darmstadt: Wissenschaftliche Buchgesellschaft.

Krausse, Helmut K. 1981. Eine neue Quelle zu drei Kantatentexten Johann Sebastian Bachs. BJ 67: 7–22.

Kreuch, Knut. 2000. Wechmar—die Heimat der Musikerfamilie Bach. In *Johann Sebastian Bach und seine Zeit in Arnstadt*, ed. Schloßmuseum Arnstadt, Stadgeschichtsmuseum Arnstadt, 21–29. Rudolstadt: Hain Verlag.

Kröhner, Christine. 1995. Johann Sebastian Bach und Johann Friedrich Bach als Orgelexaminatoren im Gebiet der freien Reichsstadt Mühlhausen nach 1708. BJ 81: 83–91.

———. 2015. Bachs Orgelbauer Wender. *Mühlhäuser Beiträge*, Sonderheft 26. Mühlhausen: Mühhäuser Geschichts- und Denkmalpflegeverein.

Langusch, Steffen. 2007. " . . . auf des Herrn Capellmeisters Bach recommendation . . . " —Bachs Mitwirken an der Besetzung des Kantorats der Altstadt Salzwedel 1743/44. BJ 93: 9–43.

Leaver, Robin A. 2009. Religion and Religious Currents. WJSB: 105–39.

———. 2016. Chorales. Routledge.

———. 2016a. Church. Routledge.

Lehmann, Peter Ambrosius. 1709. *Die vornehmsten Europäischen Reisen*. Hamburg: Neumann.

Leisinger, Ulrich. 1998. *Bach in Leipzig*, trans. Victor Dewsbery, 2nd ed. Leipzig: Edition Leipzig . . . in cooperation with Bach-Archiv, Leipzig.

Linnemann, Georg. 1935. *Celler Musikgeschichte bis zum Beginn des 19. Jahrhunderts*. Celle: Schweiger & Pick.

Loewenberg, Alfred. 1978. *Annals of Opera 1597–1940*, 3rd ed. Revised and corrected. Totowa, N.J.: Rowman and Littlefield.

Löffler, Hans. 1949/50. "Bache" bei Seb. Bach. BJ 38: 106–24.

Marshall, Robert L. 1976. Bach the Progressive: Observations on His Later Works. *The Musical Quarterly* 62: 313–57. Repr., Marshall 1989, 23–58.

———. 1979. J. S. Bach's Compositions for Solo Flute: A Reconsideration of their Authenticity and Chronology. *Journal of the American Musicological Society* 32: 463–98. Repr., Marshall 1989, 201–25.

———. 1985. *Bach's Orchestre. Early Music* 13: 176–79. Repr., Marshall 1989, 59–63.

———. 1989. *The Music of Johann Sebastian Bach: The Sources, the Style, the Significance*. New York: Schirmer Books. 11.

———. 2000. Toward a Twenty-First Century Bach Biography. *The Musical Quarterly* 84: 497–525.

Marshall, Robert L., and Traute M. Marshall. 2015. Wenig bekannte Dokumente zu J. S. Bachs Ohrdrufer Zeit. BJ 101: 157–68.

Marshall, Traute M. 2016. Wo hat Bach die Celler Hofkapelle gehört? BJ 102.

Marx, Hans-Joachim. 2004. Bericht über das Gesprächskonzert: "Finderglück: eine neue Kantate von J S. Bach? Von G. F. Händel?—'Meine Seele soll Gott loben' (BWV 223)." *Göttinger Händel-Beiträge* 10: 179–204.

Maul, Michael. 2001. "Dein Ruhm wird wie ein Demantstein, ja wie ein fester Stahl beständig sein": Neues über die Beziehungen zwischen den Familien Stahl und Bach. BJ 87: 7–22.

———. 2004. Johann Sebastian Bachs Besuche in der Residenzstadt Gera. BJ 90: 101–19.

———. 2005. "Alles mit Gott und nichts ohn' ihn"—Eine neu aufgefundene Aria von Johann Sebastian Bach. BJ 91: 7–29.

———. 2007. Neues zu Georg Balthasar Schott, seinem Collegium musicum und Bachs Zerbster Geburtstagskantate. BJ 93: 61–104.

———. 2009. *Barockoper in Leipzig (1693–1720)*. Freiburg im Breisgau: Rombach Verlag.

———. 2011. "Von Cristofori"—Zum Maler des verschollenen Porträts Anna Magdalena Bachs. BJ: 251–54.

———. 2012. *"Dero berühmbter Chor": Die Leipziger Thomasschule und ihre Kantoren (1212–1804)*. Leipzig: Lehmstedt.

———. 2013. "Welche ieder Zeit aus den 8 besten Subjectis bestehen muß." Die erste "Cantorey" der Thomasschule—Organisation, Aufgaben, Fragen. BJ 99: 11–77.

———. 2015. "zwey ganzer Jahr die Music an Statt des Capellmeisters aufführen, und dirigiren müssen." Überlegungen zu Bachs Amtsverständnis in den 1740er Jahren. BJ 101: 75–97.

Maul, Michael, and Peter Wollny. 2003. Quellenkundliches zu Bach-Aufführungen in Köthen, Ronneburg und Leipzig zwischen 1720 und 1760. BJ: 97–141.

———, eds. 2007. Preface. In *Weimarer Orgeltabulatur: Die frühesten Notenhandschriften Johann Sebastian Bachs, sowie Abschriften seines Schülers Johann Martin Schubart, mit Werken von Dietrich Buxtehude, Johann Adam Reinken und Johann Pachelbel*, xxi–xxxv. Kassel: Bärenreiter.

Meißner, Michael. 2007. Johann Sebastian Bachs Mühlhäuser Zeit (1707–1708). *Mühlhäuser Beiträge*, Sonderheft 12. Mühlhausen: Mühlhäuser Geschichts- und Denkmalpflegeverein.

Melamed, Daniel R. 2012. Johann Sebastian Bach, Johann Gottfried Walther und die Musik von Giovanni Pierluigi Palestrina. BJ 98: 73–93.

Mende, Bernd. 2008. *Bach in Weimar: Spurensuche mit Stadtrundgang*. Weimar: wtv (Weimarer Taschenbuch Verlag).

Messori, Matteo. 2010. Ein 16′-Cembalo mit Pedalcembalo von Zacharias Hildebrandt. BJ 96: 287–96.

Musketa, Konstanze, and Christiane Barth. 2012. *Musikstadt Halle: Führer durch die Ausstellung im Wilhelm-Friedemann-Bach-Haus Halle*. Halle: Stiftung Händel-Haus.

Nettl, Paul. 1951. *Forgotten Musicians*. New York: Philosophical Library.

Neumann, Werner. 1972. Johann Sebastian Bachs "Rittergutskantaten" BWV 30a und 212. BJ 58: 76–90.

Oefner, Claus. 1995. Musical Life of the Towns and Courts in Central Germany around 1700. WBC1: 35–47.

———. 2008 (?). *Musik in Eisenach: Ereignisse—Bilder—Bibliographie*. Altenburg: Verlag Klaus-Jürgen Kamprad.

Oleskiewicz, Mary. 2011. The Court of Brandenburg-Prussia. Courts: 79–130.

Osthoff, Wolfgang. 1987. "Das 'Credo' der h-moll-Messe: Italienische Vorbilder und Anregungen." In *Bach und die italienische Musik*, ed. Wolfgang Osthoff and Reinhard Wiesend, 109–40. Venice: Centro Tedesco di Studi Veneziani.

Otto, Christian F. 2009. Architectural Settings. WJSB: 141–74.

Petzoldt, Martin. 1985. "Ut probus & doctus reddar." Zum Anteil der Theologie bei der Schulausbildung Johann Sebastian Bachs in Eisenach, Ohrdruf und Lüneburg. BJ 71: 7–42.

———. 2000. *Bachstätten: Ein Reiseführer zu Johann Sebastian Bach*. Frankfurt am Main: Insel Verlag.

Pfau, Marc-Roderich. 2008. Ein unbekanntes Leipziger Kantatentextheft aus dem Jahr 1735: Neues zum Thema Bach und Stölzel. BJ 94: 99–122.

Plichta, Alois. 1981. Johann Sebastian Bach und Johann Adam Graf von Questenberg. BJ 67: 23–28.

Poenicke, G. A. 1854. *Album der Rittergüter und Schlösser des Königreichs Sachsen*. Leipzig: Poenicke.

Rampe, Siegbert. 2002. "Monatlich neue Stücke"—Zu den musikalischen Voraussetzungen von Bachs Weimarer Konzertmeisteramt. BJ 88: 61–104.

Ranft, Eva-Maria. 1985. Ein unbekannter Aufenthalt Johann Sebastian Bachs in Gotha. BJ 71: 165–66.

Rathey, Markus. 2006. Zur Datierung einiger Vokalwerke Bachs in den Jahren 1707 und 1708. BJ 92: 65–92.

———. 2016. Schools. Routledge.

Reinecke, Wihelm. 1907. Huldigungsfeste in Lüneburg. *Lüneburger Museumsblätter* 4: 23–78.

Reul, Barbara. 1999. "O vergnügte Stunden / da mein Hertzog funden seinen Lebenstag." Ein unbekannter Textdruck zu einer Geburtstagskantate J. S. Bachs für den Fürsten Johann August von Anhalt-Zerbst. BJ 85: 7–17.

———. 2011. The Court of Anhalt-Zerbst. Courts: 259–79.

Rich, Norman. 2009. The Historical Setting: Politics and Patronage. WJSB: 67–104.

Rose, Stephen. 2009. Musician-Novels of the German Baroque. WJSB: 175–90.

———. 2011. *The Musician in Literature in the Age of Bach*. Cambridge: Cambridge University Press.

Rucker, Henrike. 2014. *Mein Lied in meinem Hause. Katalog zur ständigen Ausstellung des Heinrich-Schütz-Hauses Weißenfels*. Leipzig: Lehmstedt.

Ruf, Wolfgang. 2011. The Courts of Saxony-Weißenfels, Saxony-Merseburg, and Saxony-Zeitz. Courts: 223–55.

Rust, Wilhelm. 1878. Vorwort. In *Johann Sebastian Bach's Werke*, vol. 25/2, v–ix. Leipzig: Bach-Gesellschaft.

Schabalina, Tatjana. 2008. "Texte zur Music" in Sankt Petersburg. Neue Quellen zur Leipziger Musikgeschichte sowie zur Kompositions- und Aufführungstätigkeit Johann Sebastian Bachs. BJ 94: 33–98.

Schleuning, Peter. 2014. *Vom Kaffeehaus zum Fürstenhof: Johann Sebastian Bachs Weltliche Kantaten. Studien und Materialien zur Musikwissenschaft*, 79. Hildesheim: Georg Olms Verlag.

Schrammek, Winfried. 1985. Johann Sebastian Bachs Stellung zu Orgelpedalregistern im 32-Fuß-Ton. BJ 71: 147–54.

———. 1988. Orgel, Positiv, Clavicymbel und Glocken der Schloßkirche zu Weimar 1658 bis 1774. In *Bach-Händel-Schütz-Ehrung 1985 der Deutschen Demokratischen Republik. Bericht über die Wissenschaftliche Konferenz zum V. Internationalen Bachfest der Neuen Bachgesellschaft*, ed. Winfried Hoffmann und Armin Schneiderheinze, 99–111. Leipzig: VEB Deutscher Verlag für Musik.

Schulenberg, David. 2014. *The Music of Carl Philipp Emanuel Bach*. Rochester: University of Rochester Press.

Schulze, Hans-Joachim. 1976. Melodiezitate und Mehrtextigkeit in der Bauernkantate und in den Goldbergvariationen. BJ 62: 58–72.

———. 1979. Ein "Dresdner Menuett" im zweiten Klavierbüchlein der Anna Magdalena Bach. Nebst Hinweisen zur Überlieferung einiger Kammermusikwerke Bachs. BJ 65: 45–64.

———. 1984a. *Studien zur Bach-Überlieferung im 18. Jahrhundert*. Leipzig: Peters.

———. 1984b. Studenten als Bachs Helfer bei der Leipziger Kirchenmusik. BJ 70: 45–52.

———. 1985. Johann Christoph Bach (1671 bis 1721), "Organist und Schul-Collega in Ohrdruf," Johann Sebastian Bachs erster Lehrer. BJ 71: 55–81.

———. 1994. Notizen zu Bachs Quodlibets. BJ 80: 171–75.

———. 1997. Poetry and Poets. WBC 1: 101–7.

———. 2000. Wann entstand Johann Sebastian Bachs "Jagdkantate"? BJ 86: 301–5.

———. 2004a. Johann Sebastian Bach und Zerbst 1722: Randnotizen zu einer verlorenen Gastmusik. BJ 90: 209–13.

———. 2004b. Johann Sebastian Bach und Köthen: Wege und Irrwege der Forschung. CBH 12: 9–27.

———. 2008. Johann Friedrich Schweinitz, "A Disciple of the Famous Herr Bach in Leipzig." In *About Bach*, ed. Gregory G. Butler, George B. Stauffer, and Mary Dalton Greer, 81–88. Urbana: University of Illinois Press.

———. 2010. Rätselhafte Auftragswerke Johann Sebastian Bachs. Anmerkungen zu einigen Kantatentexten. BJ 96: 69–93.

———. 2013. Anna Magdalena Wilcke—Gesangsschülerin der Paulina? BJ 99: 279–95.

Siegele, Ulrich. 1997. Bach and the Domestic Politics of Electoral Saxony. In *The Cambridge Companion to Bach*, ed. John Butt, 17–34. Cambridge: Cambridge University Press.

Siegmund, Bert. 2011. The Court of Saxony-Gotha-Altenburg. Courts: 197–221.

Smend, Friedrich. 1985. *Bach in Köthen*, trans. John Page; ed. Stephen Daw. St. Louis: Concordia Publishing House.

Snyder, Kerala. 1986. To Lübeck in the Steps of J. S. Bach. *Musical Times* 127: 672–77.

———. 2006. Music for Church and Community: Buxtehude in Lübeck. In *The World of Baroque Music: New Perspectives*, ed. George B. Stauffer, 78–104. Bloomington: Indiana University Press.

———. 2007. *Dieterich Buxtehude: Organist in Lübeck*, rev. ed. Rochester, N.Y.: University of Rochester Press.

Spitta, Philipp. 1883–85. *Johann Sebastian Bach Vol. I*, trans. Clara Bell and J. A. Fuller-Maitland. 3 vols. London: Novello. Repr., New York: Dover Publications, 1951.

Spree, Eberhard. 2012/13. Johann Sebastian Bach und der Ursula-Erbstollen. *Acamonta. Zeitschrift für Freunde und Förderer der Technischen Universität Bergakademie Freiberg* 19: 171–74; 20: 168–73.

Ständer, Manfred, and Peter Marschik. 2000. Ein Tag im Leben des 14-jährigen Johann S. Bach. *Thüringer Landeszeitung.* April 29.

Stauffer, George B. 1980. *The Organ Preludes of Johann Sebastian Bach. Studies in Musicology, No. 27.* Ann Arbor, Mich.: UMI Research Press.

———. 1993. Leipzig: A Cosmopolitan Trade Centre. LBE: 254–95.

———. 1997. Bach: *The Mass in B Minor (The Great Catholic Mass). Monuments of Western Music.* New York: Schirmer Books.

———. 2008. Music for the "Cavaliers et Dames": Bach and the Repertoire of His Collegium Musicum. In *About Bach,* ed. Gregory G. Butler, George B. Stauffer, and Mary Dalton Greer, 135–56. Urbana: University of Illinois Press.

———. 2009. Bach and the Lure of the Big City. WJSB: 243–66.

Stinson, Russell. 1985. Bach's Earliest Autograph. The *Musical Quarterly* 71: 235–63.

———. 1996. Bach: *The Orgelbüchlein. Monuments of Western Music.* New York: Schirmer Books.

———. 2001. *J. S. Bach's Great Eighteen Organ Chorales.* New York: Oxford University Press.

———. 2012. *The Complete Organ Works of Johann Sebastian Bach. Vol. I/1a: Pedagogical Works,* ed. George B. Stauffer. Colfax, N.C.: Wayne Leopold Editions.

Stockigt, Janice. 2011. The Court of Saxony-Dresden. Courts: 17–50.

Talle, Andrew. 2003. Nürnberg, Darmstadt, Köthen—Neuerkenntnisse zur Bach-Überlieferung in der ersten Hälfte des 18. Jahrhunderts. BJ 89: 143–72.

Terry, Charles Sanford. 1933. Bach: *A Biography,* 2nd ed. Oxford: Oxford University Press.

Theobald, Hans Wolfgang. 1986. Zur Geschichte der 1746 von Johann Sebastian Bach geprüften Johann-Scheibe-Orgel in Zschortau bei Leipzig. BJ 72: 81–90.

Trautmann, Christoph. 1983. Was Theodor Fontane und die Bachforschung links liegen ließen. In *Bachiana et Alia Musicologica. Festschrift Alfred Dürr zum 65. Geburtstag,* ed. Wolfgang Rehm, 325–27. Kassel: Bärenreiter.

Walter, Horst. 1967. *Musikgeschichte der Stadt Lüneburg.* Tutzing: Hans Schneider.

Weiß, Frank. 2008. *Die Bergkirche Schleiz,* 2nd ed. Regensburg: Verlag Schnell & Steiner.

Wenzel, Joachim E. 1978. *Geschichte der Hamburger Oper 1678–1978.* Hamburg: Vorstand der Hamburgischen Staatsoper.

Wessely, Othmar. 1974/1985. Der Fürst und der Tod. Zu den "Musicalischen Exequien" von Heinrich Schütz. In *Heinrich Schütz in seiner Zeit,* ed. Walter Blankenburg (*Wege der Forschung, Band 614*), 329–43. Darmstadt: Wissenschaftliche Buchgesellschaft.

Winzeler, Marius. 2010. *Die Evangelische Stadtkirche St. Peter und Paul Görlitz.* Dößel: Verlag Janos Stekovics.

Wolff, Christoph. 1981. Nachwort (postscript) to Plichta 1981. BJ 67: 28–30.

———. 1985. Johann Adam Reinken und Johann Sebastian Bach: Zum Kontext des Bachschen Frühwerks. BJ 71: 99–118.

———. 1986a. Johann Adam Reinken and Johann Sebastian Bach: On the Context of Bach's Early Works. In *Bach as Organist,* ed. George Stauffer and Ernest May, 57–80. Bloomington: Indiana University Press.

——. 1986b. *The Neumeister Collection of Chorale Preludes from the Bach Circle (Yale University Manuscript LM 4708). A Facsimile Edition*. New Haven: Yale University Press.

——. 1997. Bach's Pre-Leipzig Cantatas: Repertory and Context. WBC 1: 3–18.

——. 2000. *Johann Sebastian Bach: The Learned Musician*. New York: Norton.

——. 2002. Zurück in Berlin: Das Notenarchiv der Sing-Akademie. Bericht über eine erste Bestandsaufnahme. BJ 88: 165–67.

——. 2009. Bach in Leipzig. WJSB: 267–89.

——. GMO. Bach. List of Musicians. *Grove Music Online*. http://www.oxfordmusiconline. com.

Wolffheim, Werner. 1910. Mitteilungen zur Geschichte der Hofmusik in Celle (1635/1706) und über Arnold M. Brunckhorst. In *Festschrift zum 90. Geburtstag . . . des . . . Rochus . . . von Liliencron*, 421–39. Leipzig: Breitkopf & Härtel.

Wollny, Peter. 1994. Bachs Bewerbung um die Organistenstelle und der Marienkirche zu Halle und ihr Kontext. BJ 80: 25–39.

——. 1997. Neue Bach-Funde. BJ 83: 7–50.

——. 1998. Alte Bach-Funde. BJ 84: 137–48.

——. 1999. Das geistliche Kantatenschaffen von Bachs Zeitgenossen. WBK 3: 37–49.

——. 2000. Überlegungen zur Bach-Überlieferung in Naumburg. BJ 86: 87–100.

——. 2001. Neue Ermittlungen zu Aufführungen Bachscher Kirchenkantaten am Zerbster Hof. In *Bach und seine mitteldeutsche Zeitgenossen*, ed. Rainer Kaiser, 199–217. Eisenach: Verlag der Musikalienhandlung Dieter Wagner.

——. 2005. Über die Hintergründe von Johann Sebastian Bachs Bewerbung in Arnstadt. BJ 91: 83–94.

——. 2008. "Bekennen will ich seinen Namen"—Authentizität, Bestimmung und Kontext der Arie BWV 200, Anmerkungen zu Johann Sebastian Bachs Rezeption von Werken Gottfried Heinrich Stölzels. BJ 94: 123–47.

Wright, Craig. 2000. Bachs "Kleines harmonisches Labyrinth" (BWV 591): Echtheitsfragen und theologischer Hintergrund. BJ: 51–59.

Yearsley, David. 2012. *Bach's Feet: The Organ Pedals in European Culture*. Musical Performance and Reception. Cambridge: Cambridge University Press.

——. 2013. Hoopskirts, Coffee, and the Changing Musical Prospects of the Bach Women. *Women and Music: A Journal of Gender and Culture*, 17: 27–58.

Zehnder, Jean Claude. 1988. Georg Böhm und Johann Sebastian Bach: Zur Chronologie der Bachschen Stilentwicklung. BJ 74: 73–110.

——. 1995. Zu Bachs Stilentwicklung in der Mühlhäuser und Weimarer Zeit. In *Das Frühwerk Johann Sebastian Bachs. Kolloquium veranstaltet vom Institut für Musikwissenschaft der Universität Rostock 11–13. September 1990*, ed. K. Heller und Hans-Joachim Schulze, 311–38. Köln: Studio.

Zimpel, Herbert. 1998. Zu musikalisch-kulturellen Befindlichkeiten des anhalt-köthnischen Hofes zwischen 1710 und 1730. CBH 8: 9–51.

Zürner, Adam Friedrich. 1753. *Neue Chursächsische Post Charte*, 2nd ed.

ILLUSTRATION CREDITS

Cover, left to right, see nos. 6, 19, 20, 32, 37; lower right-hand image (Zschortau organ case) photograph by Daniel Senf, used with permission.

Cover, map background and frontispiece, *Postarum seu Veredariorum Stationes per Germaniam et Provincias Adjacentes. Neu vermehrte PostCharte durch gantz Teutschland . . . Verbesserte Auflage* (Post and Express Stations Throughout Germany and Neighboring Provinces . . . Improved Edition), first published in Nuremberg in 1709 by Johann Baptist Homann (1664–1724). From authors' collection.

1. Map of Thuringia (1680)-DE.svg. Modifications made by Furfur. From Wikimedia Commons. Licensed under the Creative Commons Attribution-Share Alike 3.0.
2. Torgau, court chapel. Photograph by Burkhard Foltz. Used by permission.
3. Grimma Postsaeule.jpg. Photograph by Joeb07. From Wikimedia Commons. Licensed under the terms of the GNU Free Documentation License. Version 1.2.
4. GrimmaPöppelmannbrH.jpg. Photograph by Jwaller. From Wikimedia Commons. Licensed under the terms of the GNU Free Documentation License. Version 1.2. Inset image: Detail of bridge marker. Photograph by authors.
5. bpk, Berlin/Musikabteilung der Staatsbibliothek Berlin. Photograph by Carola Seifert/ Art Resource NY.
6. Evangelisch-Lutherischer Kirchenkreis Eisenach-Gerstungen.
7. Photograph by authors.
8. Photograph by authors.
9. Bachhaus Eisenach, photograph by André Nestler, Eisenach.
10. Photograph by authors.
11. Photograph by authors.
12. Bach-Archiv Leipzig, Graphiksammlung.
13. Hohenlohe-Zentralarchiv GA 100 Nr. 959 (map) and Stadtverwaltung Ohrdruf (overlay).
14. Ohrdruf-Schloss-1.jpg. Photograph by CTHOE. From Wikimedia Commons. Licensed under the Creative Commons Attribution-Share Alike 3.0.
15. Private Collection, Lüneburg. Used by permission.
16. Photograph by authors.
17. Museum Lüneburg.

18. Photograph by authors.
19. Photograph by authors.
20. Photograph by authors.
21. Photograph by authors
22. Photograph by authors
23. Photograph by authors.
24. Westseite Blasiikirche Mühlhausen.jpg. Photograph by Michael Sander. From Wikimedia Commons. Licensed under the terms of the GNU Free Documentation License. Version 1.2.
25. Stadtarchiv Mühlhausen, Fotosammlung. Photograph by Tino Sieland, 2006.
26. Photograph by authors.
27. Photograph by authors.
28. Klassikstiftung Weimar, Fototek.
29. Photograph by authors.
30. Photograph by authors.
31. Gelbes Schloss, Weimar (Nordseite).jpg. Photograph by Most Curious. From Wikimedia Commons. Licensed under the Creative Commons Attribution-Share Alike 3.0.
32. Photograph by authors.
33. Photograph by authors.
34. Historisches Museum & Bach-Gedenkstätte, Köthen.
35. SchlossKöthen4-2012.jpg. Photograph by Oursana. From Wikimedia Commons. Licensed under the Creative Commons Attribution-Share Alike 3.0.
36. Photograph by authors.
37. Historisches Museum & Bach-Gedenkstätte, Köthen.
38. Historisches Museum & Bach-Gedenkstätte, Köthen.
39. 2.KöthenerBachhausMitBachdenkmal.jpg. Photograph by Georgheeg. From Wikimedia Commons. Licensed under the Creative Commons Attribution-Share Alike 3.0.
40. Der Markt in Leipzig 1845.jpg. From Wikimedia Commons. Public domain.
41. Bacharchiv, Leipzig, Graphiksammlung.
42. Leipzig Katharinenstr. 14–16, Stich um 1720. JPG. From Wikimedia Commons. Public domain.
43. Photograph by authors.
44. Bachhaus Eisenach.
45. Bachhaus Eisenach.
46. Photograph by authors.
47. Stadtgeschichtliches Museum Leipzig.
48. Photograph by authors.
49. Bachhaus Eisenach.
50. Bosehaus Leipzig Straßenfront 2.jpg. Photograph by Martin Geisler. From Wikimedia Commons. Licensed under the Creative Commons Attribution-Share Alike 3.0.
51. Thomasschule Leipzig vor 1885.jpg. From Wikimedia Commons. Public domain.

52. Schlosskirche und Schloss Altenburg.jpg. Photograph by UNi ABG. From Wikimedia Commons. Licensed under the Creative Commons Attribution-Share Alike 3.0.
53. Rosenberg Opernhaus 1773.jpg. From Wikimedia Commons. Public domain.
54. 200806 Berlin 623.jpg. Photograph by Mark Ahsman, model by Horst Düring. From Wikimedia. Licensed under the Creative Commons Attribution-Share Alike 3.0.
55. Photograph by authors.
56. Photograph by authors.
57. Photograph by authors.
58. Gemäldegalerie Alte Meister, Staatliche Kunstsammlungen Dresden. Photograph by Jürgen Karpinski.
59. Dresden 1715 Palais Flemming.jpg. Photograph © H.-P.Haack. From Wikimedia Commons. Licensed under the Creative Commons Attribution-Share Alike 3.0, image in the public domain.
60. Photograph by authors.
61. "Heinrich Schütz im Kreise seiner Hofkapelle in der Dresdner Schloßkapelle." Copper engraving by David Conrad, 1676. Heinrich-Schütz-Haus Weißenfels. Photograph by Christo Libuda.
62. Photograph by authors.
63. Photograph by authors.
64. Dresden 104201239 Katholische Hofkirche.jpg. Photograph by Michael Kranewitter, From Wikimedia Commons. Licensed under CC-by-sa 3.0/at.
65. DD-Sophienkirche1850.jpg. From Wikimedia Commons. Public domain.
66. Photograph by authors.
67. Photograph by authors.
68. Erfurt-St.-Severi-Orgel.jpg. Photograph by Misburg3014. From Wikimedia Commons. Licensed under the Creative Commons Attribution-Share Alike 3.0.
69. Altstadtbrücke und Peterskirche in Görlitz.jpg. Photograph by Schläsinger. From Wikimedia Commons. Licensed under the Creative Commons Attribution-Share Alike 3.0.
70. Photograph by authors.
71. Photograph by authors.
72. Photograph by authors.
73. MarienkircheHalle Ostseite 2.jpg. Photograph by OmiTs. From Wikimedia Commons. Licensed under the Creative Commons Attribution-Share Alike 3.0.
74. Kunstmuseum Moritzburg Halle; © 2014 Artists' Rights Society (ARS), New York/VG Bild-Kunst, Bonn.
75. 1682 Hamburg Schenk.jpg. From Wikimedia Commons. Public domain.
76. Hh-st-jacobi.jpg. Photograph by Staro 1 aus der deutschsprachigen Wikipedia. From Wikimedia Commons. Licensed under the Creative Commons Attribution-Share Alike 3.0.
77. Photograph by authors.
78. Photograph by authors.
79. Photograph by authors.

80. Bachhaus Eisenach.
81. Luebeck-St Marien vom Turm von St Petri aus gesehen-20100905.jpg. Photograph by Roland Meinecke. From Wikimedia Commons. Licensed under the terms of the GNU Free Documentation License. Version 1.2.
82. Photograph by authors.
83. Photograph by Thomas Ufert. Used by permission.
84. Schloss sanssouci potsdam von innen.jpg. Photograph by Janstoecklin. From Wikimedia Commons. Licensed under the Creative Commons Attribution-Share Alike 3.0.
85. St. Jakobi Sangerhausen 2008–002.jpg. Photograph by Tilman2007. From Wikimedia Commons. Licensed under the Creative Commons Attribution-Share Alike 3.0.
86. StörmthalKirche.jpg. Photograph by Jwaller. From Wikimedia Commons. Licensed under the Creative Commons Attribution-Share Alike 3.0.
87. Photograph by authors.
88. Photograph by Elmar von Kolson. Used by permission.
89. Bachhaus Eisenach.
90. Photograph by authors.
91. Photograph by authors.
92. Photograph by authors.
93. Photograph by authors.
94. Photograph by authors.
95. Photograph by Eberhard Spree. Used by permission.
96. Archiv des Fördervereins Schloss Zerbst e.V.
97. Photograph by authors.
98. Photograph by authors.

INDEX

G numbers. J. S. Bach's "Origin of the Musical Bach Family" (*Ursprung der musicalisch-Bachischen Familie*), compiled by the composer in 1735 and cited throughout this book as "the Genealogy," provides running numbers for every individual male family member known to him, beginning with No. 1, the patriarch, Veit (or Vitus) Bach (ca. 1555–1619). The index provides the "G numbers" ("G1," etc.) as they appear in the Genealogy for all family members mentioned in the volume. The entry for "Bach, Johann Sebastian (1685–1750; G24)" is limited to a listing of specific works.

Names of modern authors (without biographical dates) are listed here only when their writings are cited in the text commentary.

Page numbers containing images are printed in italics.

ROBERT L. MARSHALL is Sachar Professor Emeritus of Music at Brandeis University. His books include *The Compositional Process of J. S. Bach* and *The Music of Johann Sebastian Bach: The Sources, the Style, the Significance.*

TRAUTE M. MARSHALL is the author of *Art Museums PLUS: Cultural Excursions in New England* and translator of *The Classical Style* and *Brecht in America.*

The University of Illinois Press
is a founding member of the
Association of American University Presses.

_____

Designed by Dustin Hubbart
Composed in 10/12.5 Minion Pro
with Trajan Pro
by Kirsten Dennison
at the University of Illinois Press
Manufactured by Bang Printing

University of Illinois Press
1325 South Oak Street
Champaign, IL 61820-6903
www.press.uillinois.edu